SCHOLASTIC

100

2014 CURRICULUM

COMPUTING LESSONS

WITHDRAWN

Terms and conditions

IMPORTANT – PERMITTED USE AND WARNINGS – READ CAREFULLY BEFORE USING

Recommended system requirements:

- Windows: XP (Service Pack 3), Vista (Service Pack 2), Windows 7 or Windows 8 with 2.33GHz processor
- Mac: OS 10.6 to 10.8 with Intel Core™ Duo processor
- 1GB RAM (recommended)
- 1024 x 768 Screen resolution
- CD-ROM drive (24x speed recommended)
- 16-bit sound card
- Adobe Reader (version 9 recommended for Mac users)
- Broadband internet connections (for installation and updates)

For all technical support queries, please phone Scholastic Customer Services on 0845 6039091.

SCHOLASTIC

Book End, Range Road, Witney, Oxfordshire, OX29 0YD
www.scholastic.co.uk

© 2014, Scholastic Ltd

1 2 3 4 5 6 7 8 9   4 5 6 7 8 9 0 1 2 3

British Library Cataloguing-in-Publication Data
A catalogue record for this book is available from the British Library.

ISBN 978-1407-12857-3
Printed by Bell & Bain Ltd, Glasgow

Due to the nature of the web we cannot guarantee the content or links of any site mentioned. We strongly recommend that teachers check websites before using them in the classroom.

Extracts from *The National Curriculum in England, Computing Programme of Study* © Crown Copyright. Reproduced under the terms of the Open Government Licence (OGL). http://www.nationalarchives.gov.uk/doc/open-government-licence/open-government-licence.htm

Authors
Zoe Ross and Steve Bunce

Editorial team
Mark Walker, Jenny Wilcox, Kim Vernon, Lucy Tritton, Sarah Sodhi, Suzanne Adams

Cover Design
Andrea Lewis

Design
Sarah Garbett @ Sg Creative Services

CD-ROM development
Hannah Barnett, Phil Crothers, MWA Technologies Private Ltd

Illustrations
Matt Ward

Acknowledgements
The publishers gratefully acknowledge permission to reproduce the following copyright material:

David Higham Associates for the use of an extract from Fantastic Mr Fox by Roald Dahl. Text Copyright © 1970 Roald Dahl Nominee Ltd. (1974, George Allen & Unwin)

United Agents LLP for the use of illustrations from Fantastic Mr Fox by Roald Dahl. Illustrations Copyright © 1996 Quentin Blake. (1974, Puffin Books)

Brenda Williams for the use of the poem 'The legend of Robin Hood' by Brenda Williams, first published in Child Education. Poem © 2011, Brenda Williams (2011, Scholastic Ltd).

The Lifelong Kindergarten Group For the use of screenshots from the 'Scratch' program. Scratch is developed by the Lifelong Kindergarten Group at the MIT Media Lab. See http://scratch.mit.edu

Every effort has been made to trace copyright holders for the works reproduced in this book, and the publishers apologise for any inadvertent omissions.

Contents

Introduction

About the series

The *100 Computing Lessons* series is designed to meet the requirements of the 2014 Curriculum, Computing Programmes of Study. There are three books in the series, Years 1–2, 3–4 and 5–6, and each book contains lesson plans, resources and ideas matched to the new curriculum. It can be a complex task to ensure that a progressive and appropriate curriculum is followed in all year groups; this series has been carefully structured to ensure that a progressive and appropriate curriculum is followed throughout.

About the new curriculum

Computing is a subject full of opportunities for children to develop their thinking, with practical programming skills, focused on real world examples. The new 'Computing' curriculum replaces the old 'ICT' curriculum.

The National Curriculum for Computing aims to ensure that all pupils:
- *can understand and apply the fundamental principles and concepts of computer science, including abstraction, logic, algorithms and data representation*
- *can analyse problems in computational terms, and have repeated practical experience of writing computer programs in order to solve such problems*
- *can evaluate and apply information technology, including new or unfamiliar technologies, analytically to solve problems*
- *are responsible, competent, confident and creative users of information and communication technology.*

The National Curriculum Programme of Study for Computing contains guidance for Key Stages 1 and 2. The subject focuses on computational thinking with an emphasis on programming. In addition, there are other areas of computing which have equal importance. In this series, the National Curriculum has been divided into four key subject areas:
- Algorithms and programming
- Data and information
- How computers work
- Communication and e-safety

The 'Algorithms and programming' parts of the Programme of Study have been combined into one block, as they are closely related and there is a progression over the key stages. Each year there are two 'Algorithms and programming' blocks and one each for 'Data and information', 'How computers work', 'Communication' and 'E-safety'.

Terminology

In this guide, the main terms used are:

Subject areas: the area of the subject, for computing, we will use 'Algorithms and programming', 'Data and information', 'How computers work' and 'Communication and e-safety'.

Objectives: by the end of Key Stage 1 and Key Stage 2, children are expected to know, apply and understand the matters, skills and processes detailed in the relevant programme of study.

■SCHOLASTIC

About the book

This book is divided into twelve chapters; six for each year group. Each chapter contains a half-term's work and is based around a topic or theme. Each chapter follows the same structure:

Chapter introduction

At the start of each chapter there is a summary of what is covered. This includes:

- **Introduction:** A description of what is covered in the chapter.
- **Expected prior learning:** What the children are expected to know before starting the work in the chapter.
- **Chapter at a glance:** This is a table that summarises the content of each lesson, including: the curriculum objectives, lesson objectives, a summary of the activities and the outcome.
- **Overview of progression:** A brief explanation of how the children progress through the chapter.
- **Creative context:** How the chapter could link to other curriculum areas.
- **Background knowledge:** A section explaining grammatical terms and suchlike to enhance your subject knowledge, where required.

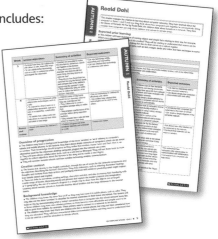

Lessons

Each chapter contains six weeks' of lessons. At the start of each week there is an introduction about what is covered. The lesson plans then include the relevant combination of headings from below.

- **Curriculum objectives:** The relevant objectives from the Programme of Study.
- **Lesson objectives:** Objectives that are based upon the Curriculum objectives, but are more specific broken-down steps to achieve them.
- **Expected outcomes:** What you should expect all, most and some children to know by the end of the lesson.
- **Resources:** What you require to teach the lesson.
- **Introduction:** A short and engaging activity to begin the lesson.
- **Whole-class work:** Working together as a class.
- **Group/Paired/Independent work:** Children working independently of the teacher in pairs, groups or alone.
- **Differentiation:** Ideas for how to support children who are struggling with a concept or how to extend those children who understand a concept without taking them onto new work.
- **Review:** A chance to review the children's learning and ensure the outcomes of the lesson have been achieved.

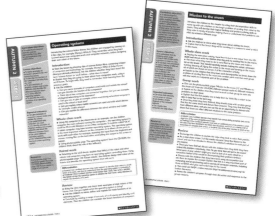

Assess and review

At the end of each chapter are activities for assessing and reviewing the children's understanding. These can be conducted during the course of the chapter's work or saved until the end of the chapter or done at a later date. They are set out the same as lesson plans with an underlying assessment focus.

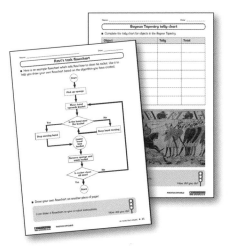

Photocopiable pages

At the end of each chapter are some photocopiable pages that will have been referred to in the lesson plans. These sheets are for the children to use. There is generally a title, an instruction, an activity and an 'I can' statement at the bottom. The children should be encouraged to complete the 'I can' statements by colouring in the traffic lights to say how they think they have done (red – not very well, amber – ok, green – very well).

These sheets are also provided on the CD-ROM alongside additional pages as referenced in the lessons (see page 7 About the CD-ROM).

Tablet appendix

At the end of the book are 16 additional lessons which have been written with a specific focus on tablet computers and other touch-screen devices.

SCHOLASTIC

About the CD-ROM

The CD-ROM contains:

- Printable versions of the photocopiable sheets from the book and additional photocopiable sheets as referenced in the lesson plans.
- Interactive activities for children to complete or to use on the whiteboard.
- Media resources to display.
- Printable versions of the lesson plans.
- Digital versions of the lesson plans with the relevant resources linked to them.

Getting started

- Put the CD-ROM into your CD-ROM drive.
  - For Windows users, the install wizard should autorun, if it fails to do so then navigate to your CD-ROM drive. Then follow the installation process.
  - For Mac users, copy the disk image file to your hard drive. After it has finished copying double-click it to mount the disk image. Navigate to the mounted disk image and run the installer. After installation the disk image can be unmounted and the DMG can be deleted from the hard drive.
- To complete the installation of the program you need to open the program and click 'Update' in the pop-up. Please note – this CD-ROM is web-enabled and the content will be downloaded from the internet to your hard-drive to populate the CD-ROM with the relevant resources. This only needs to be done on first use, after this you will be able to use the CD-ROM without an internet connection. If at any point any content is updated you will receive another pop-up upon start up with an internet connection.

Navigating the CD-ROM

There are two options to navigate the CD-ROM either as a Child or as a Teacher.

Child

- Click on the 'Child' button on the first menu screen.
- In the second menu click on the relevant class (please note only the books installed on the machine or network will be accessible. You can also rename year groups to match your school's naming conventions via the Teacher > Settings > Rename books area).
- A list of interactive activities will be displayed, children need to locate the correct one and click 'Go' to launch it.
- There is the opportunity to print or save a PDF of the activity at the end.

Teacher

- Click on the Teacher button on the first menu screen and you will be taken to a screen showing which of the *100 Computing* books you have purchased. From here, you can also access information about getting started and the credits.
- To enter the product click 'Next' in the bottom right.
- You then need to enter a password (the password is: login).
  - On first use: Enter as a Guest by clicking on the 'Guest' button.
  - If desired, create a profile for yourself by adding your name to the list of users. Profiles allow you to save favourites and to specify which year group(s) you wish to be able to view.
  - Go to 'Settings' to create a profile for yourself – click 'Add user' and enter your name. Then choose the year groups you wish to have access to (you can return to this screen to change this at any time). Click on 'Login' at the top of the screen to re-enter the disk under your new profile.

- On subsequent uses you can choose your name from the drop-down list. The 'Guest' option will always be available if you, or a colleague, wish to use this.
- You can search the CD-ROM using the tools or save favourites.

For more information about how to use the CD-ROM, please refer to the help file which can be found in the teacher area of the CD-ROM. It is a red button with a question mark on it on the right-hand side of the screen just underneath the 'Settings' tab.

Roald Dahl

This chapter engages the children in learning about computer networks. They have learned about the computer in Years 1 and 2 and now they think about how computers join together to communicate. Using the theme of *Fantastic Mr Fox* by Roald Dahl, the children think about tunnels as a network. They then consider how computers can help those children and schools in remote areas.

Expected prior learning
● The children will have experience of naming objects and simple facts relating to their size, for example, *Which one is the largest? Which one is the smallest?* They will be starting to understand that names can be sorted alphabetically, for example linking this idea to their names on a school register.
● They may know different types of data, such as text, images, audio and video, but have not begun to name them using these terms.

Chapter at a glance

Subject area
• How computers work

National Curriculum objective
• To understand computer networks including the internet; how they can provide multiple services, such as the World Wide Web; and the opportunities they offer for communication and collaboration. • To use technology safely, respectfully and responsibly.

Week	Lesson objectives	Summary of activities	Expected outcomes
1	• To understand the terminology 'computer network' (a group of two or more computers linked together). • To explain in simple terms how a network enables communication between computers.	• Children look at their friendship networks and identify connections. • They think about Mr Fox's network of tunnels and make analogies with computer networks. • They create a simple definition to describe a computer network and its function to communicate.	• Can start to understand what a basic computer network is. • Can discuss simply how computers communicate with each other.
2	• To recognise simple computer networks around them. • To sketch a simple diagram of a computer network. • To explain simply how the computers are communicating via the network.	• Children look at computers around school and identify whether a computer is using a wired, wireless or mobile network. • They sketch a picture of Mr Fox's tunnel network and a simple diagram of a computer network.	• Can describe how computers are networked in the room or school. • Can create a simple diagram of the computer network.
3	• To identify devices connected to a network including printers, mobile devices and laptops. • To add these to their simple network diagram. • To understand the simple concept that such devices can be wired to the network or be connected via a wireless network.	• In *Fantastic Mr Fox* the farmers have different products at their farms. The children make analogies with the different tools used with networks, such as printers and laptops. • They add other tools to the simple network diagram and show if they are wired or wireless.	• Can discuss how other devices can be connected to the network. • Can know that networks can be wired or wireless.
4	• To know that computers can enable communication in the classroom and beyond. • To discuss how computers have helped others in a variety of situations, such as remote schools. • To explain how computers can help people to communicate and collaborate.	• Children understand that in *Fantastic Mr Fox*, the animals join together to live in the same place. Children consider how they might communicate with another school. • They consider remote schooling, for example, in Australia, and how they communicate with other schools. • They look at initiatives like 'Skype in the classroom'.	• Can understand how computers offer opportunities for communication and collaboration. • Can explain how computers can help others.

■SCHOLASTIC

Week	Lesson objectives	Summary of activities	Expected outcomes
5	• To know how they can collaborate with others in safe, respectful ways. • To use collaborative technology, such as a wiki, to collaborate within and beyond the classroom.	• Children are prompted to notice the descriptions, behaviours, speech and hygiene of the farmers. • They discuss who the worst character was and who did the worst thing. Did they deserve to catch Mr Fox? • They discuss how Roald Dahl has captured the way the farmers speak and compare this to the children's speech and the narrator's 'voice'. • They collaborate using an online tool, to collect the features of the farmers' characters.	• Can use technology safely, respectfully and responsibly. • Can use collaborative technology to collaborate with others.
6	• To contribute to a document using collaborative technologies, such as a wiki. • To respond to others' work on a collaborative document, such as a wiki, in a supportive, constructive way. • To explain how using a wiki can help others to improve their ideas and think in new ways.	• Children create a truly horrid fourth farmer character; what do they say, look like and do? • They collaborate to create a descriptive passage using an online tool. • They prepare a performance of the passage, before giving supportive feedback. • They consider how a wiki can help others to improve their ideas.	• Can use technology to collaborate effectively with others. • Can explain how collaborative technologies can be used to help others.
Assess and review	• Assess and review the half-term's work.	• Children recognise and draw computer networks and contribute to a wiki.	• Assess and review.

Overview of progression
● The children may have a background knowledge of the terms 'wireless' or 'wi-fi' relating to computers, tablets and mobile phones. In the lessons, they learn about simple networks of computers, which can be wired or wireless. Their knowledge should progress as they realise that wireless means 'wire' and 'less', that is, an alternative could be the classroom desktop computer, plugged into the network via a wire.
● They will learn about collaborative tools, such as a wiki and an Etherpad. They will use these tools to work together to collect adjectives about the farmers in the story and to create a new rhyme.
● They will consider remote schools and how satellite technology enables communication.

Creative context
● The lessons link closely to the English curriculum, through the use of nouns for the network components and the adjectives describing the farmers' characters. They draw inferences, such as inferring characters' feelings, thoughts and motives from their actions and justifying inferences with evidence predicting what might happen from details stated and implied.
● There are links to narratives, creating settings, characters and plot, and also increasing their familiarity with a wide range of books, discussing words and phrases that capture the reader's interest and imagination.
● In geography, the use of a network diagram is a simple map to show how the objects are arranged. Learning about remote schools in Australia teaches about location and the large distances to the nearest towns.

Background knowledge
● The children may know the term 'free wi-fi' as they may have seen it in public places, such as cafes. They may also use the term 'wireless' to describe the internet connection in their home and school. The lessons will build on this by demonstrating what a 'wired' connection from a computer into the school network looks like.
● Some children may have seen wireless printers, as these become more affordable and people want to be able to print from tablets, for example. These printers need to connect to a network to be shared.
● The children may know that there are children who live in remote places, but may not have considered how they are educated. They will have encountered video communication before and they need to understand that it can be used as a tool for education in remote schools.

Curriculum objectives
● To understand computer networks including the internet; how they can provide multiple services, such as the World Wide Web; and the opportunities they offer for communication and collaboration.
● To use technology safely, respectfully and responsibly.

Lesson objectives
● To understand the terminology 'computer network' (a group of two or more computers linked together).
● To explain in simple terms how a network enables communication between computers.

Expected outcomes
● Can start to understand what a basic computer network is.
● Can discuss simply how computers communicate with each other.

Resources
Photocopiable page 17 'My networks'; interactive activity 'Naming my computer' on the CD-ROM; *Fantastic Mr Fox* by Roald Dahl; string

An introduction to networks

In these lessons about 'How computers work', the children learn about networks. We have networks of friends and we hear of social networks, so the concept of people linking together is similar to computer networks. The children look at computers in school and observe how these are linked to the school network. Desktop computers will often link via a wire. Mobile devices may use wireless technologies. Using the theme of Roald Dahl's *Fantastic Mr Fox*, the children think about networks and collaboration using networks.

Introduction
● To begin the lesson, remind the children about the parts of the computer, using the interactive activity 'Naming my computer' on the CD-ROM. Now play 'Stand up, sit down'. Explain to the children that if the answer is 'yes' they should stand up and if the answer is 'no' they should sit down. Ask questions, such as: *Do you have two eyes? Do you have a school jumper? Do you have a sister? Do you have a friend? Do you play football? Do you go to Brownies?* Highlight that they have a lot in common and they could be grouped, to show their similarities. Explain that, instead of standing up and sitting down, they are going to move from one end of the room to another. For example, ask whether they like a certain pop star, if they answer yes they move to the left, if they answer no they move to the right. Finally, ask whether they know the story of *Fantastic Mr Fox*. Ask them to explain what happens in the story.

Whole-class work
● The children may not understand what is meant by a network so, to show this, they are going to use string to represent connections within the class.
● Give each child two lengths of string, approximately two metres long. Ask the children to sit in a large circle, facing inwards. Select one child and ask them to name two friends in the class, with whom they share the same birthday month or a similar hobby. Once they have chosen, the child holds one end of the two pieces of string and the other end is given to the two friends. This process is repeated for the next child in the circle, until they have all had a turn. The network of strings will be very complex. Explain that the strings are showing a network of how they are connected together. Computers are part of networks too and need to connect to communicate.

Paired work
● Using photocopiable page 17 'My networks', the children write their name and the names of 4 classmates. They think of an activity that they do. If their friends do it too, they draw a straight line between themselves and their friend.

> **Differentiation**
> ● Challenge: More confident learners could consider something additional that they have in common with their friends, adding a line in a different colour to the network line.
> ● Support: Less confident learners may need support from adults to think of questions to ask and then help to draw the connection on the diagram.

Review
● Bring the class together and ask them to display their diagrams. Explain that networks can be very complicated. As the teacher, you have a network communicating with all of the children and they communicate back to the teacher.
● Read an extract from *Fantastic Mr Fox* to describe the network of tunnels going from the foxes to the three farms. Highlight that this can be called a network of tunnels, as it connects one place to another. Explain that computers need to connect to each other to communicate and that this is called a 'computer network'. Can they now explain to each other what a computer network is?

Computer networks in school

Inside schools, the computers are networked together to enable sharing of information, for example, to save a document that can then be accessed by other teachers on a different computer. Also, the network of computers is connected to the internet, so that sharing from those computers can occur, for example, to access a website.

Introduction
● Introduce the lesson by reading a section of *Fantastic Mr Fox*, where Mr Fox visits a farm, for example, Tunnel number one, leading to Boggis' chicken farm. Remind the children of the story, where he digs two more tunnels to reach Bunce's ducks and goose farm and Bean's cider cellar.

Paired work
● Ask the children to think about the network of tunnels in *Fantastic Mr Fox*. Using photocopiable page 18 'Tunnels network and a computer network', ask them to sketch the tunnels in the story. The den and farms are shown, the children need to add the tunnels in between.

Whole-class work
● Bring the class together and explain that they have discussed tunnel networks and now need to think about computer networks in the school. If a networked desktop computer or laptop is present, show how the cable goes out of the computer and into the socket on the wall. The computer is connected to the network and it is 'wired'. If a wireless laptop or tablet computer is present, explain that it is connected to the network, but it is 'wireless'. The children are going to look around the school to identify where they think wired and wireless computers are connected to the network.

Group work
● Working in groups of four (supervised by an adult, if necessary), the children move around the school, looking for examples of computers and deciding whether they are wired or wireless.

Differentiation
● Support: Less confident learners may need support from adults to recognise the wired and wireless computers.
● Challenge: More confident learners could compare wired and wireless computers. *Why would someone use a wired connection, when wireless was available?*

Review
● Bring the class together to discuss the tunnel pictures they have drawn. Can they see how the den connects to the three farms. Now explain that they are going to draw a simple computer network. On photocopiable page 18 'Tunnel network and a computer network', ask the children to now draw a simple network (the hub in the middle and three computers are already drawn, they need to connect the drawings). Use the interactive activity 'Simple networks' from the CD-ROM to show a solution to the drawing of a simple network.
● Conclude the lesson by stating that computers can be joined together in a network and can then communicate with each other.

Curriculum objectives
● To understand computer networks including the internet; how they can provide multiple services, such as the World Wide Web; and the opportunities they offer for communication and collaboration.
● To use technology safely, respectfully and responsibly.

Lesson objectives
● To recognise simple computer networks around them.
● To sketch a simple diagram of a computer network.
● To explain simply how the computers are communicating via the network.

Expected outcomes
● Can describe how computers are networked in the room or school.
● Can create a simple diagram of the computer network.

Resources
Photocopiable page 18 'Tunnels network and a computer network'; interactive activity 'Simple networks' on the CD-ROM; *Fantastic Mr Fox* by Roald Dahl

Curriculum objectives
● To understand computer networks including the internet; how they can provide multiple services, such as the World Wide Web; and the opportunities they offer for communication and collaboration.
● To use technology safely, respectfully and responsibly.

Lesson objectives
● To identify devices connected to a network including printers, mobile devices and laptops.
● To add these to their simple network diagram.
● To understand the simple concept that such devices can be wired to the network or be connected via a wireless network.

Expected outcomes
● Can discuss how other devices can be connected to the network.
● Can know that networks can be wired or wireless.

Resources
Photocopiable page 19 'Foxes and geese'; interactive activity 'Foxes and geese' on the CD-ROM; photocopiable page 18 'Tunnels network and a computer network' (from previous lesson); *Fantastic Mr Fox* by Roald Dahl

More networking

The children have been learning about wired and wireless computer networks. They now consider other devices that may be connected, such as printers. They also are introduced to the concept that mobile phones are connected to large networks.

Introduction
● Introduce the lesson by reading a section of *Fantastic Mr Fox* about the visit to Bunce's duck and goose farm.
● Demonstrate how to play a game of 'Fox and geese' (using photocopiable page 19 'Foxes and geese' or the interactive activity 'Foxes and geese' on the CD-ROM). On the photocopiable sheet, the children can either cut out the fox and geese pieces or use plastic counters or coins. The thirteen geese are placed on the board in the places shown, then the fox is added. The fox and geese take turns to move one square in any direction (only one goose can move each turn and cannot jump over another piece). The fox can jump over a goose on to an empty space, then that goose is removed from the board. The fox wins if all the geese are removed, or the geese can win by crowding the fox so that it cannot move.

Paired work
● Place the children into pairs to play the 'Foxes and geese' game. Let them notice that the spaces are connected by lines. Tell them that this is a network of lines and that the pieces can move along these lines.

Whole-class work
● After the children have enjoyed playing the game, bring them together to discuss how they moved their pieces. They moved around the board, following the lines of the network. Explain that this is similar to how information is moved from computer to computer in a network.
● Explain to the class that other devices can be connected to the network. The class may have a printer attached to the computer, though this may not be on the network but simply connected to that individual computer. A networked printer would be connected to more than one computer. For example, if the school has an ICT Suite, there may be a networked printer in there. Also, ask the children about printers in their homes. Wireless printers are becoming more common and the children could share how they can print from a tablet computer or laptop straight to the printer, without plugging in any cables.

Independent work
● Using photocopiable page 18 'Tunnels network and a computer network' from the last lesson, ask the children to add a picture of a printer to the diagram and draw a line to the hub.

Differentiation
● Support: Less confident learners may need support from adults to understand the rules of the game and how to play.
● Challenge: More confident learners will be able to play the 'Foxes and geese' game independently and explain their tactics.

Review
● Bring the class together and ask whether they have seen a mobile phone before. Almost certainly, the whole class will have seen one and probably used one to speak to a relative or friend. Ask them: *How does the phone connect with the other mobile phone?* The mobile phone connects to a large phone network using a wireless phone signal. Explain to the children that smart phones can usually connect to the mobile phone network and also connect to a wireless network in a house or public place, such as a cafe, to access 'free wi-fi'. In both these ways, the phone is joining a large network to communicate.

Connecting classrooms

The children have been thinking about networks and how computers can connect. What are the advantages of these connections? They consider how being able to connect could be beneficial to their lives. Also, the class discusses remote schools, where a school may be a long distance from any others. How can they stay in touch?

Curriculum objectives
● To understand computer networks including the internet; how they can provide multiple services, such as the World Wide Web; and the opportunities they offer for communication and collaboration.
● To use technology safely, respectfully and responsibly.

Lesson objectives
● To know that computers can enable communication in the classroom and beyond.
● To discuss how computers have helped others in a variety of situations, such as remote schools.
● To explain how computers can help people to communicate and collaborate.

Expected outcomes
● Can understand how computers offer opportunities for communication and collaboration.
● Can explain how computers can help others.

Resources
Materials to make string telephones: disposable cups, string, scissors, a sharp pencil; photocopiable page 20 'String telephones'; *Fantastic Mr Fox* by Roald Dahl

Introduction
● Introduce the lesson by reading *Fantastic Mr Fox*, the part at the end of the story, where Mr Fox invites all of the animals to come and live together with him. The animals can see the advantages of being together – safety from the farmers and also large food stocks, via the tunnels to the farms.
● Ask the children about their communication with each other and other classes in the school. *If your class was the only one in the school, would it be good to communicate with a class from another school? How would you do that?*

Paired work
● The children make string telephones using disposable cups and string (see photocopiable page 20 'String telephones' for instructions). Once made, they can stretch out the string in between the cups and speak and listen to each other. Give them the challenge of ordering food from Boggis, Bunce and Bean's farms. Can they communicate clearly?

Whole-class work
● Explain to the children about schools in remote areas. For example, in Australia, for many years there has been 'The School of the Air' (http://australia.gov.au/about-australia/australian-story/school-of-the-air). Initially, teaching was delivered using radios to communicate. Now, using a satellite connection, the teachers use a video camera and an interactive whiteboard in a studio to give lessons to students. The students on the network can watch and respond in real-time via a web camera attached to their computer.
● Explain that another initiative is 'Skype in the classroom' (https://education.skype.com/), where classrooms around the world can connect to share lessons and experiences.

Differentiation
● Support: Less confident learners could explain the difference between wired and wireless networks.
● Challenge: More confident learners could explain how computers can enable communication outside of the school.

Review
● Bring the class together and use a string telephone to give a message to a child. Now ask another child to join your network (the child connected to the teacher now holds one end of the new connection, so there is a line from teacher to child, then from that child to another). Send a message along the connection. So, the children can see that this network could continue, adding more and more links to the network, to cover a long distance.
● Conclude the lesson by explaining that wired networks can transport information over long distances. In Australia, they are using satellite connections to send information, over even greater distances, to the remote schools.

Curriculum objectives
- To understand computer networks including the internet; how they can provide multiple services, such as the World Wide Web; and the opportunities they offer for communication and collaboration.
- To use technology safely, respectfully and responsibly.

Lesson objectives
- To know how they can collaborate with others in safe, respectful ways.
- To use collaborative technology, such as a wiki, to collaborate within and beyond the classroom.

Expected outcomes
- Can use technology safely, respectfully and responsibly.
- Can use collaborative technology to collaborate with others.

Resources
Sticky notes; collaborative online writing pad http://shamblespad.com/ and two computers; photocopiable page 21 'Farmer rhyme'; interactive activity 'Bad farmer' on the CD-ROM; *Fantastic Mr Fox* by Roald Dahl

Farmer rhyme

The children have discussed different networks and how these connect together. They now consider how they can collaborate together to use an online tool to gather information about the farmers in *Fantastic Mr Fox*.

Introduction
- The children will be collaborating on an online 'pad'. They could use a wiki, which is similar to a web page, that can be edited by more than one person. For this chapter, they will use an online tool called an Etherpad.
- Before the lesson, set up the collaborative Etherpad document at http://shamblespad.com/. On arrival on the web page, name the pad, for example, using the school or class name. The site then creates a special pad for that address. So, if the school and class was 'Fairfield school' and 'Class 3', then on the Shamblespad home page, you could enter 'fairfieldclass3'. This will create a new online pad for sharing at http://shamblespad.com/p/fairfieldclass3. Delete the text on the page and it is ready for use.
- Introduce the lesson by saying the rhyme about the farmers from *Fantastic Mr Fox* (see photocopiable page 21 'Farmer rhyme'). Ask the children to chant the rhyme together. Ask, *How does Roald Dahl create the revolting characters?* Look at the descriptions of the farmers' behaviours, speech and hygiene.

Whole-class work
- Ask: *Who do you think is the worst farmer?* Using the interactive 'Bad farmer' on the CD-ROM, the children list each farmer's traits.

Paired work
- The children work in pairs to play 'Guess which farmer am I?'. They write the name of a farmer on a sticky note, but do not show their partner. They swap and without looking at the note, hold it against their foreheads. They ask 3 questions before guessing which farmer it is. For example, *Am I tall and thin?*

Whole-class work
- Thinking more about the characters, ask: *Who was the worst character? What was the worst thing the farmers did? Did they deserve to catch Mr Fox?*
- Discuss how Roald Dahl has captured the way the farmers speak and compare this to the children's speech and the narrator's 'voice'.
- Using the Shamblespad, show the children that when you type, it appears on the screen. The web address can be entered on another computer and a second person can now type on the screen at the same time. On the right-hand side, there is an icon with a picture of a person – this is the 'User' button. Click it and type in a name. As each person types on the page, their text has a different background colour.
- Divide the class into two groups, using two computers – computer 1 and computer 2. The children will be adding words to describe the features of the farmers. Ask group 1 for an adjective and enter it onto the online pad. Now ask group 2 for an adjective and type it in using computer two. The children should see the words appearing on the screens, as each computer is used.

Differentiation
- Support: Less confident learners may need support from adults to think of words to describe the farmers.
- Challenge: More confident learners could be typists for the online pad and add the adjectives, as the class suggests words.

Review
- Looking at the collaborative document, the children can see where each group has added adjectives. Explain that there are many different tools that can be used to collaborate and that these online tools can be accessed from anywhere in the world with an internet connection.

Curriculum objectives

● To understand computer networks including the internet; how they can provide multiple services, such as the World Wide Web; and the opportunities they offer for communication and collaboration.
● To use technology safely, respectfully and responsibly.

Lesson objectives

● To contribute to a document using collaborative technologies, such as a wiki.
● To respond to others' work on a collaborative document, such as a wiki, in a supportive, constructive way.
● To explain how using a wiki can help others to improve their ideas and think in new ways.

Expected outcomes

● Can use technology to collaborate effectively with others.
● Can explain how collaborative technologies can be used to help others.

Resources

Photocopiable page 21 'Farmer rhyme'; photocopiable page 22 'The fourth farmer'; interactive activity 'Spot the adjective' on the CD-ROM

The fourth farmer

The children collaborate to create a 'fourth' farmer. What will be his features? Will he be nice or nasty? What will he eat or drink? Using an online collaborative tool, the children will work together to design the new character. They will try to extend the rhyme to include him in the farmer rhyme.

Introduction

● Introduce the lesson by saying *There's a fourth farmer!* The children will invent a truly horrid fourth farmer character. What will they say, look like and do?
● Read the farmer rhyme of 'Boggis, Bunce and Bean' (see photocopiable page 21 'Farmer rhyme') and the children can chant it together again. Use interactive activity 'Spot the adjective' on the CD-ROM to look at the farmer rhyme and identify the adjectives describing them.

Paired work

● In pairs, the children discuss the features of the fourth farmer. Then, using photocopiable page 22 'The fourth farmer', they draw a picture of the new farmer, give them a name and add adjectives to describe them.

Whole-class work

● Bring the class together and share examples of the children's farmers.
● To create a new rhyme, similar to the last lesson, set up a collaborative online pad to gather ideas. Divide the class into two groups and nominate a typist for each one. The farmer rhyme can be modified to add in the new farmers.
● In the online pad, paste the farmer rhyme onto the page. Group 1 goes first and adds the name of a fourth farmer. For example, 'Boggis, Bunce and Bean' could become 'Boggis, Bunce, Bean and Brown'. Then Group 2 adds to the next line. For example, 'One short, one fat, one lean' could become 'One short, one fat, one lean, one scrawny'. The groups take turns to add words.

> ### Differentiation
> ● Support: Less confident learners may need support to think of more than one adjective.
> ● Challenge: More confident learners can create several adjectives, to describe the character.

Review

● Display the new rhyme, so that all the children can see it. Together, they chant the new rhyme (it may not rhyme or scan well, with the extra words, but read it all together).
● Finally, each group decide upon a comment that could be added to give feedback for the other group. Can they think of a comment that is 'kind, specific and helpful'? Add the comment to the online pad.
● Remind the children that there are many different online tools, such as wikis. In their lessons, they have used an online word processor called an Etherpad to collaborate. Explain that a large wiki, such as Wikipedia, enables large numbers of people to share their knowledge and ideas and also helps other people develop their thinking and understanding.
● Leave them with the thought that the two groups could have been in different rooms, school or countries. All they would need would be a connection to the large network, called the internet.

Curriculum objectives
• To understand computer networks including the internet; how they can provide multiple services, such as the World Wide Web; and the opportunities they offer for communication and collaboration.
• To use technology safely, respectfully and responsibly.

Lesson objectives
• To recognise simple computer networks around them.
• To sketch a simple diagram of a computer network.
• To contribute to a document using collaborative technologies, such as a wiki.

Expected outcomes
• Can know that networks can be wired or wireless.
• Can create a simple diagram of the computer network.
• Can explain how computers can help others.

Resources
Photocopiable page 23 'Networks'; *Fantastic Mr Fox* by Roald Dahl

Roald Dahl: Assess and review

In this assess and review lesson, the children describe the differences between wired and wireless networks. They think about networks and sketch a simple diagram. Finally, they think about how collaboration online can be used to help others.

Introduction
• Introduce the lesson by re-reading part of *Fantastic Mr Fox*, especially the part that describes the tunnel network and the end where the other animals are invited to live together.
• Ask: *Can you remember the network of tunnels? Can you remember what was similar between the tunnel network and the computer network?*

Independent work
• Using photocopiable page 23 'Networks', the children draw a diagram of a simple network. The aim of the activity is to see whether they can remember the diagram of a simple network, as an assessment task.

Whole-class work
• Remind the children about the tour of the school and spotting wired and wireless computer connections to the network.
• Ask: *How could you tell if the computer had a wired connection to the network?* (You could see the cable going from the computer into a network point on the wall).
• The children imagine they live in different countries, for example, the USA and the UK.
• Ask: *How could you communicate with each other in different countries? How could you use a computer network to communicate?*

Paired work
• In pairs, the children write a story, one line at a time, on the computer. If they used a wiki, such as Wikispaces (www.wikispaces.com/), they could structure a web page to contain the information. In this chapter, a simple online tool called an Etherpad has enabled collaboration.
• If there is access to two computers, each pair can share one Etherpad. They take turns to retell the story of *Fantastic Mr Fox*.
• Ask: *What is an advantage of working together online?*

Differentiation
• Support: Less confident learners could use the farmer rhyme to type one line at a time.
• Challenge: More confident learners could structure their story with headings 'Beginning', 'Middle' and 'End'.

Review
• Bring the class together, to review the learning. Ask the children to consider whether they know the answers to the questions:
• Ask: *Can you explain what a computer network is?*
Ask: *Can you explain the difference between wired and wireless networks?*
Ask: *Can you give an example of how a computer network enables people to help others?*

My networks

■ Complete the network drawing.

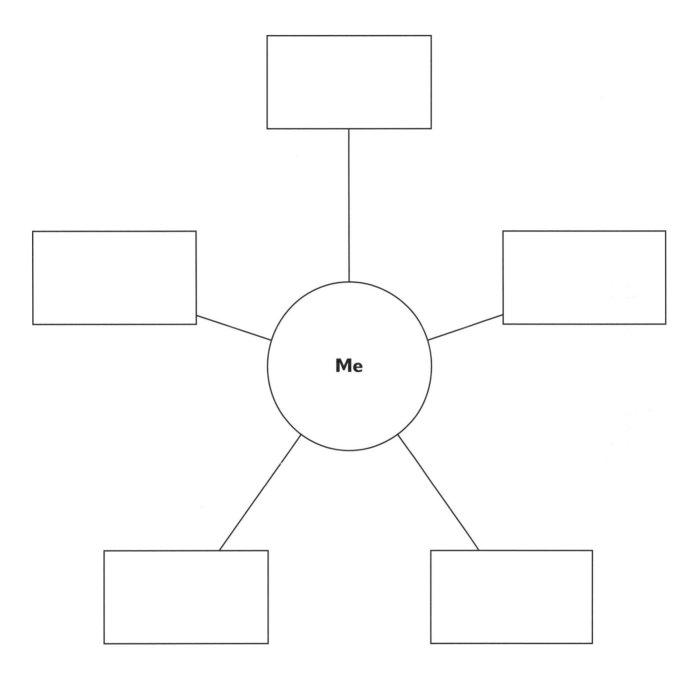

I can draw a basic network.

How did you do?

PHOTOCOPIABLE

Tunnels network and a computer network

■ Draw the tunnel network from *Fantastic Mr Fox*.

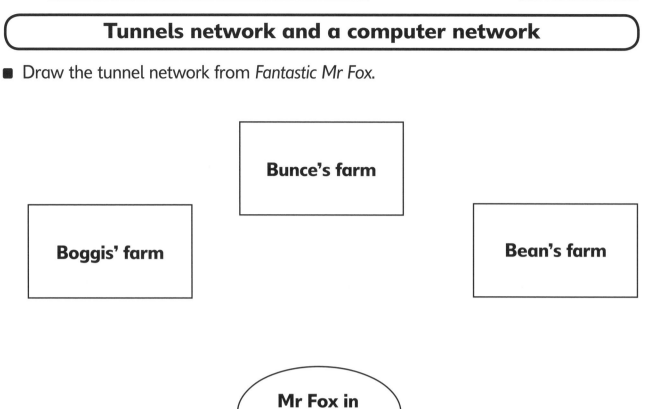

Bunce's farm

Boggis' farm

Bean's farm

Mr Fox in

his den

■ Draw a simple network drawing.

NETWORK HUB

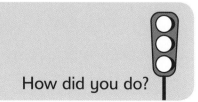

I can complete a simple network drawing.

How did you do?

PHOTOCOPIABLE

Foxes and geese

String telephones

What you need:

2 paper cups, a sharp pencil or sewing needle to poke holes, modelling clay, string.

■ Instructions:

1. Cut a long piece of string. Experiment with different lengths but perhaps 20m is a good place to start.

2. Poke a small hole in the bottom of each cup with the pencil or needle, pushing it into the modelling clay to make sure it is safe.

3. Thread the string through each cup and tie knots at each end to stop it pulling through the cup. (Or use a paper clip, washer or similar object to hold the string in place.)

4. Move into a position where you and a partner hold the cups at a distance that makes the string tight. (Make sure the string isn't touching anything else.)

5. One person talks into the cup while the other puts the cup to their ear and listens. Can you hear each other?

I can make a string telephone.

How did you do?

PHOTOCOPIABLE   ■SCHOLASTIC www.scholastic.co.uk

Farmer rhyme

■ Your teacher will read out a rhyme. Fill in the blanks.

_____ and _____ and _____

One _____, one _____, one _____.

These _____ crooks

So _____ in looks

Were none the less _____ mean.

■ Write the rhyme out again but replace the words you filled in with different words on lines two, three, four and five. Think of words with similar meanings.
■ Swap with a partner and read their words.

_____

_____

_____

_____

_____

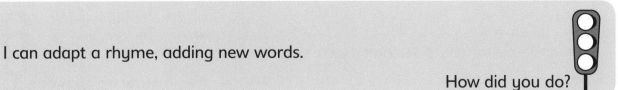

I can adapt a rhyme, adding new words.

How did you do?

The fourth farmer

■ Draw your farmer here.

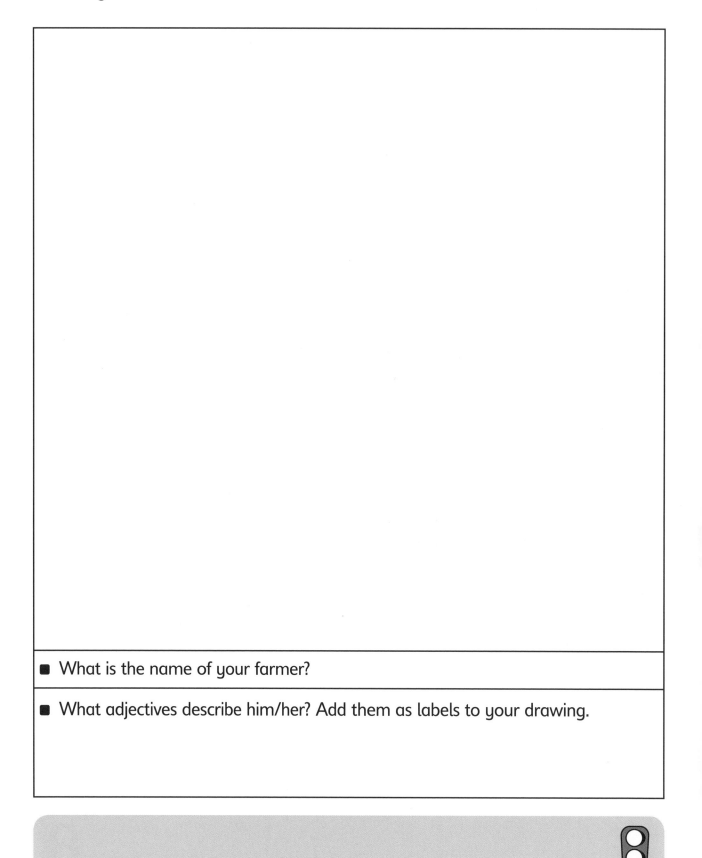

■ What is the name of your farmer?

■ What adjectives describe him/her? Add them as labels to your drawing.

I can draw a new character and describe them using adjectives.

How did you do?

Networks

- We have been looking at computer networks. Can you remember what a simple network looks like?
- Complete the diagram below.

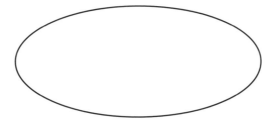

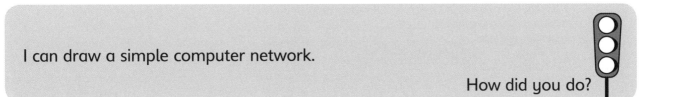

I can draw a simple computer network.

How did you do?

Robots

This chapter uses robots as a theme and builds on the knowledge and understanding of algorithms that children have developed in Key Stage 1. Key computational thinking skills such as problem solving and logical thinking are further developed together with the consolidation of algorithmic understanding around sequencing, flowcharts and repetition (loops). The concepts of composition and selection are introduced formally for the first time.

Expected prior learning

● The children have already been introduced to algorithms and programming in Key Stage 1, so have a solid understanding of algorithms and programming on which to build.

Chapter at a glance

Subject area
• Algorithms and programming

National Curriculum objective
• To debug programs that accomplish specific goals, including controlling or simulating physical systems; solve problems by decomposing them into smaller parts; use sequence and repetition in programs; use logical reasoning to explain how some simple algorithms work and to detect and correct errors in algorithms and programs.

Week	Lesson objectives	Summary of activities	Expected outcomes
1	• To understand that by breaking down larger problems into smaller parts, a problem is easier to solve. • To use logic and persistence to solve a variety of different problems and puzzles. • To begin to understand that a problem can sometimes be solved in a number of different ways. • To be able to explain the steps taken to solve the problems and puzzles.	• Children decompose the problem of sending a robot to the moon. • They solve a number of puzzles relating to sending a robot to the moon. • They discuss how they have solved the puzzle and arrived at their solution.	• Can solve problems by decomposing them into smaller parts. • Can use logical reasoning to be able to solve simple problems.
2	• To be able to break down simple goals into their composite parts in order to create an accurate algorithm, for example how to make a drink or sandwich. • To create algorithms that achieve a specific goal using repeats where appropriate, for example repeating the action of spreading butter. • To begin to understand how simple selection (if statements) can be used in algorithms. (For example, 'if the glass is full, then stop'.) • To be able to explain simply and verbally how their algorithms work.	• Children write algorithms for their robot to tell it how to eat and drink. • They add repetition and selection into algorithms. • They explain how the algorithms they have created work.	• Can use sequencing and repetition when writing simple algorithms and explain how they work. • Can use logical reasoning to include selection in simple algorithms and explain how they work.
3	• To recognise repetition and selection in algorithms in flowcharts. • To sequence flowcharts into the correct order to include repetition and selection. • To plan and create their own flowcharts using sequencing, repetition and selection. • To discuss the logical reasoning behind their flowchart.	• Children sequence flowcharts to include repetition and selection. • They create their own flowchart using repetition and selection. • They demonstrate to others how their flowchart works.	• Can use simple flowcharts to represent an algorithm. • Can use logical reasoning to explain how sequencing, repetition and selection apply to algorithms.

Week	Lesson objectives	Summary of activities	Expected outcomes
4	• To prepare accurate algorithms for a human robot to achieve specific goals. • To follow instructions given verbally and visually, through flowcharts, by their peers. • To work cooperatively to detect and correct any errors in instructions. • To explain why robots, or computers, need precise instructions to carry out specific tasks.	• Children write algorithms for a chosen task. • They follow algorithms created by others. • They debug algorithms. • They explain why computers need more accurate instructions than humans.	• Can explain how sequencing, repetition and selection work in algorithms. • Can understand that computers need more precise instructions than humans.
5	• To create a disguise for their robot using a template. • To write algorithms for their robot to achieve a range of outcomes, such as sending it to a specific place. • To understand that their algorithm will be executed by a program within the robot. • To program the robot to make it perform a variety of creative tasks, such as making it dance.	• Children create their own robot. • They write algorithms for their robot to achieve specific tasks. • They program the robot and debug their algorithm. • They explain to others that algorithms are executed by computers as programs.	• Can create programs that accomplish simple specific goals, including controlling or simulating physical systems. • Can solve problems by decomposing them into smaller parts.
6	• To recognise and correct errors in their own and peers' algorithms. • To refine algorithms and programs previously written for their robots to include repetition and selection where appropriate. • To be able to explain verbally how and why they have included repetition and selection.	• Children debug algorithms for a specific task, spotting and correcting errors. • They program their algorithms into Bee-Bots to test them out. • They add repetition and selection to algorithms. • They explain their understanding of repetition, selection and the debugging process.	• Can detect and correct errors in simple algorithms and programs. • Can use sequence and repetition in simple programs.
Assess and review	• Assess and review the half-term's work.	• Children write algorithms independently. • They draw a flowchart to represent their algorithm. • They explain how they have used repetition and selection in their algorithms.	• Assess and review.

Overview of progression

● Throughout the lessons the children build upon their knowledge and understanding of algorithms. They begin by using decomposition, problem solving and logical reasoning to solve a series of problems on a robots theme. They then write algorithms to solve their problems, using repetition and selection.

● Later on in the chapter, children implement their algorithms using a programmable floor robot (Bee-Bots) and make their robot perform a number of different commands, building on work completed in Key Stage 1.

● The children explain verbally their understanding of algorithms, using repetition and selection. This helps them become comfortable in sharing work with peers, which helps with collaborative debugging.

Creative context

● The lessons have links to the mathematics curriculum with children using logic puzzles, problem solving and flowcharts. The computing lessons also draw upon the children's learning in English, by asking them to plan and give exact instructions to their robot to make it perform the actions.

Background knowledge

● From the work completed in Key Stage 1, the children will know about sequencing, flowcharts, algorithms and programming and this understanding will be developed further in this chapter.

● From assessing children's understanding in the Key Stage 1 units, you will need to assess their capability in following and creating algorithms and provide additional support as necessary.

Curriculum objectives
● To debug programs that accomplish specific goals, including controlling or simulating physical systems; solve problems by decomposing them into smaller parts; use sequence and repetition in programs; use logical reasoning to explain how some simple algorithms work and to detect and correct errors in algorithms and programs.

Lesson objectives
● To understand that by breaking down larger problems into smaller parts, a problem is easier to solve.
● To use logic and persistence to solve a variety of different problems and puzzles.
● To begin to understand that a problem can sometimes be solved in a number of different ways.
● To be able to explain the steps taken to solve the problems and puzzles.

Expected outcomes
● Can know that networks can be wired or wireless.
● Can create a simple diagram of the computer network.
● Can explain how computers can help others.

Resources
Interactive activity 'Send Ravi Robot to the moon' on the CD-ROM; photocopiable page 'Mission to the moon (1)' from the CD-ROM; photocopiable page 'Mission to the moon (2)' from the CD-ROM

Mission to the moon

Introduce the children to this chapter by using their decomposition skills to come up with sub-solutions to the larger problem of sending their robot to the moon. They will develop their logical thinking and problem-solving skills as they solve a variety of puzzles, helping them to understand that problems can often be solved in different ways.

Introduction
● Ask the children to share what they know about visiting the moon.
● Explain that in this lesson they will be working on a mission to send a robot to the moon.

Whole-class work
● Display the interactive activity 'Send Ravi Robot to the moon' from the CD-ROM and discuss with the children that they will be sending Ravi to the moon.
● Ask them what they need to do to send Ravi to the moon and make a list on the board. This should hopefully include making the rocket, astronaut training, blasting off, flying the rocket to the moon and landing on the moon, all of which are shown on screen 3 of the interactive activity.
● Explain to the children that they have used *decomposition* to break down the problem of sending Ravi to the moon into smaller parts and that each group will now work on a separate part of the problem.

Group work
● Give out the photocopiable pages 'Mission to the moon (1)' and 'Mission to the moon (2)' from the CD-ROM. Different groups could do different missions.
● Explain to the children that they need to work in their group to solve the problems on their sheet.
● Explain that the first puzzles are to help them to 'think like a robot' to be able to help Ravi in the best way.
● Once they think they have finished, they should swap with another group that has the same sheet and discuss their answers. They may find that they have different ideas, and you can use this as an opportunity to discuss with them that there are often different solutions to the same problem.

Differentiation
● Support: Less confident learners may benefit from mixed-ability groupings and can be given one of the more straightforward tasks.
● Challenge: More confident learners could take an additional part of the problem, which the class may have identified in the initial class discussion, and work on creating a list of instructions to complete that section, or be given one of the other missions to work on too.

Review
● Encourage the children to explain the steps they took to solve their puzzles.
● As a class show screen 3 of the media resource 'Send Ravi Robot to the moon' and use it as stimulus to discuss the children's solutions to each part of the mission.
● Once you have finished, discuss with the children how they think they have solved the problem collectively. Ask: *Do you think Ravi will get to the moon? What parts of your solution might you need to look at in more detail for a successful mission?* (This would be decomposing their problem further.)
● Discuss with the children that they have been using *decomposition* and ask them to explain the concept. Explain that this is a very important part of computing and programming and is used by all computer scientists, including those at NASA who plan real rocket trips to the moon!
● You could use NASA's online resource http://trainlikeanastronaut.org/ for further discussion.
● Assess the children's progress through class discussion and responses to the group missions.

Curriculum objectives
● To debug programs that accomplish specific goals, including controlling or simulating physical systems; solve problems by decomposing them into smaller parts; use sequence and repetition in programs; use logical reasoning to explain how some simple algorithms work and to detect and correct errors in algorithms and programs.

Lesson objectives
● To be able to break down simple goals into their composite parts in order to create an accurate algorithm, for example how to make a drink or sandwich.
● To create algorithms that achieve a specific goal using repeats where appropriate, for example repeating the action of spreading butter.
● To begin to understand how simple selection (if statements) can be used in algorithms. (For example, 'if the glass is full, then stop'.)
● To be able to explain simply and verbally how their algorithms work.

Expected outcomes
● Can use sequencing and repetition when writing simple algorithms and explain how they work.
● Can use logical reasoning to include selection in simple algorithms and explain how they work.

Resources
Media resource, 'Help Ravi eat and drink' on the CD-ROM; sandwich making equipment if wished (you would need two slices of bread, butter, cheese slice, plastic butter knife, plate); photocopiable page 33 'How to make a glass of squash'

Writing algorithms for Ravi Robot

In this lesson, the children write algorithms to help Ravi the Robot eat and drink before his mission to the moon. They will identify opportunities for using repetition and selection and include these in their algorithms.

Introduction
● Remind the children of the work they completed in the last lesson in which they helped Ravi to get to the moon.
● Show screen 1 of the media resource 'Help Ravi eat and drink' and explain that before Ravi goes he wants to make sure that he has some food and drink.

Whole class work
● Explain to the children that Ravi is a robot so he only understands algorithms. Their mission today is to create an algorithm to help Ravi make a sandwich and a glass of squash.
● Ask the children to suggest instructions that Ravi would need to make a sandwich. If you wish, you could actually create a sandwich in class to help them understand the process.
● Show screen 2 of the media resource on the CD-ROM, which shows the instructions of how to make a sandwich. Highlight that the instructions are exact and in order because Ravi can only follow the instructions he is given.
● Explain that they will now create instructions for making a glass of squash.

Paired/group work
● Hand out the photocopiable page 33 'How to make a glass of squash'.
● Explain that the children's first task to help Ravi is to write down a list of instructions for what he needs to do in as much detail as possible.

Whole-class work
● Ask the children to share their instructions and remind them that often algorithms can be made more effective by using repetition and selection, for example using 'repeat this action' and 'if this happens then do this'. Explain that Ravi likes to be able to repeat instructions when he can and also likes to be told when to do, or stop something.
● Show screen 2 of the media resource. Ask the children to identify where repetition and selection could occur in the instructions (repeat action of putting the butter on both slices of bread; if the bread is covered in butter then stop).
● Show screen 3 of the media resource, which shows repetition and selection represented in the instructions.
● Ask the children to look again at their completed instructions on the photocopiable page and identify where repetition and selection could occur (repeat the action of adding water; if the glass is full, then stop).

> ### Differentiation
> ● Support: Less confident learners may benefit from mixed-ability pairings and may need further adult support in writing their instructions. They should be encouraged to write a simple list of the actions needed.
> ● Challenge: More confident learners will be able to write more detailed instructions and should be encouraged to 'think like a robot', breaking each task down into smaller tasks. For example, *How could 'spread the butter on the bread' be broken down?*

Review
● Ask the children to share their instructions with you, or a volunteer, miming the actions or using sandwich making equipment.
● Ask others in the class to debug them if needed, coming up with a final list of detailed instructions to help Ravi. Questions to assess their level of understanding include: *How did you work out what instructions to include? How did you break down the instructions into smaller parts? How did you use repetition/selection in your algorithm?*

Curriculum objectives

Curriculum objectives
● To debug programs that accomplish specific goals, including controlling or simulating physical systems; solve problems by decomposing them into smaller parts; use sequence and repetition in programs; use logical reasoning to explain how some simple algorithms work and to detect and correct errors in algorithms and programs.

Lesson objectives
● To recognise repetition and selection in algorithms in flowcharts.
● To sequence flowcharts into the correct order to include repetition and selection.
● To plan and create their own flowcharts using sequencing, repetition and selection.
● To discuss the logical reasoning behind their flowchart.

Expected outcomes
● Can use simple flowcharts to represent an algorithm.
● Can use logical reasoning to explain how sequencing, repetition and selection apply to algorithms.

Resources
Media resource 'Help Ravi eat and drink' on the CD-ROM; interactive activity 'Making a sandwich flowchart' on the CD-ROM; interactive activity 'Making a glass of squash flowchart' on the CD-ROM; completed photocopiable page 33 'How to make a glass of squash' from last lesson (if wished)

Repetition and selection in flowcharts

Building on the previous lesson's work, the children create flowcharts from the algorithms they designed in the last lesson. They start off sequencing flowcharts in the correct order and then create their own, adding repetition and selection where appropriate. This helps them to explain how their flowchart can help Ravi to eat and drink.

Introduction
● Remind the children that they have been creating algorithms and including selection and repetition in their algorithms.
● Show them screen 4 from the media resource 'Help Ravi eat and drink' to remind them how selection and repetition helped to make their algorithm for making a sandwich easier for Ravi to follow.
● Explain that in this lesson they will be giving Ravi instructions using a flowchart, which makes it even easier for him to follow the instructions they give him.

Whole-class work
● Display the interactive activity 'Making a sandwich flowchart' on the CD-ROM on the board and ask volunteers to drag and drop the instructions into the correct box.
● Highlight to the children the different-shaped boxes and the fact that they are giving Ravi instructions to repeat and where they are using selection to tell him to stop (the repeat action of putting the butter on both slices of bread, if the bread is fully buttered then stop).
● Explain to them that they are going to do the same thing but this time for making a glass of squash.

Independent/paired work
● Ask the children to access the interactive activity 'Making a glass of squash flowchart' on the CD-ROM and explain that they need to drag and drop the instructions into the correct box.
● You may find it helpful to give them back their completed photocopiable page 33 'How to make a glass of squash' from the last lesson for this task.

Differentiation
● Support: Mixed-ability pairings may be useful for the flowchart exercise and less confident learners may benefit from working with adult support to help with their flowchart.
● Challenge: More confident learners could use the same format to write an algorithm and flowchart on paper for drinking a glass of squash.

Review
● As a class, go through the interactive activity 'Making a glass of squash flowchart' on the CD-ROM, asking the children to share their reasoning as you go.
● Ask the children to review their work as you do this and identify any errors they have made. Hopefully these will be minor errors. However, if there are common misunderstandings, you may need to take time to go through the whole activity as a class.
● Questions to help you assess their progress include: *Why did you decide to put that instruction there? Why did you repeat that instruction? What is that instruction telling Ravi to do? What do you think the different shapes in the flowchart are for?*
● Review the children's progress through their discussions and the outcomes of the 'Making a glass of squash flowchart' interactive activity.

Writing and following algorithms

In this lesson children write their own algorithms, which include repetition and selection for others to follow, and follow algorithms written by others. This naturally leads to a collaborative process of debugging and to understanding that if they are acting as robots, they have to have very detailed, accurate and specific instructions to follow.

Introduction

● Remind the children that in the last lesson they were creating algorithms using flowcharts to help Ravi to eat and drink.
● Explain that in this lesson they will be writing their own algorithms from scratch and giving them to a partner, who will be acting as Ravi, to follow.
● Remind them of the term 'debug' and ask them to explain its meaning. Explain that they will be working together to debug their algorithms.

Whole-class work

● Display the photocopiable page 34 'Ravi's tasks' and explain that Ravi is now on the moon and has some jobs to do!
● Pick one of the tasks and ask for a volunteer to act as Ravi while the rest of the class give instructions to help Ravi carry out the task.
● Highlight to the children any opportunities for using repetition or selection in the task and encourage the class to debug each other's instructions. You could write down the instructions on the board as the children give them to help with this.

Independent/paired work

● Give the children photocopiable page 34 'Ravi's tasks' and ask them to pick one of the tasks to work on.
● Explain that they should first work together to create an algorithm to complete their chosen task, using selection and repetition where they think they should.
● Once they think they have finished their algorithm, they should take turns in being 'Ravi' while the other child gives instructions. Then they should debug their algorithm and swap their roles to try again with their improved algorithm.
● Once they think they have a perfect algorithm for Ravi, give them photocopiable page 35 'Ravi's task flowchart' and ask them to try to draw a simple flowchart for their algorithm, using the example as a guide.

Differentiation

● Support: Less confident learners may need support with writing the algorithm for their task and mixed-ability pairings may help. You may also wish to ask them to just write the algorithm, rather than the algorithm and the flowchart.
● Challenge: More confident learners can create algorithms and flowcharts for more than one of Ravi's tasks.

Review

● Ask for volunteer pairs to act out their algorithms with one of them giving instructions and the other being Ravi. As they do so, other pairs who have completed the same task can share how they have done it differently, again illustrating that there is often more than one way to solve a problem.
● If you have time, ask the children to draw their flowchart on the board and repeat the same process, asking the others if they did anything differently.
● Ask the children to explain why, when they were being Ravi, they needed very precise instructions and use this to emphasise that robots and computers need very clear and exact instructions to know what we want them to do.
● Review children's progress through their discussions and outcomes of their paired work.

Curriculum objectives
● To debug programs that accomplish specific goals, including controlling or simulating physical systems; solve problems by decomposing them into smaller parts; use sequence and repetition in programs; use logical reasoning to explain how some simple algorithms work and to detect and correct errors in algorithms and programs.

Lesson objectives
● To create a disguise for their robot using a template.
● To write algorithms for their robot to achieve a range of outcomes, such as sending it to a specific place.
● To understand that their algorithm will be executed by a program within the robot.
● To program the robot to make it perform a variety of creative tasks, such as making it dance.

Expected outcomes
● Can create programs that accomplish simple specific goals, including controlling or simulating physical systems.
● Can solve problems by decomposing them into smaller parts.

Resources
Bee-Bots; photocopiable page 36 'Ravi template'; variety of craft materials; photocopiable page 37 'Ravi's algorithms'; space for the Bee-Bots and children to move around

Creating and programming Ravi

In this fun lesson, the children are reminded that a program executes an algorithm as they use a Bee-Bot, or similar programmable floor robot, to implement the algorithms that they write. They are given creative scope to create a disguise for their robot and write algorithms for a variety of purposes, debugging their program as they go. They are also given the opportunity to share their work with others and explain their understanding that algorithms are executed by computers as programs.

Introduction
● Remind the children that last lesson they were creating algorithms and flowcharts for Ravi to follow and that they were 'being' Ravi.
● Explain that in today's lesson they will be creating their own Ravi using a template and the Bee-Bots (you could show them one you have prepared earlier).
● Explain that they will also then be programming their Ravi Bee-Bots to perform a variety of tasks of their choice.

Whole-class/group work
● Show the children the prepared photocopiable page 36 'Ravi template' and explain how this is like a jacket that can fit on the Bee-Bot. Show them the materials they can use and tell them they can be as creative as they wish.
● Depending on the number of Bee-Bots you have, ask the children to create their Ravi Robot disguise.
● Once they have done so, ask them to come up with some ideas for tasks that Ravi could undertake in the classroom. For example, he might feel thirsty and need to get to the sink, or he might want to hide from one of the other robots.
● Give the children photocopiable page 37 'Ravi's algorithms' and ask them to write the task they come up with and the algorithm they will use.
● Once they have shown you their algorithm and explained how it will work, they program Ravi to complete the task, debugging their program as they go.

Differentiation
● Support: Less confident learners could work in a small group with adult support to help write down their algorithms. You may also wish to give them further help in programming the Bee-Bot.
● Challenge: More confident learners could write flowcharts for their algorithms and be encouraged to design more complex tasks and algorithms, for example dodging several obstacles.

Review
● As a class, share some of the tasks and algorithms that the children have developed, asking volunteers to program the Bee-Bots.
● You could award certificates or prizes for the best disguise and the most creative algorithm.
● You could photograph the children's work for a display and assess their progress through their written algorithms and class discussion/demonstration.

Curriculum objectives
● To debug programs that accomplish specific goals, including controlling or simulating physical systems; solve problems by decomposing them into smaller parts; use sequence and repetition in programs; use logical reasoning to explain how some simple algorithms work and to detect and correct errors in algorithms and programs.

Lesson objectives
● To recognise and correct errors in their own and peers' algorithms.
● To refine algorithms and programs previously written for their robots to include repetition and selection where appropriate.
● To be able to explain verbally how and why they have included repetition and selection.

Expected outcomes
● Can detect and correct errors in simple algorithms and programs.
● Can use sequence and repetition in simple programs.

Resources
Bee-Bots with their disguises from Week 5; space for the Bee-Bots and children to move around; photocopiable page 38 'Algorithms written by Ravi'

Debugging and improving programs

In this lesson, the children build on the Bee-Bot work they completed in Week 5 and combine this with the knowledge and understanding they now have about using repetition and selection in algorithms. They will learn that while Bee-Bots can be used for simple programming, there are more effective programs for implementing algorithms that require selection and repetition.

Introduction
● Recap the last lesson with the children, reminding them that they created their own Ravi the Robot and created algorithms for him to perform different tasks in the classroom.
● Explain that in this lesson they will be using their *debugging* skills, together with repetition and selection to make their own and other people's algorithms and programs more efficient.
● Ask the children to give examples of repetition and selection and discuss why Ravi likes to use these.

Whole-class work
● Show the children photocopiable page 38 'Algorithms written by Ravi' and explain that Ravi has been trying to write his own algorithms and programs, but he has not quite got them right!
● Depending on the children's confidence, you may wish to go through the first algorithm as a class and leave them to do the second one, or you may feel happy to let them try both.

Paired/group work
● Give the children photocopiable page 38 'Algorithms written by Ravi' and explain that they need to spot the mistakes and rewrite the algorithm.
● Let them know that they can use the Bee-Bot to help them work out the correct sequence.
● Tell them that they can use repetition and selection in their algorithms, although you need to explain that the Bee-Bot will only allow them to use repetition in their actual program, not selection.
● Once the children have completed their algorithm, they should swap with a partner/other group and test and debug them. Ask: *Are there any differences? Which one is correct? What needs to be changed, if anything?* If possible, they could program their algorithms into different Bee-Bots at the same time to see whether different algorithms can solve the same problem.

Differentiation
● Support: Less confident learners will benefit from mixed-ability groupings and may need help in writing their algorithms.
● Challenge: More confident learners could help others to debug their work and could write their own algorithms for Ravi using repetition and then programming the Bee-Bot to test and debug these.

Review
● Review the algorithms the children have written for each of the tasks, programming them into the Bee-Bot and asking them to explain their use of repetition. You could create a whole-class algorithm on the board if you wish.
● Encourage the children to discuss how they approached debugging Ravi's algorithms.
● Ask them to identify where they would use selection in their algorithms and explain that it is not possible to program selection into a Bee-Bot. Discuss how there are different types of programs that can be used for different purposes and explain that the next time they study algorithms and programming they will be using the programming software Scratch (Spring 2).
● Assess the children's understanding from their group work and the review discussion.

Curriculum objectives
● To debug programs that accomplish specific goals, including controlling or simulating physical systems; solve problems by decomposing them into smaller parts; use sequence and repetition in programs; use logical reasoning to explain how some simple algorithms work and to detect and correct errors in algorithms and programs.

Lesson objectives
● To create accurate algorithms to achieve a specific outcome.
● To include repetition and selection in algorithms.
● To plan and create flowchart representations of algorithms.
● To explain the use of repetition and selection in algorithms.

Expected outcomes
● Can create accurate, precise algorithms that contain repetition and selection.
● Can explain how repetition and selection work in their algorithm.

Resources
Interactive activity 'Guide Ravi's rocket' on the CD-ROM; photocopiable page 39 'Independent tasks'; video camera/audio recording device

Robots: Assess and review

This lesson provides an opportunity to review the key learning points from the chapter. The children write an algorithm for their chosen task using selection and repetition where appropriate. They then represent their algorithm in a flowchart. Through the outcomes of children's work and observation, you can undertake teacher assessment, review aspects of the chapter and adjust future learning as necessary.

Introduction
● Remind the children that throughout this chapter they have been creating algorithms using the theme of Ravi the Robot and have been adding repetition and selection to their algorithms. You may wish to remind them of the making a sandwich/glass of squash algorithms at this point.
● Explain that in this lesson they will choose one task to work on to show you how much they know about algorithms and using repetition and selection.
● Display photocopiable page 39 'Independent tasks' and go through the tasks with the children, explaining the requirements briefly as appropriate.
● Depending on the children's confidence you may wish to give them further guidance in the steps needed for each task.

Independent work
● The children should work through their chosen task (or the appropriate task) as independently as possible.
● They can also access the interactive activity 'Guide Ravi's rocket' on the CD-ROM. This activity asks children to create an algorithm which will move the rocket to a planet. A more challenging task would be creating an algorithm which visits both planets.

Differentiation
● Support: You may wish to allocate tasks to all children, particularly less confident learners who you should ask to complete the algorithm, rather than the flowchart.
● Challenge: Encourage more confident learners to complete the flowchart as well as the algorithm. They should be able to complete the task with full independence.

Review
● Ask the children to explain their algorithm and how they have used selection and repetition. You could video or record their answers to use in assessment if possible or wished.
● Assess the children's progress by their response to the independent task and their explanation of their algorithm.

How to make a glass of squash

■ Write down how you make a drink on Earth. The first instruction is done for you.

1. Take a glass.

I can write instructions for making a glass of squash.

How did you do?

Ravi's tasks

■ Pick one of the tasks below and write an algorithm for Ravi to follow.

Collect moon rocks to bring back to Earth.

Check moon craters for aliens.

Fix the five broken pieces of his rocket with his screwdriver.

I can write instructions for Ravi to follow.

How did you do?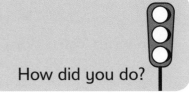

PHOTOCOPIABLE

SCHOLASTIC
www.scholastic.co.uk

Ravi's task flowchart

■ Here is an example flowchart which tells Ravi how to clean his rocket. Use it to help you draw your own flowchart based on the algorithm you have created.

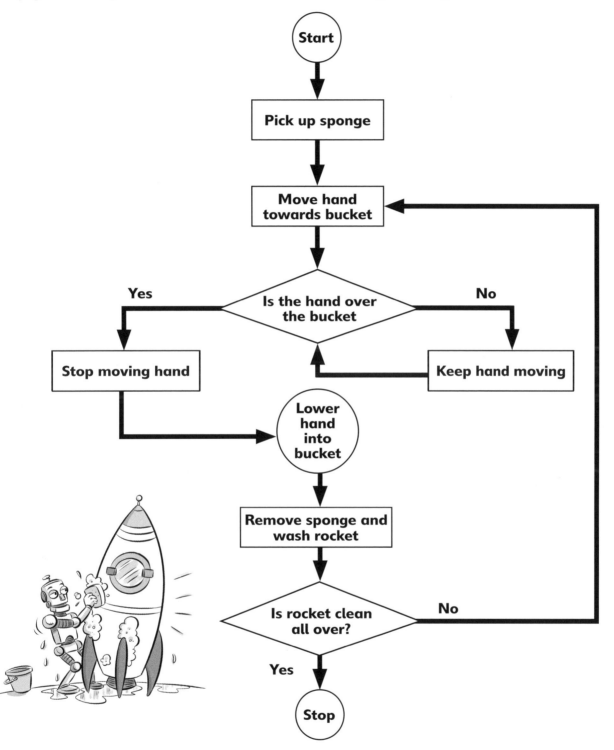

■ Draw your own flowchart on another piece of paper.

I can draw a flowchart to give a robot instructions.

How did you do?

Ravi template

■ Design your own robot here using the template.

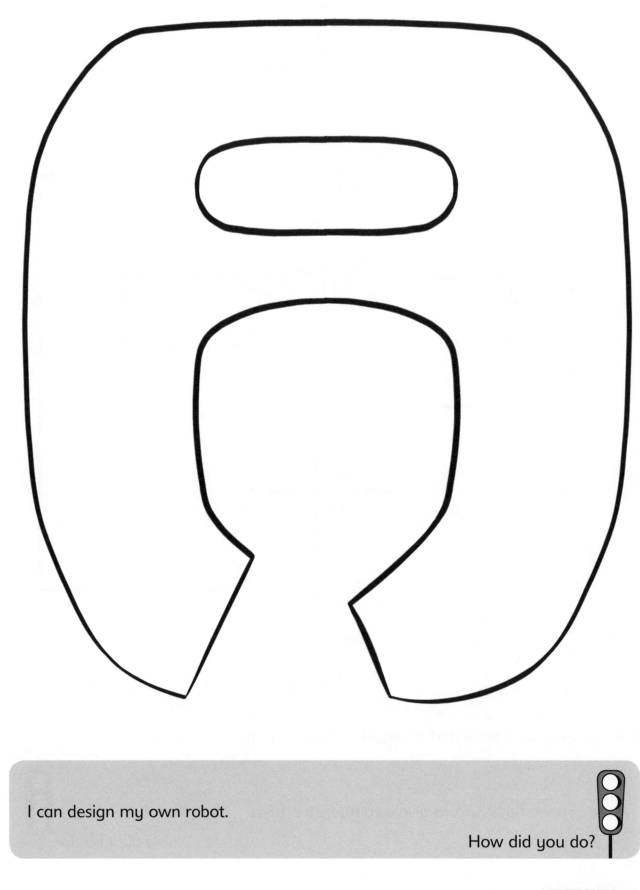

I can design my own robot.

How did you do?

PHOTOCOPIABLE

■ SCHOLASTIC
www.scholastic.co.uk

Ravi's algorithms

- Think about some tasks you can give Ravi in the classroom.
- What will your algorithm make Ravi do?
- Write your algorithm in the box below.

I can write an algorithm to ask Ravi to do things.

How did you do?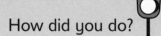

Algorithms written by Ravi

■ What is wrong with these algorithms? Can you find the problem and help Ravi?

1. Ravi wants to turn in a circle. He thinks this algorithm is correct. Can you help him?

Start
Turn right
Forward
Turn left
Stop

Write the correct algorithm here.

2. Ravi wants to go in a diagonal line across the room. He thinks this algorithm is correct. Can you help him?

Start
Go forward
Go forward
Go forward
Go forward
Go forward
Stop

Write the correct algorithm here.

3. Ravi wants to go zig zag among some obstacles. He thinks this algorithm is correct. Can you help him?

Start
Go forward
Turn left
Go forward
Turn left
Go forward
Go forward
Stop

Write the correct algorithm here.

I can give directions for Ravi to follow.

How did you do?

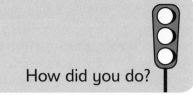

PHOTOCOPIABLE

Name: _____   Date: _____

Independent tasks

■ Choose one of the tasks below. Use extra paper if needed.

Task 1:
■ Ravi has decided to come home! Write an algorithm to tell Ravi how to fly his rocket back down to Earth.

Task 2:
■ Write an algorithm to tell Ravi how to land his rocket.
■ Can you use your algorithm to draw a flowchart for Ravi to follow? Use 'Ravi's task flowchart' from p35 to help you.

I can draw a flowchart for Ravi to follow.

How did you do?

Kings, queens and castles

This chapter engages the children in the topic of kings, queens and castles. This could be from fiction, with fairy tales, or non-fiction, looking at real castles. The children may visit a castle or use a virtual tour to think about its main features. The aim of the chapter is to think about communication. The children search for information online, thinking about the search terms they use and how they can narrow the search. The children look at presentations and decide what would improve them, before creating their own.

Expected prior learning

● The children will be familiar with searching online – most likely they say 'Google it' if they want to search for information. Also, children will be familiar with YouTube and watching videos about different topics. In this chapter, they consider how to narrow their searches.

● With presentations, the children have presented before in their English lessons, for example, about a favourite toy. So, they know that they need to speak clearly and share the information. They may not have presented using software to share their images, video, audio and text.

Chapter at a glance

Subject area
• Communication

National Curriculum objective
• To use search technologies effectively. • To use technology safely, respectfully and responsibly.

Week	Lesson objectives	Summary of activities	Expected outcomes
1	• To be able to use a child-friendly search engine accurately for simple research. • To understand how focused search terms can return the most accurate results. • To find specific information about a particular topic (their chosen king, queen or castle). • To begin to understand which websites are likely to be the most trustworthy.	• Children describe the features of castles, for example corridors, stairs, and so on. • They are asked questions about the castle, for example When was it built? • They think about where they can find out this information: person, book, online. • Using a search engine they use keywords to find out information and decide if it is trustworthy.	• Can use search technologies effectively. • Can locate specific information by using a search engine.
2	• To be able to narrow searches by type (for example, image, video) and time (most recent). • To understand how basic Boolean searching (+, -) and basic advanced tools (for example, size of image) can be used to return more accurate results. • To use basic advanced searching techniques to research more accurate information about their chosen king, queen or castle.	• With reference to the narrow staircases of a castle the children find out that their searches can be narrowed as well. • They search for an image, a video and a recent item. • They are introduced to '+' when searching to mean 'and'. • And '–' to remove an item.	• Can use search technologies effectively to search for a variety of media. • Can use Boolean and advanced searching to narrow search results in simple ways.
3	• To identify effective and poor presentations. • To devise a list of key elements of effective presentations. • To understand how to use images, text, colour and themes sparingly to enhance a presentation. • To understand the importance of paper planning. • To create a simple storyboard for a five-slide presentation.	• Children read the story The princess and the pea by Lauren Child and learn that castles are classic fairy tale settings. • They decide what the main features of the story are to prepare a five-slide presentation.	• Can identify key elements of an effective presentation. • Can plan simple, effective designs on paper.

Week	Lesson objectives	Summary of activities	Expected outcomes
4	• To use presentation software to create five slides. • To add appropriate and effective text and images to their presentation. • To give and receive effective feedback on the first drafts of presentations.	• Using the *King Midas* and *The emperor's new clothes* stories, children find out that in some stories the king is shown to be silly. • They look at a 'silly' presentation (unreadable text, clashing colours, unrelated pictures) and discuss what they would change. • They work together to identify effective text and images for their presentations. • Children are introduced to the basic function of the hard drive.	• Can create a simple five-slide presentation. • Can add simple text and images to their presentation.
5	• To enhance their presentation with colour and themes/background as appropriate. • To add animations to their work as appropriate. • To discuss why such elements should be used sparingly. • To know how to print out their presentation in different views.	• Children continue to work on their presentations and consider using animated slides. • They print out their presentation so they can use it as a prompt.	• Can add other elements, such as colour and themes to their presentation as appropriate. • Can add animation to their work if appropriate.
6	• To know how to deliver an effective presentation to an audience. • To give their presentation to their peers. • To give and receive feedback on their presentations.	• Children deliver their presentation to their peers. • They focus on 'kind, specific and helpful feedback' when reviewing the presentations.	• Can present their work to their peers.
Assess and review	• Assess and review the half term's work.	• Children research a king or queen and decide on search terms. • They give feedback on a presentation and make sure it is kind, specific and helpful.	• Assess and review.

Overview of progression
● The children progress their knowledge of using search engines by considering the search terms they use and by adding '+' and '−' in between. They begin to use the advanced search features to narrow their searches.
● They have given simple oral presentations in English lessons, so the children need to think about how they can use software to enhance their talks. They look at 'silly' presentations and think about how to improve them. This progresses their understanding of effective presentations. Finally, they respond to the presentations, developing their skills in giving 'kind, specific and helpful' feedback.

Creative context
● The lessons link closely to the English curriculum in the presentations, using simple organisational devices such as headings and subheadings, using conjunctions, adverbs and prepositions to express time and cause. They discuss and record ideas to plan their talks.
● Further links with the English curriculum involve assessing the effectiveness of their own and others' writing.
● In maths, the children consider the logic of 'adding' search terms together and also 'minusing' terms, that is, search using the key terms, but they do not include results with this term.
● Linking with history and geography, they look at castles around the UK and can compare their features.

Background knowledge
● The children will have previous experience of searching for information online, for example, 'Googling' for information on a pop star. They may not have considered advanced search tools or how to narrow the search.
● With presentations, they may have seen teachers' presentations in lessons, but may not have considered the features that make up the presentation, for example, the text and images or the video and audio. They will have some experience of using presentation software, though this will vary across the class.
● For giving feedback on presentations, the children have been told to be kind when communicating face-to-face and online, so they should think about being kind when responding to others. They may not have thought about being specific or whether their advice is helpful. Can the other person act upon the feedback?

Curriculum objectives
● To use search technologies effectively.
● To use technology safely, respectfully and responsibly.

Lesson objectives
● To be able to use a child-friendly search engine accurately for simple research.
● To understand how focused search terms can return the most accurate results.
● To find specific information about a particular topic (their chosen king, queen or castle).
● To begin to understand which websites are likely to be the most trustworthy.

Expected outcomes
● Can use search technologies effectively.
● Can locate specific information by using a search engine.

Resources
Media resource 'Castles' on the CD-ROM; photocopiable page 49 'My castle'; photocopiable page 50 'Searching'

An introduction to kings, queens and castles

To start the topic, the children think about castles they have seen and visited. They consider the common features and draw their own pictures. How could they find out more information about castles? If they searched on the web, which words might they use as the 'search terms'? When they have found the information, how do they know it is reliable?

Introduction
● Introduce the lesson by displaying a picture of a castle (or use the media resource 'Castles' on the CD-ROM). Ask the children: *Have you ever been to a castle? Can you name it and say where it was? Do all castles look the same?*

Whole-class work
● Display a virtual tour of a castle (for example, Windsor Castle virtual tour http://www.bbc.co.uk/history/british/launch_vt_windsor_castle.shtml). Ask: *What are the features of castles?* (For example, turrets, stairs, corridors or dungeons). Collect the responses and display them.

Paired work
● In pairs, the children discuss the features of castles and draw an imaginary castle on photocopiable page 49 'My castle'. Ask: *Who lived in your castle? When was it built?* They invent answers to these questions.

Whole-class work
● Ask the children to share their pictures of castles and make a castles display.
● Returning to the original image of castles, ask the children: *Who lived here? When was it built?* They will not know the answers, so ask: *Where could you find out the answers?* If the children were in the castle, there might be a person or information board to explain. If they had a book about the castle, it could contain the answers. They might suggest looking on the web.
● Using a search engine, such as Google or Bing, type in the name 'Bodiam Castle'. The results include a link to a National Trust website and a Wikipedia page. On these pages, the children can find out information about castles.
● Explain that the words they used to search can be called the 'search terms'. In this case 'Bodiam' and 'castle'. Ask the children to think which words they would use to search for information about 'Windsor Castle', they should suggest 'Windsor' and 'castle'. Explain that they want to find out when Windsor Castle was built. They could type the whole sentence into the search box, for example, 'When was Windsor Castle built?'. However, this can be shortened to 'Windsor Castle built', without the 'was' and the question mark.
● Using photocopiable page 50 'Searching', the children suggest which search terms they would use to find information about something that interests them, for example a famous person, a hobby or an interesting place.

Differentiation
● Support: Less confident learners may need support to identify the features of a castle and then help to summarise the search terms.
● Challenge: More confident learners could compare the features of their castle drawings with the images of a real castle. They could add labels to describe the features.

Review
● Bring the class together and review the search terms that the children have chosen for each of the examples on the photocopiable page 50 'Searching'. Type their suggestions into the search box of the search engine and see the results that appear. Are these what they were looking for?
● Ask the children to think about the websites that they find. How do they know they can trust the information?

Curriculum objectives
- To use search technologies effectively.
- To use technology safely, respectfully and responsibly.

Lesson objectives
- To be able to narrow searches by type (for example, image, video) and time (most recent).
- To understand how basic Boolean searching (+, −) and basic advanced tools (for example, size of image) can be used to return more accurate results.
- To use basic advanced searching techniques to research more accurate information about their chosen king, queen or castle.

Expected outcomes
- Can use search technologies effectively to search for a variety of media.
- Can use Boolean and advanced searching to narrow search results in simple ways.

Resources
Media resource 'Castle corridor' on the CD-ROM; photocopiable page 51 'and'

Narrow corridors, narrow searches

Following on from the previous lesson, the children narrow their searches to find more accurate information. If they are looking specifically for images or videos, they need to adjust their search. If they want the most up-to-date information, they need to look at websites that have been updated recently.

Introduction
- Introduce the lesson by displaying a narrow corridor in a castle (see media resource 'Castle corridor' on the CD-ROM). Castles often have narrow corridors. Remind the children that in the last lesson they were searching for information and that those searches can be 'narrowed' too.
- Remind them that they searched using Google or Bing. These search engines have features that allow the results to be filtered, protecting the children. A quick way of 'switching on' the safety tools is to use 'Safe search' (http://primaryschoolict.com/). This is a custom search, based on the Google search engine. The children type in their enquiry and the filtered results are shown.

Whole-class work
- Demonstrate how to search using Safe Search, by typing in 'castles'. A list of websites is returned, but remind them that they need an image. From the Safe Search homepage, select the 'Image search' tab and then type 'castles'.

Paired work
- Pairs look for images of a castle, a king, a queen, a drawbridge and a knight.

Whole-class work
- Bring the class together and ask one child to demonstrate looking for an image. Demonstrate searching further while still keeping the safe search filter on. At the bottom of the Safe Search results, there is a link saying 'Teachers only! Advanced image search options and more images'. By clicking on the link, you can then modify the search, by size, colour, image style (clip art), time, usage rights and, in 'More tools', display the sizes of the images. Show the class how the results can be modified (within the safe search).
- The image search can be changed to look for recent items. The 'Time' drop-down tab can filter by past 24 hours, past week or a custom range. Demonstrate searching for images of kings and queens that have been shared in the past week.
- Explain that when they type words into the web search, they can be more accurate. If they were interested in 'Beauty and the Beast', they could type that into the search. However, we have suggested that they could type 'Beauty' 'Beast' to search. So, even though we have left out the 'and the', the search engine assumes it's there. This can also be written 'Beauty + Beast', the search engine will search for the word 'beauty' AND the word 'beast'. Using photocopiable page 51 'and', ask the children to explore replacing words with '+'.

Differentiation
- Support: Less confident learners may need support to read through their search terms and guidance on where to place the '+'.
- Challenge: More confident learners could create their own examples of search terms to use and where to use '+'.

Review
- Ask: *If you wanted to find out about a certain topic, but wanted to remove a particular result, how could you do that?* If they enter 'Queen Elizabeth' into the search, then most of the top results focus on Queen Elizabeth the Second (or Queen Elizabeth II). So, if the search is 'Queen Elizabeth –II', that is, Queen Elizabeth minus II, then additional results appear for Queen Elizabeth I.
- Conclude by explaining that when searching, they can add words together with a '+' and also take away or minus words, with a '−'.

Curriculum objectives
● To use search technologies effectively.
● To use technology safely, respectfully and responsibly.

Lesson objectives
● To identify effective and poor presentations.
● To devise a list of key elements of effective presentations.
● To understand how to use images, text, colour and themes sparingly to enhance a presentation.
● To understand the importance of paper planning is an important part of the design process.
● To create a simple storyboard for a five-slide presentation on their chosen king, queen or castle.

Expected outcomes
● Can identify key elements of an effective presentation.
● Can plan simple, effective designs on paper.

Resources
The Princess and the Pea by Lauren Child; interactive activity 'Poor presentations' on the CD-ROM; photocopiable page 52 'Bad to good presentations'; photocopiable page 53 'My five slides'

Presenting: what is important?

The children think about presentations they have seen, where slides were used to support the talk. They will have given short oral presentations to their peers in English lessons, so now they explore the features of using software to enhance the experience.

Introduction
● Introduce the lesson by reading a fairy story, for example *The Princess and the Pea* retold by Lauren Child. Explain that castles are often settings for classic fairy tales.
● Ask: *What were the key points in the story?* They should point out many features, but the main point was that the princess had to detect the pea under all of the mattresses.
● Watch the short animation 'The princess and the dragon' (http://learnenglishkids.britishcouncil.org/en/short-stories/the-princess-and-the-dragon). Ask: *What is the key point in the story?*

Whole-class work
● Explain to the children that they are going to research on the web for information about castles. Once they have gathered their information, they will display it as a five-slide presentation. To begin with, they will look at some poor presentations.

Paired work
● Using the interactive activity 'Poor presentations' on the CD-ROM, allow the children to identify what is wrong with the presentations. Once complete, ask the children to identify the features of a poor presentation (using photocopiable page 52 'Bad to good presentations').

Whole-class work
● When the children have worked on a couple of the presentations on the photocopiable page 'Bad to good presentations', bring the class together and ask for examples of poor presentations. Now ask them to think of the opposite feature. For example, for the problem of images overlapping with the text, the opposite would be images not overlapping with the text. Ask for further examples, before the children return to complete the photocopiable sheet.
● Tell the children that they are going to plan a simple five-slide presentation using a paper storyboard. Explain that planning the presentation is very important and using paper can be useful. Paper planning is very familiar to the children as it is quick and focuses them on the content, rather than being initially distracted by things such as font, colours and themes.
● Using the photocopiable page 53 'My five slides', the children sketch the information or images they hope to add to their presentation.

Differentiation
● Support: Less confident learners may need support to identify two features of poor presentations and their opposites.
● Challenge: More confident learners can identify at least five features of poor presentations and their opposites.

Review
● Bring the class together and review the storyboards of three children. Looking at the storyboards, can the class identify the key information that is being shared in each slide? Ask the three children: *If you had to choose only one slide out of your storyboard, which one would it be? Why is that slide the most important?* Ask the rest of the class to consider this question with their own storyboards.

Curriculum objectives
- To use search technologies effectively.
- To use technology safely, respectfully and responsibly.

Lesson objectives
- To use presentation software to create five slides.
- To add appropriate and effective text and images to their presentation.
- To give and receive effective feedback on the first drafts of presentations.

Expected outcomes
- Can create a simple five-slide presentation.
- Can add simple text and images to their presentation.

Resources
The stories 'King Midas' and 'The Emperor's New clothes'; interactive activity 'Silly presentations' from the CD-ROM; photocopiable page 53 'My five slides' (from previous lesson)

Searching and presenting

In the previous lesson, the children started to plan their presentation. They now need to gather the information and place text and images together in a piece of software. They reflect on 'silly presentations' to review their learning about what makes an effective presentation.

Introduction
- Introduce the lesson by reading the story of 'King Midas' or 'The Emperor's New Clothes'. In those stories, the characters of the rulers are shown to be 'silly'. To reinforce the learning from the previous lesson, the children review interactive activity 'Silly presentations' on the CD-ROM. What would they change in the five slides? After the children have discussed the slides, take feedback from them. It should include changing text, images and colours.

Paired work
- Using photocopiable page 53 'My five slides' from the previous lesson, the children decide which images they will need and search to find them, download them and add them to the presentation. Then, still in pairs, they choose the text that they will use. They write this on their paper plan, as well as typing it on the screen using a program such as Microsoft PowerPoint.

Differentiation
- Support: Less confident learners may need support from adults to choose the search terms and also to write the text to accompany the images they find.
- Challenge: More confident learners could choose their own search terms and identify appropriate images for their presentation.

Review
- In the stories of 'King Midas' and 'The Emperor's New Clothes', an innocent child showed how the rulers were silly. In a similar way, can children give feedback on the presentations to make sure they are not silly? Ask the children to look at their paper plans. *Do the words make sense? Will your images match the text? What would be a kind way of suggesting an improvement?*

Curriculum objectives
● To use search technologies effectively.
● To use technology safely, respectfully and responsibly.

Lesson objectives
● To enhance their presentation with colour and themes/background as appropriate.
● To add animations to their work as appropriate.
● To discuss why such elements should be used sparingly.
● To know how to print out their presentation in different views.

Expected outcomes
● Can add other elements, such as colour and themes to their presentation as appropriate.
● Can add animation to their work if appropriate.

Resources
Interactive activity 'Silly presentations' on the CD-ROM; photocopiable page 54 'Slide plan'

Getting things moving

In this lesson, the children consider other features of presentation software, such as Microsoft PowerPoint or Apple Keynote. They can add themes to give the whole presentation a unified look. They can also add slide animations, so that images and text can appear and disappear. They consider when such animations may be appropriate.

Introduction
● Introduce the lesson by showing interactive activity 'Silly presentations' from the CD-ROM and remind the children about using text that can be seen clearly, using appropriate images and planning the key message.
● Explain that presentation software has themes, which can give a presentation a unified look – using similar colours, text sizes and positions. Demonstrate, using Microsoft PowerPoint or Apple Keynote, examples of themes (select a new presentation and the software will offer themes, with thumbnail images to show their looks).

Paired work
● The children experiment with changing the themes of their presentation. Once selected, they must be able to explain why they chose the theme and how it matches their project. The children swap partners and then justify their selection of the theme to the new partner.

Whole-class work
● Explain that presentation software has animation features. These can make text and pictures appear and disappear. Why would they want text to appear and disappear? Using photocopiable page 54 'Slide plan', the children plan a presentation slide. They draw their presentation slide on the page and then decide the order that the parts will appear. For example, the slide could have a title, a text box and a picture. The children decide in which order the parts appear by numbering each part. If the title appears first, they write '1' next to it, followed by the picture '2' and then the text '3'. This is to show how a slide could build, with the parts being animated as they appear.
● Will their slide look more interesting? Does it make it easier to understand the information? Is it better to have all of the information on the slide from the beginning?

Paired work
● The children can experiment adding animation to their text and images to their presentations. Again, once selected, they must be able to explain why they chose the animation and why it is necessary.

Differentiation
● Support: Less confident learners may need support to justify their reasons for selecting a theme and animations.
● Challenge: More confident learners could add labels to their paper-based presentation plan, to show where the theme adds consistency to their presentation.

Review
● Bring the class together and explain that, even though text and image animations can be exciting and eye-catching, it's most important that their audience can still understand the key message. Ask: *Do you think children will like lots of animations? Would adults like lots of animations?*
● To conclude, explain that a presentation is there to support someone talking. When planning the words to use, it can be helpful to have a print out of the presentation. In the hand-out view, the slides are printed approximately six slides per page, with space for notes. Demonstrate what a presentation might look like, when printed.

Curriculum objectives
● To use search technologies effectively.
● To use technology safely, respectfully and responsibly.

Lesson objectives
● To know how to deliver an effective presentation to an audience.
● To give their presentation to their peers.
● To give and receive feedback on their presentations.

Expected outcomes
● Can present their work to their peers.

Resources
Photocopiable page 55 'My criteria'; photocopiable page 'Kind, specific, helpful' from the CD-ROM

Presentations, please!

The children have been researching and refining their presentations about castles. In this lesson, they will share their presentations and justify how they have chosen themes, text, images and animations. This combines their speaking and listening skills, with their computer software skills. They then give feedback and try to make it 'kind, specific and helpful'.

Introduction
● Begin by reminding the children of their previous lessons. They have searched on the web for images and information about castles. They have planned on paper, then created presentations, using text and images. They have added a theme and chosen animations, where appropriate. Now they need to present their work, keeping the key idea very clear.

Whole-class work
● To help the children plan their talk, consider the structure of a story. Read 'King Midas' or 'The Emperor's New Clothes'. Can they see that the stories have a beginning, middle and end? Ask three children: *What happens at the beginning. What happens in the middle? What happens at the end?* In an adventure story, in the beginning something starts the adventure; in the middle the hero/heroine tries to solve the problem or carry out a trial; in the end all is solved. Ask the children to think about their talk like an adventure story.

Paired work
● Using photocopiable page 55 'My criteria', the children think about which criteria they will use with their talk. They select three criteria from the list, judging why they think these criteria are relevant and then rank them in order one, two and three.
● In pairs, the children practise their talks to go with their presentations. Their partner must listen carefully and not interrupt. Using photocopiable page 'Kind, specific, helpful' from the CD-ROM, the children write a response to their partner about their presentation. They then review it, asking whether it is kind. Next, they think about being specific – so ideally, they pick one improvement on one slide or one part of the talk relating to one slide. Finally, they reflect on their advice – is it helpful? Will the presenter be able to use the advice to improve the presentation? For example: *On slide three, I could not read the writing, because it is too dark on top of your castle picture. Could you change the colour of the writing or move the picture from behind it?*

> **Differentiation**
> ● Support: Less confident learners will need support to give specific feedback for their partner, to help them improve.
> ● Challenge: More confident learners can give kind, specific and helpful advice to their partners. They may consider how well the talk explains the content of the slides.

Review
● Bring the class together and ask one pair to describe how the review process went. Ask: *Were they kind? What was the specific point their partner identified. How were they helpful in suggesting an improvement?*
● Explain to the children that this is an early step in communicating using technology, with a talk alongside it. Tell them that in this kind of work, there are many opportunities to share and also to be kind, specific and helpful in their feedback.

Curriculum objectives
● To use search technologies effectively.
● To use technology safely, respectfully and responsibly.

Lesson objectives
● To be able to use a child-friendly search engine accurately for simple research.
● To find specific information about a particular topic (their chosen king, queen or castle).
● To give and receive feedback on their presentations.

Expected outcomes
● Can use search technologies effectively.
● Can locate specific information by using a search engine.
● Can give kind, specific and helpful feedback.

Resources
Photocopiable page 'My king and queen research' from the CD-ROM; interactive activity 'King presentation'

Kings, queens and castles: Assess and review

In this assess and review lesson, the children look at a presentation made by an imaginary child. They focus on giving kind, specific and helpful feedback to them. The children also think about searching the web and which search terms they would use to find information.

Introduction
● Introduce the lesson by playing 'Hunt the thimble', allowing the children to search around the room. Give them clues to the thimble's location, such as the key search terms 'book + door'.
● Ask: *How did you narrow your search when you were given search terms?*

Whole-class work
● Explain that the children are going to research into a king or queen of England. They need to think of the search terms, record them and think about whether they will use '+' or '−' in the search box.

Paired work
● Using photocopiable page 'My king and queen research' from the CD-ROM, the children write which search terms they will use to find out about a king or queen from history. Once decided, they can use 'Safe Search' to find out information about the king or queen and write five facts about them on the sheet.

Differentiation
● Support: Less confident learners may need support to identify the search terms they need and support to identify the information on the web page.
● Challenge: More confident learners could locate five facts about a king or queen and then explain whether the website is suitable for a child or adult to use.

Paired work
● Using the interactive activity 'King presentation' on the CD-ROM, the children identify errors. They then compose kind, specific and helpful feedback.
● *Question: Why should we be kind?*

Review
● Bring the class together and display the interactive activity 'King presentation'. Ask three pairs of children to read out their kind, specific and helpful feedback.
● Summarise the learning over the previous lessons: how they have thought about searching the web, and how there is so much information that they need to be able to navigate it well. They then thought about how they can take the information and communicate it clearly. Finally, they have thought about how they can improve by supporting each other with kind, specific and helpful feedback.

Name: _____   Date: _____

My castle

- Draw your castle in the box.
- Can you add labels to show the different parts?

[ ]

- Who lives in your castle?  _____

- When was it built? _____

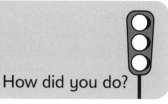

I can draw a castle and label the important parts.

How did you do?

Name: _____ Date: _____

Searching

- Choose a famous person, a place or a favourite activity you like to do.
- What would you like to find out about that person, place or activity?

- Write two questions:

Question 1:

_____

- Which words would you type into the box?

	SEARCH

Question 2:

_____

- Which words would you type into the box?

	SEARCH

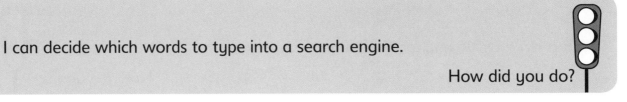

I can decide which words to type into a search engine.

How did you do?

PHOTOCOPIABLE

SCHOLASTIC
www.scholastic.co.uk

'and'

- Rewrite the search terms below using '+' instead of 'and'.

Goldilocks and the three bears

| | SEARCH |

Beauty and the beast

| | SEARCH |

Peter and the wolf

| | SEARCH |

Edinburgh Castle and its gun which is fired at one pm

| | SEARCH |

Jack and the beanstalk

| | SEARCH |

I can rewrite search terms.

How did you do?

Bad to good presentations

■ What is bad about these slides? Write how you could improve each one.

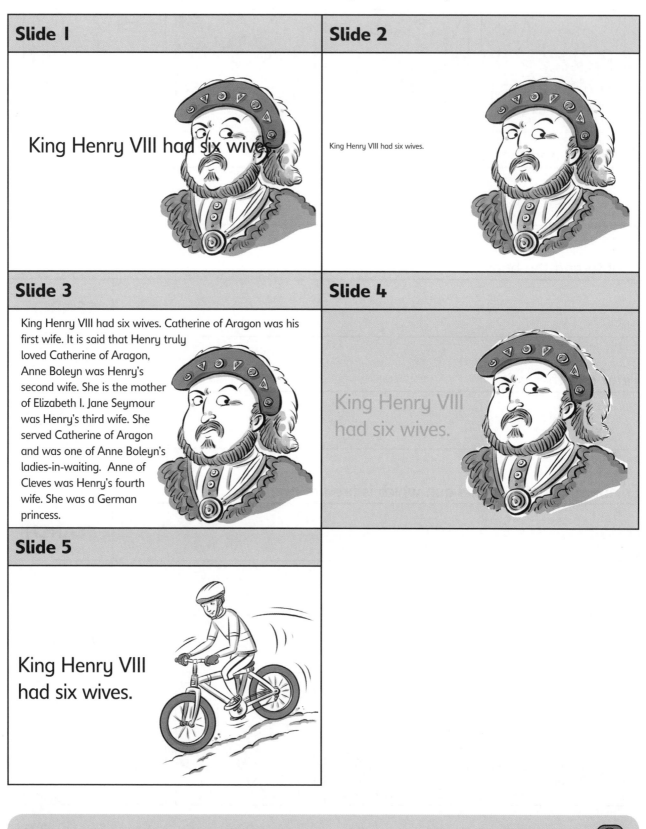

Slide 1

King Henry VIII had six wives.

Slide 2

King Henry VIII had six wives.

Slide 3

King Henry VIII had six wives. Catherine of Aragon was his first wife. It is said that Henry truly loved Catherine of Aragon, Anne Boleyn was Henry's second wife. She is the mother of Elizabeth I. Jane Seymour was Henry's third wife. She served Catherine of Aragon and was one of Anne Boleyn's ladies-in-waiting. Anne of Cleves was Henry's fourth wife. She was a German princess.

Slide 4

King Henry VIII had six wives.

Slide 5

King Henry VIII had six wives.

I can decide what makes a good presentation slide.

How did you do?

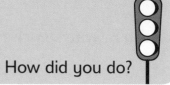

PHOTOCOPIABLE

Name: _____   Date: _____

My five slides

Sketch of slide	Notes

I can plan a presentation.

How did you do?

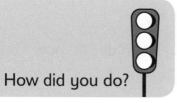

Slide plan

■ Draw your slide below. Then number each part in the order it will appear.

I can decide how I build my slide, adding each part in order.

How did you do?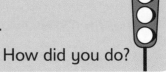

PHOTOCOPIABLE   SCHOLASTIC
www.scholastic.co.uk

My criteria

- Which of these criteria will you use?

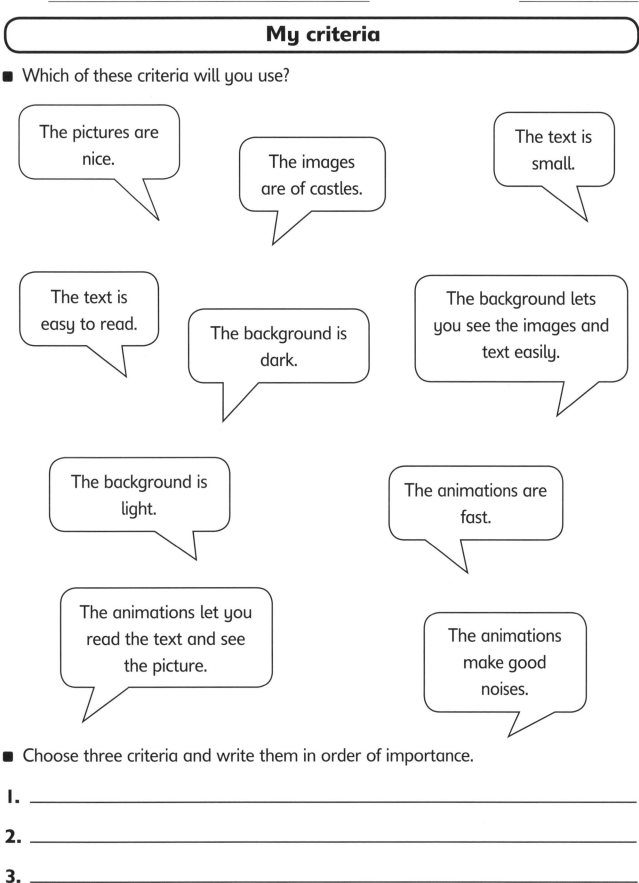

The pictures are nice.

The images are of castles.

The text is small.

The text is easy to read.

The background is dark.

The background lets you see the images and text easily.

The background is light.

The animations are fast.

The animations let you read the text and see the picture.

The animations make good noises.

- Choose three criteria and write them in order of importance.

1. _____

2. _____

3. _____

I can select criteria for my presentation.

How did you do?

Aliens

This chapter uses aliens as a theme and builds on the knowledge and understanding of algorithms that the children have developed so far in Key Stage 1 and Year 3 Autumn 2 'Robots' chapter. The children are introduced to the graphical programming language Scratch for the first time and are able to apply their computational thinking skills and the knowledge and understanding they have from the basic programming tasks they have undertaken previously.

Expected prior learning

● The children have been introduced to algorithms and programming in Key Stage 1 and Autumn 2 and are used to programming onscreen devices and floor robots, so they have a solid understanding of algorithms and programming on which to build in the new programming environment introduced in this chapter.

Chapter at a glance

Subject area
• Algorithms and programming

National Curriculum objective
• To design, write and debug programs that accomplish specific goals, including controlling or simulating physical systems; solve problems by decomposing them into smaller parts; use sequence and repetition in programs; use logical reasoning to explain how some simple algorithms work and to detect and correct errors in algorithms and programs.

Week	Lesson objectives	Summary of activities	Expected outcomes
1	• To understand that Scratch is a software program that can execute algorithms. • To navigate around the Scratch interface. • To know how to add a sprite in Scratch. • To understand how to get a sprite to complete basic movements. • To understand how to add speech bubbles to sprites. • To explain to a beginner the interface of Scratch and how to get a sprite to move and speak.	• Children are introduced to the Scratch interface. • They add sprites to the stage. • They add basic movements and speech to sprites.	• Can solve problems by decomposing them into smaller parts. • Can use programming software to execute simple algorithms.
2	• To be able to paint a new sprite using basic drawing tools. • To create a short sequence of instructions to allow their sprite to perform multiple actions. • To use repeated actions when moving their sprite. • To be able to use simple repetition to make the algorithm more efficient.	• Children create sprites using the paint tools in Scratch. • They understand how to use sequencing and repetition in Scratch scripts.	• Can use sequence and repetition in programs. • Can use basic drawing tools to create simple artwork.
3	• To fulfil a series of simple challenges using Scratch. • To understand the process of debugging code within Scratch. • To work collaboratively with their peers to debug algorithms within Scratch. • To explain to others how they have debugged their code.	• Children undertake a series of challenges using Scratch. • They debug incorrect code.	• Can use logical reasoning to explain how some simple algorithms work. • Can use logical reasoning to detect and correct errors in algorithms and programs.

Week	Lesson objectives	Summary of activities	Expected outcomes
4	• To record sounds using Scratch. • To add sounds to their code. • To use repetition and selection to achieve different outcomes with sounds in Scratch. • To be able to add backgrounds in Scratch.	• Children learn how to record sounds in Scratch. • They experiment with different ways of adding sounds to scripts. • They add backgrounds to a Scratch project.	• Can record sounds and create algorithms to play sounds. • Can use basic drawing tools to create simple artwork.
5	• To plan and create a short joke animation using a template. • To create their own sprites in Scratch for their joke. • To add a background in Scratch for their joke. • To create their own sounds to add to their joke.	• Children plan an alien joke animation. • They create sprites and sounds for an alien joke animation and adding backgrounds.	• Can plan a short joke animation in Scratch. • Can create characters, backgrounds and sounds in Scratch.
6	• To create algorithms for their joke animation. • To program their algorithms into Scratch. • To test and debug their algorithms. • To give and receive constructive feedback. • To use logical reasoning to explain how the algorithms within their joke work.	• Children create algorithms and program them into Scratch to create an alien joke animation. • They give, receive and action feedback.	• Can create and debug simple algorithms that accomplish specific goals.
Assess and review	• Assess and review the half term's work.	• Children use a 'Control tool' to undertake a series of programming challenges. • They present their work to their classmates and/or teacher.	• Assess and review.

Overview of progression

● Throughout the lessons, the children build upon their knowledge and understanding of programming using Scratch. They quickly move from an introduction to the Scratch interface to creating short animations.
● Throughout the chapter, the children apply their knowledge and understanding of algorithms by creating precise, accurate sequences of instructions to obtain their desired outcome. They are also reminded that the program is executing their algorithms, so if something is going wrong, it is because they have given incorrect instructions. The basic programs they create in this chapter give them a sound base to build on future work.
● The children are encouraged to share their work with their peers and work collaboratively to review and debug their work, an essential skill that will be further developed in future chapters.

Creative context

● The lessons have links to the mathematics curriculum as children use logical thinking and problem solving to sequence and debug their code. The children also need to be aware of the number of degrees in a circle when using the 'turn' blocks in Scratch. The computing lessons should also draw upon the children's learning in English as they type speech and record sounds for their sprites and also in the planning of their joke animation. The written feedback they are required to give is also a useful skill across the curriculum.
● The lessons also have links to the art curriculum as the children use paint tools to draw sprites, for example.

Background knowledge

● From the work they have already completed in Key Stage 1 and Autumn 2, the children will know about sequencing, flowcharts, algorithms and programming an onscreen device and floor robot. This knowledge and understanding is consolidated and developed further in this chapter as they use a graphical programming language for the first time.
● From assessing children's understanding in the Key Stage 1 units, you will need to assess the children's capability in following and creating algorithms and provide additional support as necessary.
● It is important to spend some time familiarising yourself with the Scratch interface prior to the lessons by looking at the many tutorials on the Scratch website that introduce the programming language.
● The lessons assume the use of Scratch 1.4, other versions, including the online version, could be used.

Curriculum objectives

● To design, write and debug programs that accomplish specific goals, including controlling or simulating physical systems; solve problems by decomposing them into smaller parts; to use sequence and repetition in programs; to use logical reasoning to explain how some simple algorithms work and to detect and correct errors in algorithms and programs.

Lesson objectives

● To understand that Scratch is a software program that can execute algorithms.
● To navigate around the Scratch interface.
● To know how to add a sprite in Scratch.
● To understand how to get a sprite to complete basic movements.
● To understand how to add speech bubbles to sprites.
● To explain to a beginner the interface of Scratch and how to get a sprite to move and speak.

Expected outcomes

● Can solve problems by decomposing them into smaller parts.
● Can use programming software to execute simple algorithms.

Resources

Scratch 1.4 program installed on the computers in the classroom – available from http://Scratch.mit.edu/Scratch_1.4/

Introduction to Scratch

In this lesson children are introduced to Scratch. They learn how to navigate their way around the Scratch interface, how to add sprites and program the sprites with simple yet accurate instructions. They are then asked to share their new learning. They will build on these foundations in future lessons as their understanding of programming using Scratch develops.

Introduction

● Remind the children of the work they completed in Autumn 2, where they were writing algorithms for robots.
● Discuss with them what they remember, using questions as prompts such as: *What is an algorithm? What does a program do? What programs have we used before? How did they work?*
● Explain that in this lesson they will be using a new program called Scratch.

Whole-class work

● Show the children the Scratch interface on the whiteboard.
● Encourage the children to discuss what they can see. Ask: *What do you notice? What would you like to find out more about?*
● Tell them more about each part as they discuss it; for example, showing them how the blocks can be dragged across to the script area and that the different-coloured blocks contain different groups of scripts. The most important areas to highlight are labelled in the screenshot below.

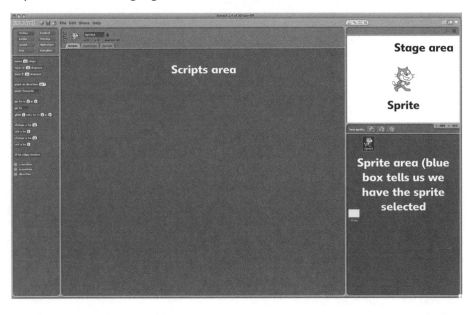

● Tell the children that the cat is fun, but that Scratch has lots of other sprites they can use too.
● Show them how to delete the cat sprite by right-clicking on it and choosing delete.
● Show them how to 'Choose new sprite from file' and add a sprite of your choice:
    ● Click 'Choose new sprite from file'.
    ● Select the folder of your choice.
    ● Select the sprite of your choice.
    ● Your sprite will show on the stage.

Independent/paired work

- Ask the children to log on to the computers and open up Scratch.
- Ask them to repeat the steps you have just completed as a class, deleting the cat sprite and then selecting and adding a sprite of their own choice.

Whole-class work

- Using a volunteer, show the children how the blocks can be used to control the sprite.
- Drag the 'move 10 steps' block across to the scripts area and explain that they also need to tell the program to 'start'.
- Go to the yellow 'control' blocks and choose 'when the green flag is clicked'.
- Show them how the blocks slot together like a jigsaw and talk through the script: *What are we telling the sprite to do? How can you tell? Where is the green flag for us to click?* (top right corner).
- Click the green flag to run the script and show the children how the sprite is moving ten steps every time the green flag is clicked.
- Show them how the white input box on the move 10 steps block can be changed to make the sprite move to the left '10 steps' and to move the number of steps they wish, for example '50 steps'.

Independent/paired work

- Ask the children to add scripts in the same way to get their sprite to move across the stage left and right and by more and fewer steps.

Whole-class work

- Using a volunteer, show the children how the sprite can be made to 'talk' using a speech bubble.
- Drag across the 'say Hello for 2 secs' block (from the purple 'Looks' blocks group) and show how it can be slotted in to the end of the script to make the speech happen *after* the movement. Show how the input box can be changed to the speech of your choice.

Independent/paired work

- Ask the children to add scripts in the same way to get their sprite to speak.
- Encourage them to try moving the speech block to *before* the move block to see the difference (it will run the script in the order they tell it to, so the speech will happen before the movement).

Differentiation
- Support: Less confident learners may benefit from additional support when putting their script together. You may wish for some learners to experiment with movement only, although the tasks here should be accessible, and fun, for most levels of learners.
- Challenge: More confident learners can experiment with other blocks to create their own sequence. They will naturally start to problem solve and work out what can be done with the program.

Review

- Using the whiteboard, ask for volunteers to share the work they have completed with the class, particularly anyone who has created different scripts for their sprite.
- You can use this as an opportunity to discuss further blocks and their functions, correct any misunderstandings and probe children's understanding. It is also a great chance for children to lead learning as they share what they have discovered about the Scratch program.

Curriculum objectives

● To design, write and debug programs that accomplish specific goals, including controlling or simulating physical systems; solve problems by decomposing them into smaller parts; to use sequence and repetition in programs; to use logical reasoning to explain how some simple algorithms work and to detect and correct errors in algorithms and programs.

Lesson objectives

● To be able to paint a new sprite using basic drawing tools.
● To create a short sequence of instructions to allow their sprite to perform multiple actions.
● To use repeated actions when moving their sprite.
● To be able to use simple repetition to make the algorithm more efficient.

Expected outcomes

● Can use sequence and repetition in programs.
● Can use basic drawing tools to create simple artwork.

Resources

Scratch 1.4 installed on the computers in the classroom.

Drawing sprites and using repetition

In this lesson the children will build on their knowledge and understanding of how Scratch works. Having been introduced to the interface and some basic blocks in Week 1, they develop their understanding of how to sequence instructions and use the repeat block. The children are also introduced to the idea that they can create their own sprites.

Introduction

● Remind the children that last week they were introduced to Scratch. If you wish you can review this with them on the whiteboard, using volunteers to talk through the main learning points from Week 1.
● Remind the children of key concepts such as why the sprite does things in that order (they have told it to with their sequence of instructions so, if the sprite does not do what they want, they need to 'debug' their scripts), what blocks the different-coloured groups contain and how they can run their scripts (using the green flag).

Whole-class work

● Explain that Scratch also lets them create their own sprites and that this week they will be creating their own alien sprites to work with.
● Delete the cat sprite and show them how the 'Paint new sprite' tool can be used to draw a simple alien sprite. Show the shape tools, change colours, fill and paint brush tools and how to undo their work if they make a mistake.
● Show the children how to name their sprite and discuss why it is important to give the sprites names rather than just leaving them as 'sprite 1', 'sprite 2' and so on (so they know exactly which sprite they are working on).

Independent/paired work

● Ask the children to draw their own alien sprite using the Paint new sprite tool.
● They should be encouraged to be as creative as they like, but ask them not to 'fill' the background of the sprite, keeping it transparent instead so the sprite does not take up the whole stage.

Whole-class work

● Explain to the children that scripts can be added to the painted sprite in the same way as before.
● Add the 'when green flag clicked', 'move 10 steps' and 'say Hello for 2 secs' blocks as used in the first lesson.
● Explain that they can use the 'repeat' block (the sixth block down in the yellow control blocks) to repeat an action, or a group of actions, a set number of times.
● Drag the repeat block round the move 10 steps and say Hello for 2 secs blocks and ask the children what they think will happen.
● Click the green flag to test whether their predictions were correct.
● You could also change the order of the blocks, moving the 'say Hello for 2 secs' block to after the repeat block and ask the children to predict what will happen. This is to get them used to the idea that the repeat block can go round a series of blocks, or round one block. Also show them how the input box can be changed to alter the number of times the action is repeated.

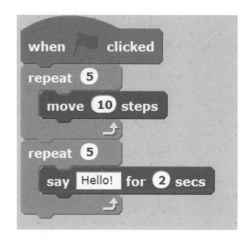

Independent/paired work

● Ask the children to try out using the repeat block with their alien sprite and their own choice of blocks, although, if they feel more comfortable, they could start with the move 10 steps and say Hello for 2 secs blocks first.
● Encourage them to test out different combinations of blocks to see how the repeat blocks work. If they are confident, this is also a good opportunity to introduce the 'wait 1 secs' block if they find they cannot tell if the script is being repeated as it's going too fast. They could also try using the 'forever' block instead of the repeat block to make something happen forever rather than repeat a set number of times.
● Show the children how to save their work, saving as 'alien Scratch project' (the location will differ according to the system you have at school).

Differentiation
● Support: Less confident learners may benefit from further adult support in understanding how the repeat block is telling the other blocks to repeat for a set number of times. They may wish to stick to adding to the original sequence without using the repeat, or repeating only one action.
● Challenge: More confident learners will be able to create more complex scripts and program their sprite with a sequence of instructions, perhaps using multiple repeats.

Review

● Ask the children to share their understanding by creating a class sequence on the whiteboard using the class alien created at the start. Each volunteer adds one block to the sequence and the rest of the class must predict what will happen.

Curriculum objectives
• To design, write and debug programs that accomplish specific goals, including controlling or simulating physical systems; solve problems by decomposing them into smaller parts; to use sequence and repetition in programs; to use logical reasoning to explain how some simple algorithms work and to detect and correct errors in algorithms and programs.

Lesson objectives
• To fulfil a series of simple challenges using Scratch.
• To understand the process of debugging code within Scratch.
• To work collaboratively with their peers to debug algorithms within Scratch.
• To explain to others how they have debugged their code.

Expected outcomes
• Can use logical reasoning to explain how some simple algorithms work.
• Can use logical reasoning to detect and correct errors in algorithms and programs.

Resources
Photocopiable page 67 'Challenge Scratch!'; photocopiable page 68 'Debug the code!'

Challenge Scratch!

Building on the previous lessons, children start to explore Scratch further by working through a series of challenges which consolidate and extend their learning from the previous weeks, but that they must work as independently as possible to solve. They are also asked to work collaboratively to debug programs that have been created incorrectly, spotting the mistake and then inputting the correct sequence of instructions.

Introduction
• Remind the children that in the previous two lessons they have been learning how to use Scratch, have added sprites and learned how to add sequences of scripts to the sprites to get them to do certain things.

Whole-class work
• Explain to the children that this week they will be given a series of challenges that they need to work through in Scratch.
• Explain that there are often different ways that the challenge can be repeated and they should experiment with different blocks.
• Emphasise that they need to try to solve the challenges themselves, using their problem-solving skills. If they get stuck, they can work collaboratively.
• You could award points/prizes to those who achieve the challenges.
• You may need to discuss with the children that a full circle is 360 degrees.

Independent/paired work
• Ask the children to open the 'alien Scratch project' file from last week.
• Give the children photocopiable page 67 'Challenge Scratch!' and talk through it with them. You may wish to complete the first challenge as a class.
• They should work through the challenges as independently as possible, trying different possibilities out until they get their sprite to do as they wish.

Whole-class work
• Go through the solutions to the challenges as a class, perhaps with children demonstrating their work for the rest of the class. Ask the children to self-assess their work using the photocopiable sheet.

Independent/paired work
• Give the children photocopiable page 68 'Debug the code!' and talk through it with them. You may wish to complete the first one as a class.
• They should work through the different problems, trying the code out using Scratch, until they have debugged it correctly. They should note the debugging they have completed on the sheet, adding in the correct code used.

> **Differentiation**
> • Support: Less confident learners may benefit from working collaboratively in mixed-ability pairings or with adult support to help with the challenges.
> • Challenge: More confident learners could design their own challenges for others.

Review
• Go through the challenges as a class, asking the children to share their reasoning as you go.
• Ask the children to review their work as you do this and identify any errors they have made. Hopefully these will be minor errors. However, if there are common misunderstandings, you may need to take time to go through the whole activity in detail as a class.
• Questions to help you assess their progress include: *Why did you decide to put that block there? Why is that block repeated? What is that instruction telling the alien to do? What other scripts could make that happen?*
• Review the children's progress through their discussions and the outcomes of the challenge activities.

Adding sounds and backgrounds to Scratch

Curriculum objectives
● To design, write and debug programs that accomplish specific goals, including controlling or simulating physical systems; solve problems by decomposing them into smaller parts; to use sequence and repetition in programs; to use logical reasoning to explain how some simple algorithms work and to detect and correct errors in algorithms and programs.

Lesson objectives
● To record sounds using Scratch.
● To add sounds to their code.
● To use repetition and selection to achieve different outcomes with sounds in Scratch.
● To be able to add backgrounds in Scratch.

Expected outcomes
● Can record sounds and create algorithms to play sounds.
● Can use basic drawing tools to create simple artwork.

Resources
Microphones

In this lesson the children learn how to record sounds in Scratch and add these to their scripts in different ways to achieve different outcomes. They also learn how backgrounds can be added to Scratch.

Introduction
● Remind the children that they have been working in Scratch, getting their alien sprites to perform certain actions using sequences of script blocks.
● Explain that this week they will be working with sound and backgrounds.

Whole-class work
● Display the Scratch interface on the whiteboard with the 'alien Scratch project' file opened. The children may already have noticed the sound blocks and the stage part of the sprite area. Ask them to point these out, discussing what they have already discovered.
● Using volunteers show the children how sounds can be *imported* from the files contained within Scratch or *recorded* by the children themselves.
● Show them how to add the sounds to the script using the 'play sound' block.
● Ensure that you emphasise that the sounds should be imported/recorded first and then added to the sprite's script.

Independent/paired work
● Ask the children to open their own 'alien Scratch project' file and import at least one sound and create their own sound.
● Once they have imported/created their sounds, they add these to a script for their alien sprite (one saved from the last lesson or a new one).

Whole-class work
● Show the children how the 'repeat' and 'forever' block can be used to play the sound a set number of times or continuously. Explain that to play the whole sound they will need to use the 'play sound until done' block with the repeat or forever blocks.

Independent/paired work
● Encourage the children to experiment with using the repeat and forever blocks to play the sound a set number of times, or continuously.

Whole-class work
● Show children how to choose a background and import it onto the stage by clicking 'Stage', then selecting the 'Backgrounds' tab, clicking 'Import' and then choosing a suitable background from one of the collections.
● At this stage, you could choose to show the children how they can also create their own background, by choosing 'Paint' on the backgrounds tab.

Independent/paired work
● Encourage the children to experiment with adding suitable backgrounds.

Differentiation
● Support: Less confident learners may need support in the process of adding sound and backgrounds to their work.
● Challenge: More confident learners can be encouraged to experiment with adding multiple sounds in different places within their script to achieve different outcomes.

Review
● Have a 'who can show me' activity using the whiteboard where you ask questions such as: *Who can show me how to import a sound?, Who can show me how to make that sound play continuously?* and so on.

Curriculum objectives

● To design, write and debug programs that accomplish specific goals, including controlling or simulating physical systems; solve problems by decomposing them into smaller parts; to use sequence and repetition in programs; to use logical reasoning to explain how some simple algorithms work and to detect and correct errors in algorithms and programs.

Lesson objectives

● To plan and create a short joke animation using a template.
● To create their own sprites in Scratch for their joke.
● To add a background in Scratch for their joke.
● To create their own sounds to add to their joke.

Expected outcomes

● Can plan a short joke animation in Scratch.
● Can create characters, backgrounds and sounds in Scratch.

Resources

Photocopiable page 69 'Joke plan template'; sample 'Alien joke' Scratch file on the CD-ROM; microphones (if required)

Planning a Scratch animation

This lesson sees children consolidate and develop their learning from the past four lessons as they plan and start an alien joke animation. They will work on their joke over the next two lessons and it provides them with a fun opportunity to be creative while demonstrating their knowledge, skills and understanding of programming using Scratch.

Introduction

● Ask the children whether they know any good alien, or space, jokes to share with the class.
● Explain to the children that over the next two lessons they will have the opportunity to show what they have learned about using Scratch by creating an alien joke animation.

Whole-class work

● Show the children the sample 'Alien joke' Scratch file (opened from the Quick links section of the CD-ROM) and explain that they will be creating their own version.
● Highlight to them that while one sprite is speaking, the other one 'waits'.
● Explain that the children can either use the same alien joke, or create their own if they wish.
● Give out the photocopiable page 69 'Joke plan template' and discuss why a plan is important.
● Show them how the plan works, completing the first box as an example together if you wish. Highlight that they should include a simple sketched image showing what happens and a short text description describing what is happening, for example; 1. Alien and spaceman on moon, Alien says to spaceman, 'What is an alien's favourite chocolate?' 2. Spaceman says 'I don't know'. 3. Alien says 'A mars bar'. Sound 'haha' plays, and so on.

Independent work

● The children should complete the plan check with you when they think they have finished.
● They can then begin to create their sprites, add a suitable background and create/add suitable sounds.

Differentiation

● Support: Encourage less confident learners to use the same joke but create their own version of it. They can also use the sample file as a guide for completing their plan.
● Challenge: Encourage more confident learners to come up with their own joke for the animation and to be as creative as they like when planning.

Review

● Review with the children their progress during the lesson and ensure that they know what they need to do at the start of the next lesson. Hopefully they will be ready to go on to programming their sprites, but they may need to finish creating their sprites or sounds. You could get them to write this on the back of their planning sheet if you wish.

Curriculum objectives
● To design, write and debug programs that accomplish specific goals, including controlling or simulating physical systems; solve problems by decomposing them into smaller parts; to use sequence and repetition in programs; to use logical reasoning to explain how some simple algorithms work and to detect and correct errors in algorithms and programs.

Lesson objectives
● To create algorithms for their joke animation.
● To program their algorithms into Scratch.
● To test and debug their algorithms.
● To give and receive constructive feedback.
● To use logical reasoning to explain how the algorithms within their joke work.

Expected outcomes
● Can create and debug simple algorithms that accomplish specific goals.

Resources
Photocopiable page 70 'Feedback'

Programming and debugging a Scratch animation

This week, the children complete their joke animations, programming their sprites to perform their desired outcomes and debugging any errors in their code. They also give and receive constructive feedback and action the feedback given to improve their work, getting them used to the idea that others' opinions are valuable in improving their work.

Introduction
● Recap the work the children completed last week in which they were creating the elements for their alien joke animation.
● Explain to them that in this lesson they will be programming their sprites to complete their joke and then giving feedback to help each other to improve their animation.

Whole-class work
● Show the sample joke animation again and emphasise the important point that when one sprite is speaking, the other needs to wait.
● If you wish, you could emphasise this point further by asking two volunteers to 'act out' the joke, so the children understand that in order to make the two sprites work together, one needs to 'wait' while the other 'speaks'.

Independent work
● The children should program their sprites with their joke, using movement, repetition and sounds as they have planned, although it is also fine for them to include elements they have not planned.
● They will most likely need to debug their work, as things may not always go as they expect. Encourage them to work with a partner to debug their code.
● Once they think they have finished, they should swop with a partner and give each other feedback using photocopiable page 70 'Feedback'. You may need to talk through how to give constructive feedback to others if you have not done so in other areas of the curriculum.
● Once they have received their feedback, they should make the changes suggested by their partner and write what they have changed on the feedback sheet.

Differentiation
● Support: Less confident learners may benefit from writing out the algorithms they wish to program first that is, what they want to happen exactly as a list of instructions in addition to the plan they have created. They may also need some assistance in debugging their code.
● Challenge: Encourage more confident learners to create a more sophisticated joke with, for example, additional movements, sounds and multiple repetitions.

Review
● Bring the children together and select some of the animations to show (saving their work in a shared area will be helpful for this as will noting which children have included aspects in their animation that will be interesting to show). Ask the children to talk through their animations as they are shown to explain how and why they have programmed their animation in that way.
● You may have time to show all the animations, and discuss their animation with each child, which will help with assessment of the chapter's work.
● Assess the children's understanding from their Scratch work and the review discussion.

Curriculum objectives

● To design, write and debug programs that accomplish specific goals, including controlling or simulating physical systems; solve problems by decomposing them into smaller parts; to use sequence and repetition in programs; to use logical reasoning to explain how some simple algorithms work and to detect and correct errors in algorithms and programs.

Lesson objectives

● To apply their knowledge and understanding of programming to another programming tool.
● To fulfil a series of challenges using the control tool.
● To present their work to others.

Expected outcomes

● Can use programming software to execute simple algorithms.
● Can create and debug simple algorithms that accomplish specific goals.
● Can use logical reasoning to explain how some simple algorithms work.

Resources

Interactive activity 'Finding planets' on the CD-ROM; photocopiable page 71 'Finding planets challenges'

Aliens: Assess and review

This lesson sees the children apply the knowledge, skills and understanding they have developed using Scratch to a different programming tool. This will help to consolidate their learning and provide an opportunity for them to demonstrate their understanding of programming and of implementing algorithms with different programs. Assessment and observation of the children's work will allow you to make adjustments to future learning of this topic, as you deem appropriate.

Introduction

● Remind the children that they have been using Scratch and explain that this is known as a graphical programming language.
● Explain that many of the skills they have already learned can be transferred to different programming languages and that this is an important skill for a computer programmer.
● Explain that this week they will be using a software 'control tool' to work through a number of challenges.
● Access the interactive activity 'Finding planets' from the CD-ROM. The children should remember using a similar activity in earlier units.

Independent work

● Give out the photocopiable page 71 'Finding planets challenges' and go through the instructions with the children.
● You may wish to complete the first challenge together so they know what is required of them.
● The children should work through the challenge sheet, using paper to plan their algorithms then using the 'Finding planets' interactive activity to try out the algorithms.

Differentiation

● Support: You may wish to allocate tasks to all children according to their level, particularly less confident learners who you should ask to focus on the first few tasks, which are less complex.
● Challenge: Encourage more confident learners to work through the tasks as independently and accurately as possible, or give them only the more complex tasks to complete.

Review

● The end of this chapter is an ideal opportunity to get the children to present the work they have created, whether this is their joke or the programs they have created during this lesson.
● Videoing them explaining their work, for example how the program is executing their algorithms, or how they debugged their code, could be used for assessment.
● Similarly, you could use screenshots of their work and print outs of their code for display purposes.
● Assess the children's work through the outcomes of their challenges and make adjustments to future algorithms and programming work based on these assessments.

Challenge Scratch!

■ **Challenge 1:**

Can you make your alien move to the right and then to the left ten times?

■ **Challenge 2:**

Can you make your alien go round in a circle?

■ **Challenge 3:**

Can you make your alien sing?

■ **Challenge 4:**

Can you combine challenges 1, 2 and 3 to make your alien look like it's dancing?

I can program a sprite in Scratch to perform a variety of actions.

How did you do?

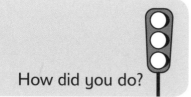

Name: _____ Date: _____

Debug the code!

- Can you detect the errors in the code below?
- Use Scratch to help you find and correct the mistakes.
- Write the correct sequence in the box provided.

1. Make the sprite move ten steps ten times then say hello once.

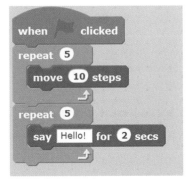

2. Make the sprite turn in a full circle.

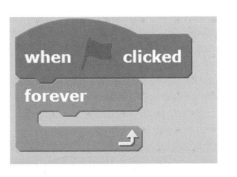

3. Make the sprite move round in a circle forever.

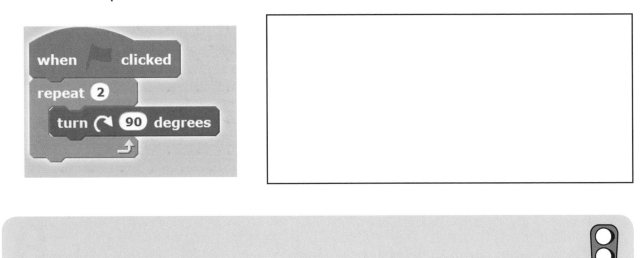

I can debug Scratch code.

How did you do?

PHOTOCOPIABLE

Name: _____ Date: _____

Joke plan template

■ Plan your Scratch joke animation using the template below.

_____

_____

_____

_____

_____

_____

I can plan an animation using a template.

How did you do?

100 COMPUTING LESSONS ■ 69

Feedback

■ Watch your friend's animation and give them helpful feedback in the space below.

My name _____

My friend's name_____

■ What did you like about your friend's work?

_____

_____

■ How could your friend improve their work?

_____

_____

■ What changes have you made after receiving feedback?

_____

_____

I can give constructive feedback to help my friend to improve their work.

How did you do?

PHOTOCOPIABLE

Finding planets challenges

■ Complete these challenges using the 'Finding planets' interactive activity.

Challenge 1:
Can you make your spaceship visit the red planet then the yellow planet?

Challenge 2:
Can you make your spaceship visit the green planet then the red planet?

Challenge 3:
Can you make your spaceship visit all three planets?

■ Jump commands
You may notice the grid has coordinates around the sides. If you want to make your spaceship move directly to a grid square, you can use a 'Jump' command. For example *Jump 2 2* would make the spaceship jump straight to the square with those coordinates.

Challenge 4:
Can you make your spaceship visit the red planet using a 'Jump' command?

Challenge 5:
Can you make your spaceship visit all three planets using 'Jump' commands?

Challenge 6:
Can you make your spaceship visit all three planets then return to its starting position using 'Jump' commands?

I can carry out a series of control tool challenges.

How did you do?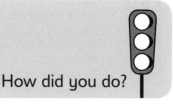

Chocolate factory

This chapter engages the children in data and information with a chocolate theme. Building on the previous lessons, where the children designed and used a tally chart for data collection, they represent the data in different ways. The lessons focus on identifying errors and cleaning up 'dirty data' – where obvious errors are corrected. Linking to the lessons in Year 3 Spring 1, the children present to their peers, giving constructive feedback.

Expected prior learning

● The children will be familiar with searching online – most likely they say 'Google it' if they want to search for information. Also, children will be familiar with YouTube and watching videos about different topics. In this chapter, they consider how to narrow their searches.

● From giving presentations in, for example, English lessons, children will know that they need to speak clearly and share the information. They may not have presented using software to share their images, video, audio and text.

Chapter at a glance

Subject area

• Data and information

National Curriculum objective

• To select, use and combine a variety of software to design and create a range of content that accomplish given goals, including collecting and presenting data and information.

Week	Lesson objectives	Summary of activities	Expected outcomes
1	• To design a simple tally sheet for data collection. • To collect data from relevant people (about chocolate preferences) using a tally sheet. • To organise data in simple ways. • To represent data pictorially using chocolate bar wrappers. • To draw simple initial conclusions from the data collected.	• Children are introduced to the 'chocolate' theme and discuss their favourite chocolate bars. • They design a tally sheet and collect data. • They organise the data and display the information in a bar chart, drawing conclusions.	• Can collect data using a tally sheet. • Can organise collected data in an effective way.
2	• To look at simple 'dirty' data and identify obvious errors. • To explain how errors can occur when collecting data. • To explain the reasons why data was identified as being incorrect (in relation to the data set).	• Children use the story Charlie and the Chocolate Factory to look at errors in data. • They look at the five children characters in the story and discuss which are bad and which are good. • They find errors in data and consider how errors can occur when collecting data.	• Can analyse simple 'dirty' data to check for errors. • Can explain why errors can occur when collecting data. • Can explain reasons for correcting errors in simple data.
3	• To look at simple block graphs and identify obvious errors. • To explain how errors can occur when collecting data. • To explain the reasons why data was identified as being incorrect (in a block graph).	• Children look at the story Charlie and the Chocolate Factory and make analogies with data telling a story. • They find errors in block graphs. • Based on the Oompa Loompas' song they create their own data checking song.	• Can analyse simple block graphs to check for errors. • Can explain reasons for correcting errors in simple block graphs.
4	• To collect data about chocolate using software to collate the responses. • To use software to organise the data. • To create simple graphs using the software. • To demonstrate that they have checked for errors.	• Children invent a new chocolate bar, thinking about name, slogan, packaging, ingredients, and so on. • They use a tally chart to collect opinions about their chocolate bar and transfer this information to graphs.	• Can collect data using software. • Can organise collected data in an effective way. • Can create simple graphs using software.

Week	Lesson objectives	Summary of activities	Expected outcomes
5	• To learn to work on projects with their peers cooperatively. • To identify how larger tasks can be broken down into smaller tasks (decomposition) and distributed throughout the group to achieve a goal. • To identify an area to research on the process of making chocolate bars, from bean to bar. • To collect relevant information to contribute to a presentation. • To use more than one piece of software to create the presentation.	• Children write a pitch for their new chocolate bar. They work in groups: • Group 1 develop the wrapper • Group 2 think about ingredients • Group 3 research the process of making the chocolate bar.	• Can work collaboratively with peers on a project. • Can collaborate to create a presentation. • Can contribute information for a presentation, from gathered data. Can combine different software to create a presentation.
6	• To deliver a chocolate presentation to their peers in an effective way. • To receive and give feedback in the form of two stars and a wish, or similar, from their peers. • To explain verbally or in simple written form as appropriate how they would improve their approach to a similar project in the future.	• Groups prepare their pitch. Each presentation includes data and a graph. • They explain how they have checked the data. • Children give constructive feedback after the presentations.	• Can deliver a presentation to their peers. • Can give and receive constructive feedback on presentations.
Assess and review	• To assess the half term's work.	• Children collect and organise data, producing bar charts and checking for errors.	• Assess and review.

Overview of progression

• The children recap on their learning from Year 2, where they began to use tally charts to record the data.
• The children display the data using paper and pencil methods to draw pictographs and bar charts. They progress to using software to display the data as a block graph or bar chart.
• There is a clear focus on checking the data for errors throughout the chapter, whether the data is numerical or presented as a graph.
• The children progress their skills in drawing conclusions from the data, in order to tell a story.

Creative context

The lessons link closely to the English curriculum, as the children:

• retrieve and record information from non-fiction and fiction texts
• research and present on a topic
• draw inferences such as characters' feelings, thoughts and motives from their actions and justifying inferences with evidence predicting what might happen from details stated and implied
• discuss words and phrases that capture the reader's interest and imagination.

In maths, the chapter links very closely to 'Reading and interpreting pictograms', as the children:

• read, interpret and present data using pictograms and bar charts with scales
• solve problems using information presented in pictograms, bar charts and tables. (This can include: solving one-step and two-step questions such as 'How many more?' and 'How many fewer?')

In science and geography, the chapter links to where our food comes from.

Background knowledge

• The children will have collected data in Year 2 and also in their maths lessons. They will be aware of the range of chocolate bars available. In the lessons, they gather data about which chocolate bars are most popular by recording votes from their friends.
• The children will have seen simple bar charts and may have drawn them on paper; however, they may not have used software to display the data.

Curriculum objectives
- To select, use and combine a variety of software to design and create a range of content that accomplish given goals, including collecting and presenting data and information.

Lesson objectives
- To design a simple tally sheet for data collection.
- To collect data from relevant people (about chocolate preferences) using a tally sheet.
- To organise data in simple ways.
- To represent data pictorially using chocolate bar wrappers.
- To draw simple initial conclusions from the data collected.

Expected outcomes
- Can collect data using a tally sheet.
- Can organise collected data in an effective way.

Resources
Photocopiable page 81 'Favourite chocolate bars'

Chocolate

These data lessons follow a chocolate theme, where the children take surveys and present their findings. Using a tally chart, they ask each other about their favourite chocolate bars and then create bar charts.

Introduction
- Introduce the lesson by asking: *Who likes chocolate?* After the children put up their hands, count them and say, for example: *In our class, 29 out of 31 children like chocolate.* Explain that they have collected data and remind them of their previous lessons on data collection.
- Ask the children to name types of chocolate bars and choose four examples. Instead of putting their hands up, point to the four corners of the room and say: *If you like [name of chocolate bar] go to that corner.* To support this, you could write the name of the bar on a drywipe board and one child could hold it, so the other children can see it. Once the children have chosen a corner, rearrange the first group to stand in a line that comes out from one side of the room. Now, line the second group up next to them, and continue until the four groups are standing in the four lines. Is it easy to see which is most popular?
- Ask the longest line to squash together and the shortest line to spread out. Ask: *Has this changed the results?*

Whole-class work
- The children use photocopiable page 81 'Favourite chocolate bars' to design their tally chart. Check that they can remember how to record the results using tally marks. Once created, they can begin data collection, by asking ten other children for their favourite chocolate bar name. There is no limit on the types of bar that can be suggested, there will probably be more than the four types used in the class example.

Paired work
- Using the results from the data collection, the children count the tallies and write them as an integer. In their pairs the children compare their results. Is the most popular bar the same for both of their sets of results?
- The children organise the data by sorting the chocolate types into order from the most popular to least popular.
- The children draw a bar chart on the photocopiable sheet.

> **Differentiation**
> - Support: Less confident learners may need support to organise their tally chart and to draw the bar chart, to the correct scale.
> - Challenge: More confident learners could collect data from 20 children and arrange the data from most popular to least and least popular to most.

Review
- Bring the class together and ask the children to describe the process of collecting the data. Ask different children to report their results and their conclusions about the most and least popular chocolate bars.
- Had they been collecting from all the children in the school, how would it be different? (The process would be more complicated and errors would be more likely to occur). Explain that, in the following lessons, they will be looking at errors in data and how to spot them.

Curriculum objectives

● To select, use and combine a variety of software to design and create a range of content that accomplish given goals, including collecting and presenting data and information.

Lesson objectives

● To look at simple 'dirty' data and identify obvious errors.
● To explain how errors can occur when collecting data.
● To explain the reasons why data was identified as being incorrect (in relation to the data set).

Expected outcomes

● Can analyse simple 'dirty' data to check for errors.
● Can explain why errors can occur when collecting data.
● Can explain reasons for correcting errors in simple data.

Resources

Charlie and the Chocolate Factory by Roald Dahl; interactive activity '*Charlie and the Chocolate Factory* characters' from the CD-ROM; photocopiable page 'Dirty data' on the CD-ROM; photocopiable page 'Class dirty data' from the CD-ROM

Into the factory

Continuing the chocolate theme, the children recall the story *Charlie and the Chocolate Factory* by Roald Dahl and think about the main characters of the five children. They are either good or bad and their actions portray their characters. Then, looking at data, which contains obvious errors, they clean up the 'dirty' data and justify their decisions.

Introduction

● Introduce the lesson by asking whether the children know the *Charlie and the Chocolate Factory* story. Can they remember that five children were chosen, but something goes wrong and they make mistakes or errors, except for Charlie? Can they name the five children in the story? (Augustus Gloop, Veruca Salt, Violet Beauregarde, Mike Teavee and Charlie Bucket). Read the part of the story to describe the children just before they enter the chocolate factory.
● Ask the children to think about the characters. Can they classify them as either completely good or bad? Using interactive activity '*Charlie and the Chocolate Factory* characters' on the CD-ROM, the children decide whether the characters are good or bad and label them with the bad event from the story and the outcome of their actions.

Whole-class work

● In the story, bad events or mistakes can happen. Explain that the same can happen when collecting and recording data. Using photocopiable page 'Dirty data' from the CD-ROM, ask the children to look at the results from a survey about Willy Wonka's chocolate bars. Explain that ten people were asked which their favourite was. One of the results in the data reads 36, so it should stand out from the other figures. Ask the children: *Which one do you think might be an error? Why do they think that?*

Paired work

● In pairs, the children look at the other examples of data collected. Can they identify the errors and give a reason for their choice?

Differentiation
● Support: Less confident learners may need support to create an explanation, as to which value is the error.
● Challenge: More confident learners can identify the errors and suggest a more accurate value for the data, with an explanation.

Review

● Bring the class together and review the answers from different groups. Can they explain their reasons for the errors they have spotted?
● Finally, look at the example of dirty data on photocopiable page 'Class dirty data' from the CD-ROM. Can they spot the errors and explain why?

Curriculum objectives
● To select, use and combine a variety of software to design and create a range of content that accomplish given goals, including collecting and presenting data and information.

Lesson objectives
● To look at simple block graphs and identify obvious errors.
● To explain how errors can occur when collecting data.
● To explain the reasons why data was identified as being incorrect (in a block graph).

Expected outcomes
● Can analyse simple block graphs to check for errors.
● Can explain reasons for correcting errors in simple block graphs.

Resources
Interactive activity 'Our pets' on the CD-ROM; photocopiable page 'Spot the error on the graph' from the CD-ROM; *Charlie and the Chocolate Factory* by Roald Dahl

Oompa-Loompa cleaning up the data

The children focus on the graphical representation of the data. They look at block graphs and see whether they can identify errors in the data. Using the *Charlie and the Chocolate Factory* story, they spot the errors and justify their decisions. Finally, the children create a song related to cleaning up the data.

Introduction
● Begin the lesson by reading the 'Oompa-Loompa' rhyme about Augustus Gloop from *Charlie and the Chocolate Factory* (Chapter 17). Let the children enjoy hearing about his bad character.
● Explain to the children that they will follow the story of Charlie in the book and then they are introduced to the other children. Can they predict what happens next after Augustus Gloop is naughty? (The next child is naughty). The text tells a story. Emphasise to the children that data tells a story too.
● Display the graph from interactive activity 'Our pets' on the CD-ROM. The graph shows favourite pets in an imaginary class. Ask: *What story does the data tell us? Which is the most popular pet? Why do you think dogs are the most popular?* Explain that if they repeated the survey in a year's time, the numbers could change. For example, if a new pet shop opened nearby that sold lizards and snakes, then these animals might appear on the graph – this tells a story.

Whole-class work
● Looking at photocopiable page 'Spot the error on the graph' from the CD-ROM, the children can look at a graph and try to identify whether there is a mistake. Looking at the first graph, there is a large number of children who have a bike (over 40 children), but the graph says 30 children were asked which mode of transport they use, so there is an error.

Paired work
● In pairs, the children look at the second graph and decide if they think there is an error. Simply because a graph has one category with a higher value does not mean it is an error, but it may look suspicious. Also, if one category is lower than expected, the children may need to check it. The aim is to get the children thinking about the data and checking whether they think it is incorrect. In the case of the second graph, 1000 people were surveyed but the data does not add to 1000. The error here is that the figure for football should have been 500, not 50. If children are struggling to work out the error, prompt them to think about which sport they would have expected to be most popular.

Differentiation
● Support: Less confident learners may need support to identify errors in the data and structured sentences to explain their answers, for example, 'I think that the _____ is an error, because it is too _____ (high or low), when looking at the others.'
● Challenge: More confident learners could check the data in the graph and write their explanations for their decisions.

Review
● Ask the children in turn to share their ideas about correct and incorrect data. Some of the answers may be open to interpretation, so it is important for them to explain their reasoning.
● Ask whether it was easier to spot errors in the graphs, rather than the numerical data or the tally charts. They may say that the graphs are pictorial and so a particularly high or low value may stand out.
● Finally, the children could create a 'Data checking' Oompa-Loompa song. If possible, show a clip of the Oompa-Loompas singing in the film *Willy Wonka and the chocolate factory*. Ask children to add a line about checking the data. For example, 'Oompa-Loompa, do-bitty-do, if I were wise, I'd listen to you, Check-the, check-the, data today, it will make the errors go away!'

Curriculum objectives
● To select, use and combine a variety of software to design and create a range of content that accomplish given goals, including collecting and presenting data and information.

Lesson objectives
● To collect data about chocolate using software to collate the responses.
● To use software to organise the data.
● To create simple graphs using the software.
● To demonstrate that they have checked for errors.

Expected outcomes
● Can collect data using software.
● Can organise collected data in an effective way.
● Can create simple graphs using software.

Resources
Interactive activity 'Data graphs' on the CD-ROM; photocopiable page 82 'The new chocolate bar'; photocopiable page 83 'New chocolate bar survey'; Charlie and the Chocolate Factory by Roald Dahl; the films Willy Wonka & the Chocolate Factory and Charlie and the Chocolate Factory

Mmm, what shall we make?

In this lesson, the children imagine that they are Willy Wonka, thinking up a new idea. What shall the new chocolate bar be called? What will it taste like? The children design their new bar and sketch it, before carrying out surveys with their peers. They check for errors and present the data they find.

Introduction
● Read the description of Willy Wonka (when he appears outside the factory in chapter 14). The children imagine what he looks like. If possible, watch an extract from either of the films based on the story (Willy Wonka & the Chocolate Factory or Charlie and the Chocolate Factory). Tell the children that today they are going to be Willy Wonka and invent a new chocolate bar!
● Ask them to think about the new bar: What will you call it? What will it taste like? What ingredients and nutrients will it have? For the wrapper, which colours and writing will you use?

Paired work
● In pairs the children discuss their ideas, before sketching the bar and the wrapper on photocopiable page 82 'The new chocolate bar'. The children talk with their partner to refine their ideas, by asking each other questions from the photocopiable sheet.

Independent work
● The children survey the class to find out their opinions of the new bar. They must choose one aspect to survey, for example, the name, the wrapper or the ingredients. Once decided, they use photocopiable page 83 'New chocolate bar survey' to create a tally chart and refine their question. The children then ask 15 other children to respond (writing the names of the children on the sheet, to avoid asking the same child more than once).

Paired work
● Demonstrate to the class how to use interactive activity 'Data graphs' on the CD-ROM. The children enter the name of the categories and then add the number for that category. When finished, they can display a bar chart. In pairs, allow the children time to explore the software and to enter their data.

Differentiation
● Support: Less confident learners may need support to construct their question and tally chart. They may also need help using the software.
● Challenge: More confident learners could ask more than 15 children their opinions and then organise the data to rank it in order from smallest to largest and vice versa. They could compare using a bar chart to using a pie chart as ways of displaying the information.

Review
● Bring the class together and ask one pair to present their survey. Ask: What was your question? How did you organise the data? Was it easy to use the interactive tool to create the graph? Did you check for errors in the numerical data? Did you check for errors, once it was displayed as a graph. Finally, what is your conclusion from the graph?

Curriculum objectives
• To select, use and combine a variety of software to design and create a range of content that accomplish given goals, including collecting and presenting data and information.

Lesson objectives
• To learn to work on projects with their peers cooperatively.
• To identify how larger tasks can be broken down into smaller tasks (decomposition) and distributed throughout the group to achieve a goal.
• To identify an area to research on the process of making chocolate bars, from bean to bar.
• To collect relevant information to contribute to a presentation.
• To use more than one piece of software to create the presentation.

Expected outcomes
• Can work collaboratively with peers on a project.
• Can collaborate to create a presentation.
• Can contribute information for a presentation, from gathered data.
• Can combine different software to create a presentation.

Resources
Interactive activity 'Yummy chocky' on the CD-ROM; Interactive activity 'Data graphs' on the CD-ROM; photocopiable page 84 'New bar ingredients'; photocopiable page 85 'New bar wrapper design'; photocopiable page 86 'From bean to bar'

Working together

The children work together on a project about the new chocolate bar. The project is split into smaller parts for different groups to do, and then they come together to collaboratively achieve the goal of presenting a pitch. Each group carries out a survey and prepares to present the results, which they will do in the next lesson.

Introduction
• Begin by asking the children to explain what they did in the previous lesson, creating a new chocolate bar. Display the interactive activity 'Yummy chocky' on the CD-ROM and ask the children to think of persuasive words to describe the chocolate bar. Look at examples of slogans for other bars, 'Have a break, have a...', 'Why have cotton, when you can have silk?'
• Explain that the large project of 'pitching' the new chocolate bar will be divided into smaller parts. Explain that a pitch is where they have to convince someone to like their idea. This can be backed up with data from surveys, to show that other people like their idea too.

Whole-class work
• Divide the children into 3 groups to prepare the pitch and give them their tasks: Group 1 wrapper design, Group 2 chocolate bar ingredients and Group 3 the process of making chocolate.

Group work
• Group 1 develop the wrapper design – the children will use the wrappers they designed in the previous lesson. Using photocopiable page 85 'New bar wrapper design', they choose three examples and then collect opinions on their suitability for the new bar. They display the results using interactive activity 'Data graphs' on the CD-ROM.
• Group 2 focus on the chocolate bar's contents, collecting opinions on people's tastes. The group decide upon the taste and ingredients of three example bars. Using photocopiable page 84 'New bar ingredients', they design their data collection tally sheet and then collect the opinions from the class. They display the results using interactive activity 'Data graphs' on the CD-ROM.
• Group 3 research the process of making chocolate bars, from bean to bar. They will use the web to find out about the process of making chocolate bars. To guide their research, they could use the Cadbury's website description: www.cadbury.com.au/about-chocolate/chocolate-making.aspx. They make notes about the production process, using photocopiable page 86 'From bean to bar'. To collect data, they collect opinions on whether the children think Willy Wonka or Mr Cadbury really had factories and really existed. They display the results using interactive activity 'Data graphs' on the CD-ROM.
• Each group should take a screen-grab of their results, using the 'print screen' key on the keyboard, so they can refer to it in the next lesson.

Differentiation
• Support: Less confident learners may need support to decide upon the question to ask the children in their survey and support to enter the information into the software.
• Challenge: More confident learners could draw conclusions from the data collection and prepare the results for presentation, by placing them into the software.

Review
• Bring the groups together and ask a spokesperson to feed back to the class about the process. Ask Groups 1 and 2 how they decided upon the three chocolate wrappers or three ingredients to survey upon. Ask Group 3, where they researched the information and what they found? Can they simply describe the process of making chocolate bars?
• From the survey by Group 3, does the class think that Willy Wonka and Mr Cadbury existed and really had factories?

Curriculum objectives
● To select, use and combine a variety of software to design and create a range of content that accomplish given goals, including collecting and presenting data and information.

Lesson objectives
● To deliver a chocolate presentation to their peers in an effective way.
● To receive and give feedback in the form of two stars and a wish, or similar, from their peers.
● To explain verbally or in simple written form as appropriate, how they would improve their approach to a similar project in the future.

Expected outcomes
● Can deliver a presentation to their peers.
● Can give and receive constructive feedback on presentations.

Resources
Interactive activity 'Data graphs' on the CD-ROM; photocopiable page 87 'Pitch'

Putting it all together

The children use the information gathered in the previous lesson to create a 'pitch' for a new chocolate bar. Each group presents their data to show the chosen wrapper, ingredients and the process of producing a chocolate bar. They give feedback to each other, using the 'Two stars and a wish' and remembering from their learning that feedback must be 'kind, specific and helpful'.

Introduction
● Explain that it is time to present the pitch for the new chocolate bar. The children are going to work in their groups to prepare what they will say and present their graph.

Group work
● The children separate into their groups and use photocopiable page 87 'Pitch' to construct their presentation.
● Group 1 display the three wrappers that they originally chose and prepare a description of each one. Then they show the bar chart they created in the last lesson and, from this graph, say which wrapper was chosen and why.
● Group 2 display the three chocolate bars they chose and describe the tastes and ingredients of each. They show the bar chart they created in the last lesson and, from this graph, explain which bar was chosen and why.
● Group 3 describe the process of making a chocolate, from bean to bar. This could be divided between the children, for example, each child could write one of the steps in the process on a drywipe board. They then could extend the final step to show how their new chocolate bar would be produced in the factory. (This group shared their data handling in the previous lesson, deciding whether Willy Wonka and Mr Cadbury existed.)

Differentiation
● Support: Less confident learners may need support to construct their presentations and draft the words they will say.
● Challenge: More confident learners could present the information as a bar chart and explain how the results may have been different if they had asked a larger number of people or a different group, for example adults.

Review
● Bring the class together to prepare to present. Each group can present to the class. It might be that all the children have a role or they may choose a spokesperson. The children observing the presentation will give 'Two stars and a wish' – that is two things they liked about the presentation and one thing they would improve upon. After each presentation, take examples of two stars and a wish from the children. Remind them that they need to be kind, specific and helpful in their feedback.
● When all the presentations have been given, ask the children how they found the process: *Was it easier or harder to work in a group than in pairs or on your own? Was it better to divide the whole pitch into three groups, than to do all of the parts yourself?* Ask for their reasons, highlighting that they benefitted from each others' expertise. Also it may be quicker for groups to do the tasks at the same time, rather than individually collecting data and analysing it all themselves.

Curriculum objectives
● To select, use and combine a variety of software to design and create a range of content that accomplish given goals, including collecting and presenting data and information.

Lesson objectives
● To collect data from relevant people using a tally sheet.
● To use software to organise the data.
● To create simple graphs using the software.
● To demonstrate that they have checked for errors.

Expected outcomes
● Can collect data using a tally sheet.
● Can organise collected data in an effective way.
● Can create simple graphs using software.

Resources
Interactive activity 'Data graphs' on the CD-ROM; photocopiable page 'My favourite gum' from the CD-ROM; interactive activity 'Let's check the data' on the CD-ROM; *Charlie and the Chocolate Factory* by Roald Dahl

Chocolate factory: Assess and review

To assess and review the learning, the children carry out a survey, present it as a pictograph and also use software to create a bar chart. They use the *Charlie and the Chocolate Factory* theme to think about which foods they would put into the bubblegum (that Violet Beauregarde eats in the story). They also look at example 'dirty' data and identify errors. Finally, they draw conclusions about their findings.

Introduction
● Introduce the lesson by reading the 'Violet Beauregarde eats the gum' section from *Charlie and the Chocolate Factory* (Chapter 21). In the story, she is warned not to, but she eats the gum containing a three-course meal. The gum is meant to taste of tomato soup, roast beef and blueberry pie. Which three foods would the children put in their gum?

Whole-class work
● Explain to the children that they are going to decide upon the menu for the gum. They will need to survey their friends to find the most popular foods for the starter, main and desert.
● Ask: *How are you going to organise the data collection?*
● Ask: *How are you going to display the data?*

Paired work
● In pairs, using photocopiable page 'My favourite gum' from the CD-ROM, the children choose three types of food for the starter, three types of food for the main and three types of food for the desert. They complete their tally charts, before collecting the data from at least ten people.
● Once collected, the children check the data for errors, before entering it into the software and viewing the graphs.
● To complete the process, they decide which of their foods are the most popular to create the 'perfect' gum.

Differentiation
● Support: Less confident learners may need support to select their questions to ask the class and to create the tally charts.
● Challenge: More confident learners could consider if there is a pattern between the types of food for each course, for example, do the same people who like soup also like fish and chips?

Review
● Bring the class together and display interactive activity 'Let's check the data' on the CD-ROM. The data collected from another set of children for their favourite meals is displayed.
● Ask: *Can you spot any errors in the numbers or on the graph? Why do you think that?*
● Conclude the lesson by asking the children to share their 'perfect' gum combinations of food. Do they sound delicious?

Favourite chocolate bars

- Add headings to the tally chart.
- Then enter your chocolate bar data.

- Draw a bar chart of your results here.

 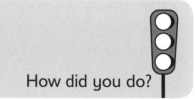

The new chocolate bar

- Draw your new chocolate bar here.

- What is it called? _____

- What will it taste like? _____

- How big is it? _____

Ingredients:

-
-
-
-
-
-
-

I can design a new chocolate bar.

How did you do?

PHOTOCOPIABLE

■ SCHOLASTIC
www.scholastic.co.uk

Name: _____   Date: _____

New chocolate bar survey

■ Complete the tally chart and add the names of the children surveyed.

Like	
Dislike	

Children who liked:	Children who disliked:

■ Draw a bar chart of your results here.

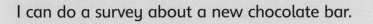

I can do a survey about a new chocolate bar.

How did you do?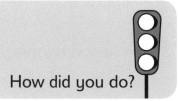

Name: _____   Date: _____

New bar ingredients

■ Decide on ingredients for three bars of chocolate.

List of ingredients:

Bar A	Bar B	Bar C

■ Do a survey. Which bar do your classmates prefer?

Bar A	
Bar B	
Bar C	

■ Draw a bar chart of your results here.

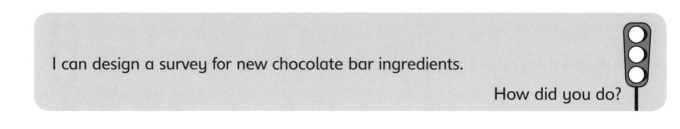

I can design a survey for new chocolate bar ingredients.

How did you do?

PHOTOCOPIABLE   SCHOLASTIC www.scholastic.co.uk

Name: _____   Date: _____

New bar wrapper design

- Design wrappers for three chocolate bars. Label them A, B and C.

- Do a survey. Which wrapper do your classmates prefer?

Bar A	
Bar B	
Bar C	

- Draw a bar chart of your results here.

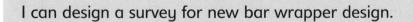

I can design a survey for new bar wrapper design.

How did you do?

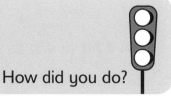

From bean to bar

How to make chocolate
1.
2.
3.
4.
5.
6.
7.
8.
9.
10.

■ Do a survey.

Ask your classmates:

- Did Willy Wonka really have a chocolate factory? Did Mr Cadbury?
- Draw a tally chart and bar chart on a separate piece of paper to show your results.

I can do a survey to find the answer to a question.

How did you do?

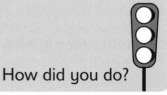

Name: _____   Date: _____

Pitch

- Use this storyboard to plan your pitch presentation.

I can use a storyboard to plan a presentation.

How did you do?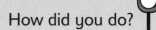

Superheroes

This chapter uses a superheroes theme to engage children in the subject of e-safety. They think about what makes a superhero and superhero characteristics. The children are introduced to the term 'social media' and look at the example of Facebook. Even though users need to be 13 years old to have a Facebook account, the children will know friends and family who are using the network. The children think about the information they may share on their profile and in the messages they may post.

Expected prior learning

● The children will have learned about avatars and basic profile information from the lessons in Key Stage 1. They will have considered the differences between communicating when face-to-face, compared with online. They will be aware of sharing personal information and that sharing has many benefits, though they need to be careful not to give away personal details.

Chapter at a glance

Subject area
• Safety

National Curriculum objective
• To use search technologies effectively.
• To use technology safely, respectfully and responsibly; recognise acceptable/unacceptable behaviour; identify a range of ways to report concerns about content and contact.

Week	Lesson objectives	Summary of activities	Expected outcomes
1	• To understand what is meant by the term 'social media'. • To know the main social media channels. • To discuss the main, age-appropriate, potential issues surrounding social media. • To start to understand how social media can be a positive source of communication.	• Children discuss what a superhero is and film and TV superheroes. • They draw character profiles of superheroes. • Children are introduced to the term social media and examples are discussed. • They begin to think about the positives of social media as well as the negatives.	• Can use technology safely, respectfully and responsibly. • Can recognise acceptable/ unacceptable behaviour.
2	• To learn what Facebook is. • To know how Facebook is used by individuals and organisations. • To understand Facebook age limits and the reasons behind the age limits. • To understand what information and media can be safely shared on Facebook and what is best kept private.	• Children look at the ancient superhero, Heracles. What are his super powers and weaknesses? • Facebook is used as an example of a social media site. Children are not allowed a Facebook page until they are aged 13. They discuss how it is used by individuals and businesses. • They discuss what information should be shared/kept private. • They create a superhero profile.	• Can use social media safely, respectfully and responsibly. • Can identify a range of ways to report concerns about content and contact.
3	• To use basic 'advanced searching' techniques to research information about their chosen superhero. • To be able to narrow searches by type (e.g. image, video) and time (most recent). • To use basic Boolean searching (+, -) and basic advanced tools (e.g. size of image) to return more accurate results. • To save text information in text editing software for inclusion on their superhero Facebook page. • To save images in a folder for use in their superhero Facebook page.	• Children search online using Safe Search, for real-life superheroes. • They use Boolean search methods. • They copy and save text and images to add to superhero profile page.	• Can use search technologies effectively. • Can save and retrieve documents effectively.

Week	Lesson objectives	Summary of activities	Expected outcomes
4	• To create a paper design for a superhero Facebook page. • To combine images, text and other media in a visually effective way. • To include relevant content that is appropriate to share.	• Children build up the profile of their superhero, with sidekick and villain. • They look at the 'back story'.	• Can plan on paper an effective superhero Facebook page. • Can combine different media to create an effective social media page.
5	• To open a saved template in a shared area. • To save a template in their own area. • To insert saved images into their superhero Facebook page. • To add suitable text to their superhero Facebook page. • To add other media as appropriate to their superhero Facebook page.	• Children use a template for inserting profile information. • They use the templates to insert information about the villain, sidekick and superhero to make profiles which can be saved in a shared area.	• Can use a template to create an effective superhero Facebook page.
6	• To discuss their superhero Facebook page and demonstrate how they have created it. • To explain verbally why they have included certain content and left out other information. • To create five top tips on using Facebook. • To discuss how their learning on Facebook can be applied across other social media.	• Children review their learning about superheroes and their characteristics. • They discuss how to be safe online and to think about what information can be shared and what can't be. • They create five top tips to using Facebook.	• Can explain why they have included and excluded information from their Facebook page. • Can explain how to use social media safely, respectfully and responsibly.
Assess and review	• Assess and review the half term's work.	• Children create a template for a social media type page and explain what information to include and how to stay safe.	• Assess and review.

Overview of progression
● The children are reinforcing their learning about profiles, avatars and sharing personal information. They learn more about profiles and posting information on social media websites.
● Using online software, the children experience using the template, before developing their skills to create their own templates on the computer.

Creative context
● The lessons link closely to the English curriculum, by drawing inferences such as characters' feelings, thoughts and motives from their actions. They retrieve and record information from fictional and non-fictional texts. They understand how a character can be described by what he or she does or says.
● Linking to maths, the children study time by using dates of birth and also the time and date of the posts on the social media page.
● Linking to art, the children look at many images of superheroes, mostly in a comic book style, which encourages them to think about the colours, layout and text being used.

Background knowledge
● The children will be aware that parents and older siblings have Facebook accounts, so in the lessons they learn about more about social media, with the main example being Facebook.
● They will have created profiles in the previous lessons, so they should have an awareness of the information they will include. Children can sometimes get 'caught up' in gathering as many friends as possible when using social media sites, so it is important that they understand to be careful with the information they share, as well as being careful about whom they are friends with.

Curriculum objectives
● To use search technologies effectively.
● To use technology safely, respectfully and responsibly; recognise acceptable/ unacceptable behaviour; identify a range of ways to report concerns about content and contact.

Lesson objectives
● To understand what is meant by the term 'social media'.
● To know the main social media channels.
● To discuss the main, age-appropriate, potential issues surrounding social media.
● To start to understand how social media can be a positive source of communication.

Expected outcomes
● Can use technology safely, respectfully and responsibly.
● Can recognise acceptable/ unacceptable behaviour.

Resources
Interactive activity 'Superhero' on the CD-ROM; photocopiable page 97 'About my superhero'

Introduction to superheroes

● This chapter focuses on superheroes in order to consider safety online. The children find out about social media and share examples they may have encountered. Though they are too young to have their own Facebook account, they think about how good and bad news can be spread on such accounts.

Introduction
● In previous lessons, the children have been taught about being careful online. They may have played online games and understand that they have to be careful about their personal information. Watch the 'Lee and Kim's adventure Animal Magic cartoon' (which can be downloaded from www.thinkuknow. co.uk/teachers/resources/). In the video, the characters are introduced to 'SID' a superhero. Ask: *How do you know he is a superhero?*
● Continue the lesson by asking: *Can you name a superhero? Why are they a superhero?* Collect the names of the superheroes and display them. Can they name any supervillains?
● Share and read examples of superheroes from comic strips. An example of a comedy superhero is Captain Underpants (www.scholastic.com/ captainunderpants/). Can the children describe the stories? The children could create their own comic strip using the comic creator tool on the Scholastic website (www.scholastic.com/captainunderpants/comic.htm).

Whole-class work
● Using interactive activity 'Superhero' on the CD-ROM, ask for superhero characteristics, for example, super powers, costume, a motif and secret identity. Add their ideas to the list on the interactive, for example, 'Spiderman wears blue and red and climbs walls.'

Paired work
● Using photocopiable page 97 'About my superhero', the children sketch a picture of their chosen superhero (they could invent their own or use a known one and add labels to describe them).

Whole-class work
● Bring the class together and ask three children to share their examples. Explain to them that superheroes often have a strong moral code – they are very clear about what is right and wrong.
● Introduce the children to the term 'social media'. Ask: *Has anyone heard that before?* Ask them whether they have heard of Facebook, Twitter, Google+, Snapchat, Instagram, for example. In this and the following lessons, the example for the social media tool is Facebook, as it is the most familiar. The intention is not to encourage the children to use Facebook, but to think about how they might see others portrayed online and to think about themselves and how they behave.

Differentiation
● Support: Less confident learners may need support to think of the characteristics of the superhero. By retelling a superhero story, they could note the good deeds.
● Challenge: More confident learners could label their superheroes with more information about the superhero's moral code – what do they do that displays their code? How do people know whether they are good or evil?

Review
● Can the children think of some good news they have heard? When they heard the good news, what did they do?
● Ask the class whether they have ever gossiped. Have they ever heard a story about someone else, which maybe is not nice, but they have told others?
● This sharing of good and bad news is similar online. Using social media can be a great way to spread good news, but shouldn't be used to spread gossip.

Curriculum objectives
● To use search technologies effectively.
● To use technology safely, respectfully and responsibly; recognise acceptable/ unacceptable behaviour; identify a range of ways to report concerns about content and contact.

Lesson objectives
● To learn what Facebook is.
● To know how Facebook is used by individuals and organisations.
● To understand Facebook age limits and the reasons behind the age limits.
● To understand what information and media can be safely shared on Facebook and what is best kept private.

Expected outcomes
● Can use social media safely, respectfully and responsibly.
● Can identify a range of ways to report concerns about content and contact.

Resources
Interactive activity 'Heracles' on the CD-ROM; Photocopiable page 98 'Heracles' online profile'; photocopiable page 99 'My online profile'

More superheroes

The children look at the superhero Heracles and read his myths. They decide upon his super powers and his weaknesses. Using the example of Facebook as a social media site, they consider the minimum age restriction and what information is safe to share online.

Introduction
● Begin the lesson by introducing Heracles, a superhero from ancient Greece (the Romans named him Hercules). Read a short version of his myths and how he completed tasks using his powers. What were his strengths and weaknesses? Use interactive activity 'Heracles' on the CD-ROM to collect their examples.

Whole-class work
● In the previous lesson, the children thought about social media. For this lesson, Facebook will be used as the main example of social media. Explain that Facebook is a way of sharing information for individuals and also for companies. The companies might use Facebook to send out information about special offers or to offer another way of getting in touch for their customers. The children will probably know someone who uses Facebook as an individual.

Paired work
● Using photocopiable page 98 'Heracles' online profile', the children create a profile page for Heracles, in the style of Facebook. This includes a profile picture, name, age, address and interests.

Whole-class work
● Bring the class together and ask: *How old do you need to be to have a Facebook account?* Collect opinions from the class, before explaining they need to be 13 years old. Explain that the minimum age of 13 is due to American laws (COPPA – Children's Online Privacy Protection Act of 1998 www. coppa.org/coppa.htm). The law says that if a child under 13 wanted to use Facebook, then they would need to be verified by their parents and their information would need to be viewable by their parents. Facebook does not allow this and so users need to be over 13 years old. In addition, younger children would be exposed to interaction from adults, as well as other children, so adding to the risks.
● Explain to the children that, as they get older, they may want a Facebook account to share things with their friends. However, they need to remember that they need to be 13 years old. Before they reach that age they will probably encounter other social media sites, where they need to be careful about the information they share.

Differentiation
● Support: Less confident learners may need support to write the imaginary address and interests of Heracles.
● Challenge: More confident learners will be able to create a Facebook-style profile, including the interests of Heracles and even create a post – this can be an update to say what he is doing during one of his 12 tasks.

Review
● Conclude the lesson by sharing the Marvel Comics profile of Heracles (http://marvel.com/universe/Hercules_(Heracles))
● Watch the cartoon, 'Hector's world' episode 1 (www.thinkuknow.co.uk/5_7/ hectorsworld/). This is a short cartoon about Hector the dolphin and his friends, one of whom put their personal details online. The characters discuss how they need to be careful about what they share.
● Using photocopiable page 99 'My online profile', the children decide which parts of their personal information they should share. This is reinforcing learning from Years 1 and 2.

Curriculum objectives
● To use search technologies effectively.
● To use technology safely, respectfully and responsibly; recognise acceptable/ unacceptable behaviour; identify a range of ways to report concerns about content and contact.

Lesson objectives
● To use basic advanced searching techniques to research information about their chosen Superhero.
● To be able to narrow searches by type (e.g. image, video) and time (most recent).
● To use basic Boolean searching (+, −) and basic advanced tools (e.g. size of image) to return more accurate results.
● To save text information in text editing software for inclusion in their superhero Facebook page.
● To save images in a folder for use in their superhero Facebook page.

Expected outcomes
● Can use search technologies effectively.
● Can save and retrieve documents effectively.

Resources
Photocopiable page 100 'Searching for people'

Real superheroes

By searching on the web, children find stories of real-life superheroes. Using search terms and the operators '+' and '−' can they narrow the search? Also, can they change the search to include only recent stories?

Introduction
● Introduce the lesson by asking: *Do you know a hero?*
● In the news, there is often talk of heroes. Ask: *What actions would they carry out to be called a hero?* They may think of armed services or the emergency services, fire, ambulance, coast guard or police. They may think of survival stories, where somebody heroically saved another climber or explorer.

Whole-class work
● Type 'hero' into Safe Search (http://primaryschoolict.com/) and see the results (it is advisable to check this prior to the lesson, as some news stories may not be suitable for the children).
● Now type 'Nelson Mandela' into Safe Search. Demonstrate that typing 'Nelson+Mandela' returns the same results. The search engine assumes that the space between the words is a '+'. The '−' operator can be demonstrated by search for 'Nelson−Mandela'. Different results are returned, where websites are found with the word 'Nelson' and NOT with 'Mandela'.

Paired work
● The children practise searching for people or characters they know, using photocopiable page 100 'Searching for people'.

Whole-class work
● Demonstrate on the display some examples from the photocopiable sheet, to show the effect of adding a '+' or '−' on the results.
● Switch to the main Google UK home page (www.google.co.uk/). Type 'Nelson Mandela' into the search box and click search. Show the children the number of results. They can narrow the search by using the advanced tools.
● On the right of the page is a cog icon. Click on it and select 'Safe search'.
● Select 'Advanced search'. Look at the list of options. There is an option for 'none of these words', which is the same as placing the '−' before a word.
● The following section says, 'Then narrow your results by...' and more options can be chosen. Select 'Last update' to choose a date in the previous 24 hours. This returns the recently changed web pages.
● Perform a new search for 'hero rescue'. (Test the searches before the lesson, as the pages will keep changing.) Show the children the results, as the time period is changed from past hour, past 24 hours, past week, past month, past year.
● Select a suitable story of a hero and allow the children to think of some questions about them.
● The children could begin to save images into a common folder for future use. They can find an image using the search term in 'Safe Search' and use the right button on the mouse to 'Save image as...' into their folder on the computer or shared folder. They can select, copy and paste text too.

Differentiation
● Support: Less confident learners may need support from adults to write sentences about their hero and to identify the information in the text.
● Challenge: More confident learners could edit the text to make it appropriate for a Year 3 child.

Review
● Remind the class how the lesson began, asking about real-life heroes. They searched online to find real heroes and narrowed their searches. They then collected information to create a profile. Explain that they are developing important digital skills to make sense of the information available online.

■ SCHOLASTIC

Curriculum objectives
● To use search technologies effectively.
● To use technology safely, respectfully and responsibly; recognise acceptable/ unacceptable behaviour; identify a range of ways to report concerns about content and contact.

Lesson objectives
● To create a paper design for a superhero Facebook page.
● To combine images, text and other media in a visually effective way.
● To include relevant content that is appropriate to share.

Expected outcomes
● Can plan on paper an effective superhero Facebook page.
● Can combine different media to create an effective social media page.

Resources
Photocopiable page 101 'My superhero/sidekick/villain profile'

Raising the profile

In this lesson, the children will create their superhero profile, and add information about them. Then they will create their sidekick and arch villain's profile too. They think about what the superhero might post online. Does it display his or her moral code?

Introduction
● Introduce the lesson by showing 'Fakebook' on the display (www.classtools. net/_FAKEBOOK/gallery/index.php). Explain to the children that these are not the real profile pages for the people shown, they have been created to look like real ones. Choose a few examples to show the children the format.
● Ask the children about superheroes, their sidekicks and the villains: *What is their back story? Why have they become the people that they are?*

Paired work
● Using photocopiable page 101 'My superhero/sidekick/villain profile', the children plan and draw the profile for their chosen superhero. They need to think about the hero's name, age and super powers. Then they could create a profile for their sidekick and their associated villain.

Whole-class work
● The children share their new superheroes, sidekicks and villains. Choose three children to try acting out the role of their superhero. The other children can ask them questions and they answer in the style of their character.

Paired work
● In pairs, the children can research images to develop the backstory of the character. For example, they might choose a city, forest or desert, as a base for their character. They save the pictures into a folder for use later.
● The children make notes on their photocopiable sheet about the details of the backstory.
● Once the children have made notes and collected appropriate images, they return to the Fakebook website and create a new page for their superhero (www.classtools.net/FB/home-page). There is a video on the page to show them how to add information.
● The children add a name and the page will search for a photo to match that name (it can be changed later). They can add a birth date and then any family names. If they have a background picture, they can select 'Click here to add a cover picture' and choose a file from the folder.
● Before the Fakebook can be saved, at least three posts should be added. The children think about who would post a message – they could add messages from the villain, sidekick or from a person the hero has rescued.
● When the children select Save, the page gives them advice to write down the web address and also create a password for the page. The children can add the details to the bottom of the photocopiable sheet.

Differentiation
● Support: Less confident learners may need support to identify important information on the web pages and to create posts on behalf of the sidekick and villain.
● Challenge: More confident learners will be able to make notes from the web pages and add the personal details of the superhero to the Fakebook site.

Review
● Bring the class together and choose one child's Fakebook to display.
● Ask the children to review the Fakebook page. Do the posts sound like the words of a sidekick and arch villain? Can the children see the format of the profile? The profile has a name, date of birth or age, background information and then posts from other people plus their own posts.

Curriculum objectives
● To use search technologies effectively.
● To use technology safely, respectfully and responsibly; recognise acceptable/ unacceptable behaviour; identify a range of ways to report concerns about content and contact.

Lesson objectives
● To open a saved template in a shared area.
● To save a saved template in their own area.
● To insert saved images into their superhero Facebook page.
● To add suitable text to their superhero Facebook page.
● To add other media as appropriate to their superhero Facebook page.

Expected outcomes
● Can use a template to create an effective superhero Facebook page.

Resources
Photocopiable page 101 'Superhero/sidekick/villain profile

Putting it all together

Following on from using the Fakebook template in the previous lesson, the children create a simple template of their own for a social media profile page. They think about the elements that form the page and then carefully put them together. Using this template, they create profile pages for the sidekick and villain.

Introduction
● Introduce the lesson by displaying a Fakebook page made by one of the children from week 4. Can the children identify the main features? It has a place for a name, photo, background image, date of birth, family names and posts. The children can draw an outline of the page on a piece of paper, (referring back to the photocopiable page 101 if they need help). This can be called a 'wireframe' (similar to making a papier-mâché model, the main structure can be made of wire, before the detail is added).

Paired work
● The children have sketched their wireframe and can now add detail. In pairs, they can discuss their sidekick and villain's details. Using the web, they could research and make notes, for example, about a particular place in the world that their character comes from.
● Using the computer, the children can create an outline template to represent their sketched layout. Using word processing software, such as Microsoft Word, or a drawing package, the children can add text boxes or shapes on to the page. At this stage, they do not add the detail. They save the page with a file name, such as 'My Fakebook template'. If they are using word processing software, they can change the file extension from .docx to .dot by selecting Save as... and changing the format to Word template. This means that they can access it again as a template. For most Year 3 children, simply saving a file and calling it a template is acceptable. The more confident may save it as a different format.
● To create a new profile, the children can open the file they called their template and immediately select Save as... and save a new version for their sidekick. They can use their notes to add details to the outline, such as name, date of birth, friends' names and family names. Then they can open the template file again and save it as their villain page, before filling in the details.

Differentiation
● Support: Less confident learners may need support to organise their page, identifying the main features of the social media page and adding text boxes.
● Challenge: More confident learners could save their outline as a template and start a new document from a template.

Review
● Bring the class together and display one of the children's pages, as an example. Ask: *Does it have all of the features of a Facebook or Fakebook page? Does it make the person sound interesting?*
● Using 'two stars and a wish', ask the children to think of two parts they like about the page and one part they would change.
● Ask the children: *Was it easier to create the second profile, once you had made the template for the first person?* Explain that when repeating a task, a template can give structure and save time when creating the final product.

Curriculum objectives
● To use search technologies effectively.
● To use technology safely, respectfully and responsibly; recognise acceptable/ unacceptable behaviour; identify a range of ways to report concerns about content and contact.

Lesson objectives
● To discuss their superhero Facebook page and demonstrate how they have created it.
● To explain verbally why they have included certain content and left out other information.
● To create five top tips on using Facebook.
● To discuss how their learning on Facebook can be applied across other social media.

Expected outcomes
● Can explain why they have included and excluded information from their Facebook page.
● Can explain how to use social media safely, respectfully and responsibly.

Resources
Photocopiable page 102 'Top tips'

Read all about it!

To conclude the lessons, the children reflect upon their learning. They have thought about superheroes (fictional and non-fictional) and their traits. They have considered how the hero might be portrayed in a social media page and added the information. They have used an online profile creation tool and created their own templates. Now, they review the content of the profile page and think about being careful about the information they share.

Introduction
● Introduce the lesson by displaying a fictional superhero, so that the whole class can see and comment upon it. What are the main characteristics of the superhero? The children should be able to explain about the features, such as super powers, costume, moral code and so on.
● Using the Fakebook website (www.classtools.net/FB/home-page), the class can collaboratively create the profile for the superhero. They can add as much detail as possible.
● Once complete, explain that social media can be a really useful tool. It can help people to stay in touch over long distances; it can bring groups of people together, who would not have met; and it can be great for groups of friends to communicate. Explain that, when a group of friends talk together, they need to be kind.

Whole-class work
● Display on the screen the Hector's World cartoons for episodes 2 to 5 (www.thinkuknow.co.uk/5_7/hectorsworld/), pausing after each one to ask the children to think of online top tips for other children.

Paired work
● In pairs, the children think about the information they might share on a profile page. The cartoons will have got the children thinking about different aspects of sharing information, so they need to transfer their learning to their superhero example.
● Can the children think of five top tips for sharing information on social media? They can record their ideas on photocopiable page 102 'Top tips'.

Differentiation
● Support: Less confident learners may need support to think of three tips for using social media. They may need support to construct their sentences.
● Challenge: More confident learners could think about five tips for using social media and protecting themselves online.

Review
● Bring the class together to review the learning. Ask the children to share their top tips for sharing information.
● Now ask the children to think about the posts. What sort of things should they be saying? Focus on being kind, as though they were face-to-face. Also, make sure that they understand not to give away important information about their movements, for example, *See you at football practice at St Matthew's playing field at 4.00pm on Thursday.* They need to think carefully about who may see that information.

Curriculum objectives
● To use search technologies effectively.
● To use technology safely, respectfully and responsibly; recognise acceptable/ unacceptable behaviour; identify a range of ways to report concerns about content and contact.

Lesson objectives
● To insert saved images into a social media style page.
● To add suitable text to their social media style page.
● To add posts to their social media-style page.

Expected outcomes
● Can use a template to create an effective social media style page.
● Can explain why they have included and excluded information from their Facebook page.
● Can explain how to use social media safely, respectfully and responsibly.

Resources
Photocopiable page 103 'All about my famous friend'

Superheroes: Assess and review

In this lesson, the children think about being kind online. They have learned about social media and how people can post text and pictures on to social media sites, such as Facebook. The children think about how being kind online should be similar to how they should behave when face-to-face.

Introduction
● Remind the children that they have been learning about social media. Thinking of different superheroes, they have constructed a 'Fakebook' profile page for a superhero. To review the learning, ask them to create a profile page for a partner, who is pretending to be a famous person.

Paired work
● In pairs, one child pretends to be a famous person (and then they can switch). They interview each other to gather information, using photocopiable page 103 'All about my famous friend'. They gather information about their names, date of birth, friends and family. Once complete, they can go to the Fakebook website and create a profile page for their partner (in the role of the famous person).

Whole-class work
● Explain that, on a social media site, people post comments and pictures. They need to be careful about what they post, as it may give away personal information. Each pair invents three posts to add to the page. These posts could be from the partner, from their friends or a conversation between them.

Paired work
● In pairs, the children review the profile that their partner has constructed for them. Looking at the information, would they want to share it? Are there pieces of information that might give away their location or school name? They may have hobbies, which are good to talk about, but do they need to check that the information is safe? For example, *I like riding my bike every night at Front Street.*

Differentiation
● Support: Less confident learners may need support to gather the personal information and to transfer that to the Fakebook webpage.
● Challenge: More confident learners could add a conversation between two or more people to the posts, one replying to the other.

Review
● Bring the class together and display on the screen the Hector's World cartoon episode 6 (www.thinkuknow.co.uk/5_7/hectorsworld/). In the cartoon, a nasty picture is shared, which upsets one of the characters. The children need to think about social media, the positives and the negatives: (it gives them the ability to communicate and share great news; however, it could also be misused, such as someone sharing a nasty picture).
● Thinking about social media, the children focused on Facebook in the lessons, which is a great way of sharing pictures and information. However, if someone shared a picture that the children were not happy with, what should they do?
● Ask: *What would you do if a picture of you was being shared, without your permission and people were making fun of you?*
● Remind the children that if something or someone online upsets them, they must tell someone.

About my superhero

■ Choose a superhero. Draw them here.

■ Label your superhero. Think about their costume, their character, their super powers, and so on.

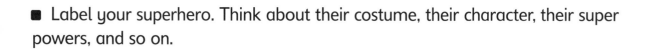

I can draw and label a superhero.

How did you do?

Name: _____   Date: _____

Heracles' online profile

■ Fill in Heracles' profile.

My face	Search
Friends	**Education**
	Books
	Music and films
	Sports

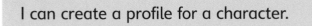

I can create a profile for a character.

How did you do?

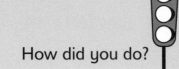

PHOTOCOPIABLE

■SCHOLASTIC
www.scholastic.co.uk

Name: _____   Date: _____

My online profile

- Look at the list of information.
- Which things should you share on social media?

First name

Age

Address

Full name of friends

Country where I live

Full name

Interest/ hobbies

Bank details

Places where you do your hobby

Favourite singers/ bands

Favourite colour

I can decide what I should share on social media.

How did you do?

Searching for people

- Search for the people below online.
- Use + and – to narrow your search.

Nelson Mandela

Queen Elizabeth II

Sherlock Holmes

Charles Darwin

I can search for people online.

How did you do?

PHOTOCOPIABLE

■ SCHOLASTIC
www.scholastic.co.uk

My superhero/sidekick/villain profile

Superhero

Search

Friends

Name

Date Of birth

About

Posts

I can plan a profile page for a superhero.

How did you do?

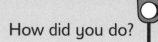

Name: _____   Date: _____

Top tips

My top tips for using Facebook are:

1. _____

_____

_____

_____

2. _____

_____

_____

_____

3. _____

_____

_____

_____

4. _____

_____

_____

_____

5. _____

_____

_____

_____

I can give my top tips for using Facebook.

How did you do?

PHOTOCOPIABLE

Name: _____   Date: _____

All about my famous friend

- Ask your friend to pretend to be a famous person.
- Interview them for a profile page.

Name: _____

Date of birth: _____

Family names: _____

Friends' names: _____

Interesting fact: _____

Hobbies: _____

I can plan a profile page for my friend's character.

How did you do?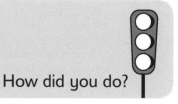

Myths and legends

To begin Year 4, the children use a 'Myths and legends' theme, based around the story of Robin Hood. They think about how they might use search technologies to find information and then – the main focus – to be discerning in evaluating digital content. They consider spam messages, biased information and fake websites through the Robin Hood theme, and reinforce their learning from the previous years.

Expected prior learning

● The children will have used search engines to locate information and will have learned simple ways of narrowing a search. They have considered keeping personal information safe and so, when learning about spam messages, should be able to use this knowledge to protect themselves.
● The children will have used software to lay out simple pages and they can use these skills to create simple webpage templates.

Chapter at a glance

Subject area
• Communication and e-safety

National Curriculum objective
• To use search technologies effectively and be discerning in evaluating digital content.

Week	Lesson objectives	Summary of activities	Expected outcomes
1	• To define a myth and legend. • To re-tell a simple myth and legend. • To identify the main steps in a story. • To use a search engine to locate basic information. • To know there are many different search engines. • To use at least two search engines. • To evaluate located information using given simple criteria.	• Children are introduced to the Robin Hood theme to discuss myths and legends. Do they know who Robin Hood was and what he did? • They decide whether Robin Hood was real or not and define a myth and legend. • They use a search engine to find more information about Robin Hood. • Using more than one search engine, the children compare results.	• Can give a simple definition of a myth and legend. • Can use search technologies to locate and evaluate information.
2	• To know a spam email or message can be misleading. • To give a simple definition of a spam message. • To make analogies with April Fool's Day hoaxes and spam messages. • To know that some spam messages may be dangerous. • To begin to recognise the features of a spam message. • To know what to do if they suspect a message to be spam.	• Children find out about spam emails, how people receive these emails which can deceive and trick, for example April Fool's Day hoaxes. • They discuss how when they receive suspicious emails they should look out for certain features. • They find out what to do if they do receive a suspicious email.	• Can define a spam email or message. • Can explain what to do when receiving a spam email or message.
3	• To know that websites may not contain truthful information. • To make analogies with fake stories in books and misleading websites. • To read myths and legends and identify information that may or may not be truthful.	• Children discuss how there are websites with false information. Myths and legends may not contain fully truthful stories. • They discuss 'wanted' posters for Robin Hood and his men and create a 'wanted' poster for a character who makes false websites.	• Can explain that websites may not contain truthful information. • Can read myths and legends, identify information and discuss if it is truthful.
4	• To create a fake website based on a myth. • To combine software tools to create the design of a website. • To evaluate other children's websites, using given criteria.	• Following on from the previous lesson, the children decide who the villain of the piece is. Is it the Sheriff, King John or King Richard? • They create a webpage to make the villain look like a hero.	• Can create a fake website based on a myth using different software. • Can evaluate peers' websites, using given criteria.

Week	Lesson objectives	Summary of activities	Expected outcomes
5	• To search for fictional inventions (for example, Boilerplate robot chindogu). • To describe the features of a trustworthy website. • To evaluate images to state whether they are truthful and justify decisions.	• Children consider websites for trustworthiness and look at examples of fictional inventions. • They create new images by cutting part of one image out and placing it on top of another. • They evaluate the features of images on the websites to decide whether they are truthful and justify their decisions.	• Can search for images of fictional inventions. • Can evaluate the images to state whether they are truthful.
6	• To know that websites may contain misleading information. • To explain what bias means. • To know and explain that websites may contain bias. • To recognise types of organisations by their website address.	• Children read The Ballad of Robin Hood and decide whether it is biased towards or against Robin Hood. • They discuss what bias means and use a 'Word cloud' tool to look at content of websites to see whether they have bias. • Finally they look at website address extensions, for example, .com or .ac.uk, to recognise organisations and consider whether they are trustworthy.	• Can explain that websites may not contain truthful information or may have a bias. • Can identify the general type of a website, based on the address.
Assess and review	• Assess and review the half term's work.	• Children review their learning on communication and being discerning in evaluating digital content. • They imagine they are a villain sending a spam email.	• Assess and review.

Overview of progression

● The children will progress their knowledge of searching online, by seeing that there are search engines other than Google or Bing.
● They will develop their understanding of spam messages, bias and fake websites and discover hints on how to identify these.
● They will consider the use of persuasive language in digital publications and how it can influence the reader.

Creative context

● The lessons link closely to the English curriculum, through studying myths and legends and identifying themes and conventions in a wide range of books. The children retrieve and record information from the text. They draw inferences, such as characters' feelings, thoughts and motives from their actions; justifying these inferences by creating fake websites and spam messages.
● Linking to the history curriculum, the children learn about the period of the Crusades, about the roles in society of peasant, yeoman, sheriff, knight and king. They learn about the weapons used and about the taxing of the people to raise funds.
● Linking to geography, the children use the ballads and stories to locate where Robin potentially lived and where Sherwood Forest is located. They can look for place names containing Robin Hood, including the airport.

Background knowledge

● The children will already know the name of Robin Hood from stories, films and television, though they may not know much about the other characters and the period in history. They may know the phrase 'Robbed from the rich to give to the poor'. In the lessons it is important to share the different stories and information about Robin Hood and how much can be proven.
● The children may know what a spam email or message is, but will not know the signs to identify one. Similarly, they may know that not all information online is true, but identifying fake websites will be new to them and is a very difficult skill to develop. Therefore, it is important to begin this learning early.

Curriculum objectives
● To use search technologies effectively and be discerning in evaluating digital content.

Lesson objectives
● To define a myth and legend.
● To retell a simple myth and legend.
● To identify the main steps in a story.
● To use a search engine to locate basic information.
● To know there are many different search engines.
● To use at least two search engines.
● To evaluate located information using given simple criteria.

Expected outcomes
● Can give a simple definition of a myth and legend.
● Can use search technologies to locate and evaluate information.

Resources
Photocopiable page 113 'Robin Hood story'; photocopiable page 114 'About the characters'

The story of Robin Hood

The first lesson is an introduction to the story of Robin Hood, as a myth and legend. What are the main features of the story? What is a myth and legend? Can we trust the details to be true? The children then search for information on the web, using more than one search engine. They evaluate their findings to see if they believe the facts are true.

Introduction

● Introduce the lesson by asking whether the children know the story of Robin Hood. They probably know that he used a bow and arrow and robbed the rich to pay the poor. There have been films and dramatisations on television, which may influence their answers.
● Ask: *How do you know if the story is true?* They may say because it has been written about or because lots of people know the story.
● Ask them if they can explain what a myth or legend is.
● Ask: *Do you think that the 'legend of Robin Hood is true?*
● Explain that in the lessons they will be searching for information online, looking at spam emails and also fake websites, which may look real, but they need to consider the evidence to decide.

Paired work

● The children complete a storyboard on photocopiable page 113 'Robin Hood story'. They sketch out the main scenes and add text to describe what is happening. If some children don't know the story well, provide a copy.
● Using a search engine, for example, the Safe Search (http://primaryschoolict. com/), the children search for information about the main characters.
● The children make notes using a word processor or by using photocopiable page 114 'About the characters'.

Whole-class work

● Bring the class together and ask the children to share their notes.
● Now ask about the process of searching for information: *Did you find it easy to find information? Were the websites you selected on the first or second page of the search results? Do you think the information you have found is true?*
● Ask whether they know of any other search engines, for example Bing.
● Use both Bing and Google to search for Robin Hood and compare results.

Paired work

● Using both Bing and Google, the children search online for information about: key characters, key settings (castle and forest) and key events in the story.
● The children observe how two search engines find information differently.

> **Differentiation**
> ● Support: Less confident learners may need support to think of keywords to search with and to then evaluate if the results from the two search engines are different.
> ● Challenge: More confident learners could search for information using the two different search engines and critically compare the order of results found. Ask: *Which engine found the most relevant results about the characters? Can you remember how to narrow a search?*

Review

● Bring the class together and share a list of search engines (http://www. thesearchenginelist.com/). Explain that there are many search engines that could be used to look for information, not just Google or Bing but to be aware these other search engines may not be safe without the Safe search feature.
● A legend may contain some truths, but there may be some information that is not truthful. They need to decide, when searching for information on a website, whether the information is truthful.

Curriculum objectives
● To use search technologies effectively and be discerning in evaluating digital content.

Lesson objectives
● To know a spam email or message can be misleading.
● To give a simple definition of a spam message.
● To make analogies with April Fool's Day hoaxes and spam messages.
● To know that some spam messages may be dangerous.
● To begin to recognise the features of a spam message.
● To know what to do if they suspect a message to be spam.

Expected outcomes
● Can define a spam email or message.
● Can explain what to do when receiving a spam email or message.

Resources
Photocopiable page 115 'April Fools'; photocopiable page 'Spam messages' from the CD-ROM; interactive activity 'A message from the Sheriff' on the CD-ROM

Spam, spam, spam, spam

In this lesson, the children learn about spam messages. What are they and who might send them? They also think about their personal information and keeping it safe. They consider the features of a spam message and how to recognise them.

Introduction
● Introduce the lesson by reminding the children of their learning last week. Ask them: *What is a legend? Did Robin Hood exist?* They should explain that there may be some truth in the story, but there may be some made-up facts too.
● Ask whether they have heard of a spam email or message. A spam email can be an unwanted email, for example, from a company trying to sell something to someone, but that person did not ask the company to get in touch and neither did they give permission or details for the company to contact them. A more dangerous type of spam email is one which looks to be genuine, but has been adapted to trick the person into clicking on a link (which could contain a virus) or to give away personal information.

Whole-class work
● To begin with, the children will look at April Fool's Day hoaxes. These are meant to be fun, to trick people into believing that something is true.
● Show on the display the 'Swiss spaghetti harvest' April Fool (www. museumofhoaxes.com/hoax/archive/permalink/the_swiss_spaghetti_harvest).
● Ask the children: *Do you think it is real? Why would people believe it to be real?* This was an April Fool from a trusted source (the BBC), so people believed it. With spam emails, they may look like they are from someone trustworthy, but they could still be fake.

Paired work
● Using photocopiable page 115 'April Fools', the children look at other examples of April Fool's Day hoaxes.

Whole-class work
● Explain that when receiving a suspicious email or message, they should look for certain features. Ask the class to identify what would make them suspicious of a message or email.
● Write their responses, so they can read them as a list. Support them by using photocopiable page 'Spam messages' from the CD-ROM. This contains suggested warning signs, for example, a message from someone they do not know asking for their personal details, asking for money or saying they have won a prize to a competition that they have not entered.

Differentiation
● Support: Less confident learners may need support to read the text on the web pages, and help to explain why some are hoaxes.
● Challenge: More confident learners could explain the reasons why they think the April Fool's hoaxes are fake and also why do they think people would believe them.

Review
● Bring the class together and ask them to imagine that they are Robin Hood and they have received a message from the Sheriff of Nottingham.
● Using interactive activity 'A message from the Sheriff' on the CD-ROM, the children try to identify why the message may be trying to trick them into giving away personal information or trapping them by following a link in the message.

Curriculum objectives
● To use search technologies effectively and be discerning in evaluating digital content.

Lesson objectives
● To know that websites may not contain truthful information.
● To make analogies with fake stories in books and misleading websites.
● To read myths and legends and identify information that may or may not be truthful.

Expected outcomes
● Can explain that websites may not contain truthful information.
● Can read myths and legends and identify information and discuss if it is truthful.

Resources
Photocopiable page 116 'Wanted – Robin Hood'; photocopiable page 117 'Wanted – Fake Frank'; interactive activity 'Wanted' on the CD-ROM

'Wanted'

Robin Hood was a wanted criminal, so the children imagine what his 'wanted' poster might look like. They identify the features of the posters and create one for Robin. Thinking about modern times, they create a photofit of a fictional character called Fake Frank, who makes fake websites. Using the photofit, they go on to create a wanted poster for him.

Introduction
● Introduce the lesson by reviewing the children's learning about myths and legends and spam messages. Reinforce that information may look correct, but it may not be truthful.
● Explain that they are going to think about the people behind the spam message or fake website and why they might want to trick people.

Whole-class work
● Explain that behind a spam message or a website with false information, there needs to be a person or group of people who want to trick others. This could be for fun, however, it could also be motivated by a wish to gain information about a person and get access to their personal details or money.
● Using interactive activity 'Wanted' on the CD-ROM, the children look at the picture of Robin Hood on a wanted poster. It has a certain style, with the word *wanted* in large type, then the name of the person, what crime they have committed, a reward price and a signature from an official.

Individual work
● Using photocopiable page 116 'Wanted – Robin Hood', the children design their own wanted posters.

Whole-class work
● Ask the children to share their posters with each other. Do they look official? If they saw a poster like theirs on a lamp-post, would it look real? They may respond with answers, such as it would need to be typed on a computer or have a police badge or crest on it.
● Explain that the police often use a photofit to show how a criminal looks.
● Show the children the Open University's Photofit me website (http://www. open.edu/openlearn/body-mind/photofit-me) and demonstrate making a face.
● Explain that they will create a wanted poster for Fake Frank, a criminal who makes fake websites to trick people into sharing personal information.

Paired work
● Allow the children time to play with the 'Photofit me' website and create their own faces.
● In pairs, the children then design a 'wanted' poster using photocopiable page 117 'Wanted – Fake Frank'. They can sketch the picture of Fake Frank onto the page or plan on paper and make a digital poster.
● They must include the fact that Fake Frank tries to trick people into sharing personal information.

> **Differentiation**
> ● Support: Less confident learners may need support to structure the wanted poster to include a reason why Fake Frank is wanted and to think of a suitable reward value.
> ● Challenge: More confident learners could create their wanted posters and add additional information, such as the details of Fake Frank's crimes.

Review
● Bring the class together and share examples of the wanted posters.
● Remind the children that there are lots of genuine people in the world, who are honest and make truthful websites. However, the children need to be careful as there are others who are not honest.

Curriculum objectives
● To use search technologies effectively and be discerning in evaluating digital content.

Lesson objectives
● To create a fake website based on a myth.
● To combine software tools to create the design of a website.
● To evaluate other children's websites, using given criteria.

Expected outcomes
● Can create a fake website based on a myth, using different software.
● Can evaluate peers' websites, using given criteria.

Resources
Interactive activity 'Persuasive words' on the CD-ROM; photocopiable page 118 'Sheriff's website'

Fakey fakey

This week the children think in more detail about websites – can we trust them, is all of the information correct? The children consider the myths and legends and how they may have some information that is not true. The children create fake websites, using persuasive words to make the Sheriff look like a 'goodie' and Robin to look like a 'baddie'.

Introduction
● Introduce the lesson by re-reading the story of Robin Hood. Ask: *Who do you think is the hero of the story? Who is the villain?*
● Ask them to consider the characters. The Sheriff and King John are often seen as the baddies. However, what about King Richard? He left England to go fighting in another country, should he have not stayed to protect his people? Take responses from the class about their opinions.
● Ask the children to consider that if Robin Hood was stealing, then surely he was a baddie. Explain that it could depend on the persons point of view, as to who was a goodie or baddie. This can be portrayed in different ways, for example, the Sheriff could portray himself as the goodie, if he shares information in a certain way.

Whole-class work
● Explain that the children are going to create a website to portray the Sheriff as a goodie and Robin Hood as the baddie.
● Using interactive activity 'Persuasive words' on the CD-ROM, the children recognise which words try to persuade the reader.

Paired work
● Using photocopiable page 118 'Sheriff's website', the children plan their webpages. These pages will contain persuasive words to convince the reader, that the Sheriff is being honest and Robin Hood is the criminal.
● The children can add drawings of crimes that Robin Hood has committed and drawings of the kind deeds that the Sheriff has done.
● Using a word-processing program or collage program, the children could create a digital version of the web page, using text boxes and rectangles to represent the spaces where images could be added.

Differentiation
● Support: Less confident learners may need support to change the Sheriff's words to make him look honest and lawful and to change Robin Hood's words to make him unlawful.
● Challenge: More confident learners could add further descriptions of the kind acts by the Sheriff and the unlawful acts of Robin Hood. They can include the persuasive words and descriptions.

Review
● Bring the class together and ask them to share their examples of the web pages.
● The children evaluate each website with the question: *Does the Sheriff sound like a goodie and does Robin Hood sound like a baddie?*
● Explain that a fake website may be quite obvious at times, but in some cases it can be very subtle and people do not realise that it is fake.

Curriculum objectives
● To use search technologies effectively and be discerning in evaluating digital content.

Lesson objectives
● To search for fictional inventions (for example, Boilerplate robot or chindogu).
● To describe the features of a trustworthy website.
● To evaluate images to state whether they are truthful and justify decisions.

Expected outcomes
● Can search for images of fictional inventions.
● Can evaluate the images to state whether they are truthful.

Resources
Photocopiable page 'Cut me out' from the CD-ROM; camera; scissors; magazines

'I don't believe it!'

April Fool's Day hoaxes have been used to trick people and the most convincing ones have come from reliable and trustworthy organisations. The children look at fake websites and inventions to see how they trick people. They especially look at images which have been manipulated and they have a go themselves at doing this. How can they spot a fake?

Introduction
● The children have thought about websites containing false or misleading information. In this lesson, they will look at how images and videos can be misleading too.
● Share the 'Chindogu' website, to see made-up inventions (http://www. chindogu.com/). Does it seem like a genuine website?
● Display to the class the 'Boilerplate' website and watch the movie trailer (http://www.bigredhair.com/boilerplate/book.html). Does it look real? Explain that the images are false and have been manipulated on the computer.
● Explain that the children can create their own new images, by cutting out photographs of themselves and placing a new background behind them. This can be done by physically cutting out images or by using digital tools.

Independent work
● Explain that images can be cut out and added to a picture. Using photocopiable page 'Cut me out' from the CD-ROM, the children draw an image of themselves, cut it out and add it to the background.
● The activity could be enhanced by taking photographs of the children and printing them out onto paper. They could cut the photographs out and place them on different backgrounds.
● They could collect additional backgrounds from magazines.

Whole-class work
● Demonstrate to the children how to use digital tools to remove part of an image from one photo and add it to another. For example, paint package software and interactive whiteboard software has a 'cut out' or 'lasso' tool built in. Take a photo of a child and open it in the software. Using the lasso tool, drag the cursor around the child's outline. Copy the selected shape and then open a new background image (for example, a castle). Paste the image on top of the background. It now looks like the child is in a different place.
● Another way to change a background is to use 'green screen' software. This is similar to how TV weather reports are shown. You put a green background behind the children and the computer replaces it with an image or video.

Paired work
● The children use a computer program to cut out an image and place it on new backgrounds.
● They can use pictures of themselves or of Robin Hood.

Differentiation
● Support: Less confident learners may need support to select an image using the lasso tool and pasting it, using a simple paint package.
● Challenge: More confident learners could use online image editing software, such as Pixlr (http://pixlr.com/editor/), where they can lasso their image and copy it, before opening a new background image – adding a new layer – then pasting the image. This introduces the concept of layers in images.

Review
● Share the children's examples. What are the signs that the images are fake? The children's examples will probably look fake because the edges are rough. However, if people have skill, time and modern technology, this may be harder to identify.

Curriculum objectives
● To use search technologies effectively and be discerning in evaluating digital content.

Lesson objectives
● To know that websites may contain misleading information.
● To explain what bias means.
● To know and explain that websites may contain bias.
● To recognise types of organisations by their website address.

Expected outcomes
● Can explain that websites may not contain truthful information or may have a bias.
● Can identify the general type of a website, based on the address.

Resources
Photocopiable page 'The Ballad of Robin Hood' from the CD-ROM; photocopiable page 'Spotting fake websites' from the CD-ROM

Biased ballads

The children should know that websites may contain misleading information. In this lesson, they try to look for bias, through the words used in a ballad and on websites. They use 'word cloud' tools to organise the words and see which ones are used most often. Finally, they look at the clues to spot fake websites.

Introduction
● Introduce the lesson by reading photocopiable page 'The Ballad of Robin Hood' from the CD-ROM and hearing about his story. Do the children think it makes Robin Hood and his men sound good or bad?

Whole-class work
● As a class, read through the ballad. The children underline the words they think make Robin Hood and his men sound good and have a positive point of view.
● Explain that the positive point of view of Robin Hood, from the writer of the ballad, can be called a 'bias'.
● Explain that in the Spring 2 topic 'Normans and the Bayeux Tapestry' topic, the children will look at the tapestry's account of the Battle of Hastings. The Normans were the winners of the battle and they created the tapestry, so people say it is biased towards them.
● Do the children think that websites have a bias if the person or company behind them want to share their point of view?
● Biased websites generally share opinions from only one side of a discussion or argument.
● Show the children a 'word cloud' tool, such as 'Wordle' (http://www.wordle. net/) or 'Tagxedo' (http://www.tagxedo.com/).
● Copy the text from the ballad and paste it into the word cloud tool.
● This displays the text as a 'cloud'. The more often a word appears in the text, the larger it appears in the cloud.
● Does this help identify if there is a bias to the text?
● Now repeat the activity, by pasting text from websites into the word cloud tool. Do the websites use particular words that might indicate a bias towards the people who created it?
● Moving on from looking at bias, focus the children on spotting fake websites.
● Explain that looking at the website address extensions can help spot a fake. For example, .com or .ac.uk can help recognise organisations by their address. This can help the children decide whether the sites would be trustworthy.

Paired work
● Using photocopiable page 'Spotting fake websites' from the CD-ROM, the children decide which features might suggest a website is fake.

> **Differentiation**
> ● Support: Less confident learners may need support to read the hints and apply them.
> ● Challenge: More confident learners could use read the hints to identify the fake websites and they could also explain their decisions.

Review
● Bring the class together to discuss the possible features of fake websites.
● Explain that it is very difficult to identify fake websites, so the children must be careful when online. Emphasise that there are many great websites to enjoy and so the fake ones should not stop them using the web.
● Tell them that if they have any concerns about content they find, they should tell someone they trust.

Curriculum objectives
● To use search technologies effectively and be discerning in evaluating digital content.

Objectives
● To know a spam email or message can be misleading.
● To give a simple definition of a spam message.
● To begin to recognise the features of a spam message.
● To know what to do if they suspect a message to be spam.

Expected outcomes
● Can define a spam email or message.
● Can explain what to do when receiving a spam email or message.

Resources
Photocopiable page 119 'King John's spam message'

Myths and legends: Assess and review

The children review their learning about communication and about being discerning in evaluating digital content. They return to their lesson on spam messages and try to imagine themselves being the villain sending one. As King John or the Sheriff, they create a spam message to trick Robin Hood. Will it work?

Introduction
● Begin the lesson, reminding the children of the characters in the Robin Hood story: the hero, Robin Hood and the villains King John and the Sheriff. Tell the children to imagine that Robin Hood has a computer and King John wants to trick him with a spam message.
● The children think about spam messages and then in pairs, decide upon a simple definition for a spam message.
● Ask: *Can you define a spam message?*

Whole-class work
● Explain that they need to think like evil King John. He wants to trick Robin into giving away his personal details, including his address or location in the forest. Ask the children to decide which information they wish to gather.
● Now, explain that they must create a trap to trick Robin. How can they do that in a message? For example, it could be a competition they say he has won and that the prize must be delivered. It could be an invitation to an archery tournament.

Paired work
● Using photocopiable page 119 'King John's spam message', the children think about the words they could use to trick Robin.
● Will they use any images, for example, a crest or official-looking stamp?
● Will they use hyperlinks to other websites?
● Ask: *What are the features of a spam message?*

Differentiation
● Support: Less confident learners may need support to create their message and think about how they are going to invite Robin to the castle to receive a prize in order to capture him.
● Challenge: More confident learners can create a spam message and use the correct punctuation and persuasive language for their message.

Review
● Bring the class together and share examples from at least three children. Do the other children think their ideas will work?
● How did the children make their messages look real? Ask them to describe the key features again.
● Explain to the children that there are many good people sending messages everyday and it is a real benefit to be able to communicate like this, across the world. However, sometimes there are bad people, who try to trick others.
● Ask: *What should you do if you suspect a message to be spam message?*
● Reinforce with the children that if they suspect a message is spam they must not give away any personal information or open any links – they should tell someone they know and trust.

Name: _____   Date: _____

Robin Hood story

■ Use the boxes below to tell the story of Robin Hood. Draw the major events in the story and add text to describe what is happening.

I can remember the Robin Hood story and its sequence of events.

How did you do?

Name: _____   Date: _____

About the characters

■ Search the web for information about the characters in the story.

Name of character	Words I used to search online	What I found out
Robin Hood		
Maid Marian		
Little John		
Sheriff of Nottingham		
King John		
King Richard		

I can search online and locate information about characters in a story.

How did you do?

PHOTOCOPIABLE

April Fools

- Search the web to find examples of April Fool's Day hoaxes.
- Write the name of the hoax and a short description in the table below.

Name of April Fool's Day hoax	Short description

I can spot a hoax.

How did you do?

Wanted – Robin Hood

■ Draw a Robin Hood 'wanted' poster below.

I can design a 'wanted' poster.

How did you do?

PHOTOCOPIABLE   **SCHOLASTIC**
www.scholastic.co.uk

Wanted – Fake Frank

■ Draw a Fake Frank 'wanted' poster below. Mention how he tricks people online.

WANTED

I can design a 'wanted' poster and describe how someone might try to trick others online.

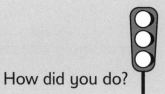

How did you do?

Sheriff's website

- Design the Sheriff's website below.
- Add a title, navigation buttons and three news stories. The stories should show the Sheriff as good and Robin as bad.

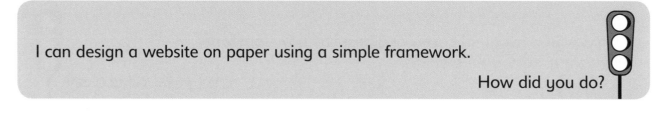

I can design a website on paper using a simple framework.

How did you do?

PHOTOCOPIABLE

SCHOLASTIC
www.scholastic.co.uk

King John's spam message

- Design a spam message for Robin Hood from John.
- Try to trick Robin into giving away his location tempt him to come to the castle.
- Will you use any images, for example, a crest official-looking stamp?
- Will you include hyperlinks to other websites

To:
From:
Message:

I can recognise the features of a spam message.

How did you do?

Science fiction

This chapter engages the children in a science fiction theme to think about 'How computers work'. The children have learned about the computer hardware, including the keyboard, mouse and central processing unit (CPU). Now they learn about the operating system (the main software on the computer) which enables the different parts to communicate with each other.

The children consider how they use software for different purposes. They then focus on apps on mobile phones and tablets. Using the science-fiction theme, the children design an 'app of the future'.

Expected prior learning

● The children will know about the hardware in a computer (the CPU, hard drive, screen, mouse, keyboard and printer). They may recognise operating systems, such as Microsoft Windows or Mac OS X.
● The children will have used many different pieces of software at school and at home. However, they may not have thought about the purpose of each one.

Chapter at a glance

Subject area
• How computers work

National Curriculum objective
• To understand computer networks and the opportunities they offer for communication and collaboration.

Week	Lesson objectives	Summary of activities	Expected outcomes
1	• To name examples of computers present inside and outside the school. • To describe the function of the computers and why they are used. • To give examples of physical, wireless and mobile networks and describe the difference between them. • To name different operating systems. • To describe the main functions of an operating system.	• Children recap on learning about 'How computers work'. • They think about the computers they use, recognising and naming different operating systems and describing their functions. • They are introduced to the theme of science fiction and how computers are portrayed. • They consider the future functions of computers.	• Can give examples of computers present inside and outside the school. • Can understand why computers are used. • Can identify examples of physical, wireless and mobile networks and know the difference between them. • Can name different operating systems. • Can understand the main functions of the operating system.
2	• To use a sci-fi theme to describe different operating systems for the same hardware. • To explain why different computers use different operating systems. • To identify software on a computer. • To describe how different software can have different functions.	• Children describe how the same hardware can use different operating systems. • They think about the different tasks computers are used for and consider the packages installed in the classroom.	• Can explain why different computers might use different operating systems and application software for the same hardware. • Can identify software on a computer and describe its function. • Can explain why different pieces of software may be used for different functions.
3	• To describe an app and its functions. • To describe the mobile technology the children may use, for example, mobile phones or tablet devices. • To explain how people may use apps every day for specific tasks. • To know that apps can be downloaded from an app store. • To create a model tablet or mobile phone and identify its main features.	• Children understand that apps are pieces of software related to mobile phones and tablet devices. • They discuss where they have seen apps and explain how they are used for specific tasks. • They understand the process of downloading apps from an online app store. • They design and make a model tablet or mobile phone and identify its main features.	• Can describe and define the functions of an app for a mobile phone or tablet computer. • Can explain that app stores are used to download an app onto a phone or tablet device. • Can create a model tablet or mobile phone and identify the main features.

Week	Lesson objectives	Summary of activities	Expected outcomes
4	• To discuss what new things might be around in the future. • To discuss what the children would like to see in the future. • To imagine the impact of new technologies on their lives. • To design an app for a sci-fi story. • To invent the functions for a future sci-fi app. • To add the imaginary app to their mobile device model.	• Children use the sci-fi theme to think about inventions of the future. • They discuss what they would like to see in the future and think about the impact it may have on their lives. • In role play they act out how to download an app to a mobile device and show how its features can benefit their lives.	• Can design an app for a fictional sci-fi story. • Can describe and define the functions of an app for a mobile phone or tablet computer. • Can add a fictional app to a model mobile phone or tablet device.
5	• To look at example newspaper reports and analyse them to highlight direct speech, the use of captions and text layout. • To plan an imaginary sci-fi newspaper article. • To write an imaginary sci-fi newspaper article using an online tool. • To collaborate on one document with other children, using an online tool.	• Children analyse newspaper reports to identify the particular style of writing: headlines, direct speech, captions, etc. • They imagine a news story covering a sci-fi event and write a newspaper article using an online tool. • Concluding the lesson, the children collaborate on one document using an online tool.	• Can use a collaborative web tool to compose a newspaper report. • Can collaborate on one document with other children, using an online tool.
6	• To present to an audience to describe the sci-fi app. • To describe the function of the sci-fi app. • To explain how more than pupil can collaborate on one document. • To demonstrate how to use a collaborative tool. • To use a collaborative tool to demonstrate the class's progress of learning over the topic.	• Children work in groups to invent a new sci-fi app. • They work together using face-to-face and online methods to plan a joint presentation. • They use an online 'sticky note' tool to demonstrate their learning progress.	• Can present to an audience to describe an app and its function. • Can explain how more than one pupil collaborated using an online tool. • Can record progress of learning, using an online tool.
Assess and review	• Assess and review half term's work.	• Children recap on their software learning. • They use a space shuttle theme to write a children's story using different types of software.	• Assess and review.

Overview of progression
● The children progress their knowledge of computers by learning about the operating system that enables the hardware (which they have learned about in the previous lessons) to communicate together.
● They will consider the software programs they use and think about why they use particular programs.
● They will learn about apps and how these are used for specific purposes on mobile phones and tablets.

Creative context
● The lessons link closely to the English curriculum, through discussing and recording ideas, composing and rehearsing sentences orally (including dialogue), progressively building a varied and rich vocabulary and an increasing range of sentence structures to describe the use of software.
● Also linking with English, the children choose nouns or pronouns appropriately for clarity and cohesion. In the newspaper activities, the children use and punctuate direct speech.
● Linking with history, the children consider time periods and people's views and predictions about the future.

Background knowledge
● The children will have encountered different types of operating systems before. They may have used tablet computers and smart mobile phones, which have operating systems too; however, the children may not have realised this.
● They will have used many types of software, though they may not have considered why they would use different types at school and at home. The children should think about how and why they use software.

Curriculum objectives
● To understand computer networks and the opportunities they offer for communication and collaboration.

Lesson objectives
● To name examples of computers present inside and outside the school.
● To describe the function of the computers and why they are used.
● To give examples of physical, wireless and mobile networks and describe the difference between them.
● To name different operating systems.
● To describe the main functions of an operating system.

Expected outcomes
● Can give examples of computers present inside and outside the school.
● Can understand why computers are used.
● Can identify examples of physical, wireless and mobile networks and know the difference between them.
● Can name different operating systems.
● Can understand the main functions of the operating system.

Resources
Photocopiable page 'The operating system' from the CD-ROM; photocopiable page 129 'Future robots'; a range of sci-fi stories

Operating systems

Introducing the science fiction theme, the children are engaged by viewing sci-fi film clips, for example, Disney's *WALL-E*. They remember what they have learned about how computers work and computer networks, before designing their own robot of the future.

Introduction
● Start the lesson by showing clips of science-fiction films, containing images of computers and technology, for example, Disney's *WALL-E* (http://www.disney.co.uk/wall-e/#videos). Ask the children whether they have heard the term 'science fiction' or 'sci-fi' before – what does it mean?
● Explain that they are going to think about how computers work, using a sci-fi theme. To begin with, they need to remember their learning from the previous years.
● Ask the children:
  ● *Can you name examples of computers used inside and outside the school? Can you describe the function of the computers?*
  ● *Think about how computers are connected together. Can you see examples of physical networking in the classroom?*
  ● *Can you see, or give an example, where a wirelessly networked computer is used in the school or local area?*
  ● *Can you explain where mobile networks are used and with which devices, for example, mobile phones?*
  ● *Can you explain the differences between the wired, wireless and mobile networks?*

Whole-class work
● Using the computer in the classroom as an example, can the children recognise the main software running the computer – the operating system? It could be Microsoft Windows or on a Mac computer, it could be called 'OS X'. A tablet computer may have another operating system. The operating system is the most important software on the computer, as it allows all the parts to work with each other, for example, receiving the input from the keyboard and mouse, moving files on the hard drive, controlling the output to the screen or printer.
● Using photocopiable page 'The operating system' from the CD-ROM, the children think about the role of the software.

Paired work
● Returning to the sci-fi theme, explain that WALL-E the robot and other robots and computers may have an operating system controlling them. Using photocopiable page 129 'Future robots', the children design their robot of the future and describe the operating system that will run it.

Differentiation
● Support: Less confident learners may need support to describe their robot, in simple terms of its parts, and then to understand that the operating system is controlling it.
● Challenge: More confident learners could design their robot, then write a detailed description of how the operating system is adapted for their robot, using adjectives to explain the functions of its parts.

Review
● Bring the class together and share their examples of their robots of the future. Ask: *Can you explain what the operating system is doing?*
● Ask the children to name, define and explain the main functions of an operating system.
● Conclude by reading a range of extracts of sci-fi stories and identify sci-fi elements. Then the children can consider the future functions of computers.

SCHOLASTIC

Curriculum objectives
● To understand computer networks and the opportunities they offer for communication and collaboration.

Lesson objectives
● To use a sci-fi theme to describe different operating systems for the same hardware.
● To explain why different computers use different operating systems.
● To identify software on a computer.
● To describe how different software can have different functions.

Expected outcomes
● Can explain why different computers might use different operating systems and application software for the same hardware.
● Can identify software on a computer and describe its function.
● Can explain why different pieces of software may be used for different functions.

Resources
Photocopiable page 130 'What do I do?'; science fiction music

What do I do?

On home and school computers, there are many different pieces of software. Children think about how they use the software and for what purposes. They take screenshots of the software in action and describe the tools. With the sci-fi theme, the children imagine future software and what it could do.

Introduction
● Begin by playing science fiction music, for example, from *Star Wars* or *Dr Who*. Explain that the same music player or computer was able to play more than one piece of music, but that it was the same hardware playing it.
● Explain that there are operating systems which they may not have seen. For example, a PC desktop or laptop can run a free operating system called 'Linux'. Also, Apple computers can be set up to run Windows, as well as OS X.
● Explain that the same hardware can run different operating systems.
● Ask children to name an operating system and explain what it does.

Whole-class work
● Explain that in addition to the operating system, many other pieces of software are used on a computer. Examples are a paint program, a game or an internet browser – the children will have used some of these before.
● Ask the children to describe the types of activities they do on the computer in their lessons: *Can you name the piece of software you use?*

Paired work
● The children use photocopiable page 130 'What do I do?' to describe the activities they do on the computer in school and identify the software.
● They describe the activities they do on computers outside of school. What do they do and which pieces of software do they use?

Whole-class work
● Bring the class together and ask the children: *What activities do you do? Which piece of software do you use to do it? Can you explain why it is suited to your purpose? Can the software perform more than one job?* For example, a paint program can be used to draw shapes but it can also be used to resize pictures.
● Open a paint program or similar software and draw the children's attention to the menu or toolbar. Can they see the different tools?

Independent work
● On the computers, the children take a screenshot of their activity using the software (for example, if the computer has a 'printscreen' or 'PrtScr' button, this captures the whole screen). They then paste the image into a paint program or word-processing document.
● Once they have identified the tools, can the children explain how the software can carry out more than one function?

Differentiation
● Support: Less confident learners may need support to remember the activities they do on the computer, to identify them and to spell the names of the pieces of software.
● Challenge: More confident learners could describe the activities they do on the computer and describe why it is fit for purpose.

Review
● Bring the class together and share pictures. Can they explain which piece of software they used and what they are able to do with it?
● Ask the children to think of all the different pieces of software they use and for what different purposes.
● To conclude, play the sci-fi music again and ask the children: *If you could imagine a piece of software in the future, what would it do?*

Curriculum objectives
● To understand computer networks and the opportunities they offer for communication and collaboration.

Lesson objectives
● To describe an app and its functions.
● To describe the mobile technology the children may use, for example, mobile phones or tablet devices.
● To explain how people may use apps everyday for specific tasks.
● To know that apps can be downloaded from an app store.
● To create a model tablet or mobile phone and identify its main features.

Expected outcomes
● Can describe and define the functions of an app for a mobile phone or tablet computer.
● Can explain that app stores are used to download an app onto a phone or tablet device.
● Can create a model tablet or mobile phone and identify the main features.

Resources
Photocopiable page 'There's an app for that' from the CD-ROM

Appy day

In this lesson, the children focus on apps and where they have seen them. They think about the purposes they have used apps for and how fit for purpose they are. They discuss how they load apps on to phones and tablets via an app store. The children make a model mobile phone and describe the apps they would place on to it.

Introduction
● Ask the children if they know what an app is and where have they seen one. Tell them that apps are pieces of software, often related to mobile phones and tablet devices.
● The children can list the names of apps and explain the locations, such as on their parents' mobile phones or on a tablet computer.
● Explain that there is a phrase 'There's an app for that', what do they think it means? (It implies that any need can be solved by a particular app.)

Paired work
● The children think about apps they have used and record their experiences on photocopiable page 'There's an app for that' from the CD-ROM.
● Bring the class together and ask them to share an example of an app and describe its function. The apps are often used for specific purposes, compared with software on the computer, which can be used for many purposes.
● The children may be aware of the idea of downloading apps from an online app store. For example, on the iPad there is the App Store and on the Android system Google Play is used.
● To use the app stores to purchase an app, the user (an adult) could either log into the store, using a username and password, then select the app. More often, the user selects an app first, then logs in to purchase.
● To pay for the apps, credit cards are often linked to the account or a gift card can add money to the account.
● To practise using an imaginary app store, the children design and make a model tablet or mobile phone, using cardboard boxes or recycled plastic items.
● The children role play using their model mobile phone to download an app from the app store, identifying the main features of the app and describing what they intend to use it for.

> ### Differentiation
> ● Support: Less confident learners may need support to write down the purpose of the apps and help to understand the process for downloading apps to a device.
> ● Challenge: More confident learners could describe the apps in more detail to explain what the app does and why it is fit for purpose.

Review
● Bring the class together and ask three children to show their model mobile phone and to role play how they would download an app.
● Explain that there are often free apps in the store, especially games, but that these will have adverts and extra items to buy within the app (in-app purchases). The game developers have spent money, time and expertise making the app, so they should be able to recoup some of the money. As long as they are upfront about the purchases, it should be fair that they can make money back on the app.
● With in-app purchases, there can often be a misunderstanding that the features or items bought in the game do not cost real money, whereas actually they do.
● On many tablets, the in-app purchases can be switched off in the device's settings.
● Emphasise that the children should always ask an adult before following free app links.

Curriculum objectives
● To understand computer networks and the opportunities they offer for communication and collaboration.

Objectives
● To discuss what new things might be around in the future.
● To discuss what would the children like to see in the future.
● To imagine the impact of new technologies on their lives.
● To design an app for a sci-fi story.
● To invent the functions for a future sci-fi app.
● To add the imaginary app to their mobile device model.

Expected outcomes
● Can design an app for a fictional sci-fi story.
● Can describe and define the functions of an app for a mobile phone or tablet computer.
● Can add a fictional app to a model mobile phone or tablet device.

Resources
Photocopiable page 131 'Inventions of the future'; photocopiable page 132 'Communicating in the future'; photocopiable page 133 'App of the future'

To the future

The children think about the future and what new technologies they might see. They think about how apps are used and imagine what an 'app for the future' might look like and what it might do. They design their app and describe the impact it may have on people's lives.

Introduction
● Begin the lesson by showing an old film clip, which includes an invention in the future, for example, the cartoon *The Jetsons* (http://en.wikipedia.org/wiki/The_Jetsons). Explain that many of the old sci-fi movies look ridiculous, because technology has moved on so quickly.
● In the film *Back to the Future Part II*, there were a large number of futuristic inventions, for example, self-tying shoelaces, an automatic drying jacket, an automatic dog walker and a weather controlling service. The film was released in 1989 and these inventions were set for the year 2015. Explain to the children that 1989 may seem a long time ago, but to the people living in that year 2015 seemed a long time in the future.
● Tell the children that they are going to invent a device for the future and think about its potential impact on their lives.

Paired work
● Thinking about the school of the future, the children use photocopiable page 131 'Inventions of the future', to describe an invention for the school of the future. It could be anything, for example, a sweet that helps them learn their times tables, a pencil that draws for them or a computer that replaces the teacher.
● They then think of a phone or communication device in the future. Ask: *Will you have a phone in the future or some type of wristwatch? Will it be implanted into you?* Give the children time to discuss and design their invention. They record their ideas on photocopiable page 132 'Communicating in the future'.
● Finally, ask the children to think about the nearer future, maybe two years ahead. Can they think of an app of the future? Using photocopiable page 133 'App of the future', they design their new app and think about the impact it could have on their lives.
● The children could add their app to their model mobile phone, by adding an icon to the screen.

Differentiation
● Support: Less confident learners may need support to design the invention and app and then to think of and spell words to describe its impact on their lives.
● Challenge: More confident learners could describe the impact of technology on their lives, sharing where they might use computers and how they can be helpful.

Review
● Bring the class together and select children to share their ideas and role play how to download the app. Ask them what impact they think their invention will have on their lives.
● Tell the children about medical apps. There are many apps that can help to monitor sleep, exercise, heart rates, for example. This could really develop in the future to monitor blood sugar for diabetics or to monitor the children's vitamin intake. Doctors could remotely see their patients by video and examine data about their health, via their phone.
● Can the children imagine having their lessons at home, learning via an app and a teacher using a video communicator?

Curriculum objectives
● To understand computer networks and the opportunities they offer for communication and collaboration.

Lesson objectives
● To look at example newspaper reports and analyse them to highlight direct speech, the use of captions and text layout.
● To plan an imaginary sci-fi newspaper article (using 'who, what, why, when and how').
● To write an imaginary sci-fi newspaper article using an online tool.
● To collaborate on one document with other children, using an online tool.

Expected outcomes
● Can use a collaborative web tool to compose a newspaper report.
● Can collaborate on one document with other children, using an online tool.

Resources
Photocopiable page 134 'Sci-fi school story'; newspaper

Future news

Using newspapers, both paper and online, the children look at the structure of the pages. They can see the way the text is laid out, including headlines, captions and direct speech. They compare online and offline news to identify the differences. They create an online newspaper for an imaginary sci-fi story and look at a collaborative online tool.

Introduction
● Begin the lesson by showing an online newspaper and holding up a real paper newspaper. Can the children read the headlines? Ask: *How is the page laid out on the paper newspaper?* For example, headlines, images, captions, text, speech marks.
● Now look at the online newspaper on the computer. Ask the children whether it is different and if so, how it is different. They may notice that there is a different layout, but also that videos, animations and sound recordings may be present.

Whole-class work
● Explain that a strange sci-fi event has just occurred on the school playground. Ask the children to think for a minute about what has happened. It could be an alien spacecraft has crash-landed or a huge worm-like creature crawled out of the school kitchen.
● Ask one child to share their idea. Can the other children think of questions based upon 'who, what, why, when and how'?
● Tell the children that today they are going to write their own news report on paper and then digitally.

Paired work
● Using photocopiable page 134 'Sci-fi school story', the children plan out their news story, using 'who, what, why, when and how' to structure the piece.
● They check with the layout of the newspaper that they have included a headline, direct speech and images with captions.
● Display the online newspaper again and remind the children to look at the layout and features.
● Using a word processing program such as Microsoft Word, the children create their story to lay it out like an example online page. They fill in the text boxes and drag the images into place.

Differentiation
● Support: Less confident learners may need support to write their stories in the style of a news report. They need to include facts, as they use the 'who, what, why, when and how' structure.
● Challenge: More confident learners could look at the use of direct speech in interviews and news reports. They should include direct speech and organise their writing into paragraphs with captions.

Review
● To conclude the lesson, the children collaborate on one document, using an online tool.
● Display an etherpad (for example, http://beta.primarypad.com/). Share the link for the page with another computer in the classroom. Ask one of the children to imagine that they are an eyewitness to an event. Ask them questions using the main classroom computer and allow the child on the second computer to respond.
● Explain that each of the children could be gathering information and placing it in the online document. This could be a method of jointly gathering information for their stories.

Sci-fi app invention

The children have considered future apps and designed their own. In this lesson, they work as a group to plan and design a new app, before voting on the design they want to pitch. They then come together to present their pitch to the class.

Introduction

- Introduce the lesson by telling the children that they are going to design a new sci-fi app and present the idea to the class. Last week, they planned an app by themselves. In this lesson, they will collaborate to create an idea.
- In small groups of four to six, the children use photocopiable page 135 'Our app idea' to structure their planning.

Group work

- Using photocopiable page 135 'Our app idea', the children interview each other to define and then come up with ideas for their app. Each child should come up with one idea.
- Using photocopiable page 'Voting time' from the CD-ROM, they write the list of app ideas down and each person quickly describes their idea. Children vote for their favourite idea by placing a tick on their sheet. The sheets are collected and the votes counted. If there is a draw, then choose the two with the most votes and all the children vote again.
- When the idea is chosen, the group must organise its pitch by splitting it into four parts: Introduction to the app, What is it for? How does it work? What is the impact on our lives?
- They plan using photocopiable page 'Our presentation' from the CD-ROM.
- The group can communicate using 'Primary Wall'. This is a sticky note website on which children can post messages to share their ideas.
- To set up the Primary Wall, go to http://primarywall.com/ and select 'Create wall'. This makes a new wall, but with random letters and numbers in the web address (URL). By deleting the letters and numbers after the forward slash, an easier to understand address can be written, for example, http://free.primarywall.com/100computinggroup1. Share this address with the group.
- Once the children have planned their part, they can join back together, face-to-face to practise the pitch. They could create a presentation using software such as Microsoft PowerPoint or Apple Keynote if they have time in the lesson.

Differentiation
- Prompt cards can support more and less confident learners during their presentation.
- Support: Less confident learners may need support to create their sentences.
- Challenge: More confident learners could think about the words they are going to use. Are their words persuasive and clear?

Review

- Each group presents their pitch for the new sci-fi app.
- The class evaluate the presentations by using the criteria on photocopiable page 'Presentation evaluation' from the CD-ROM. Was it clear what the app was called? Could they explain in simple words what it did? Could they explain what the impact on the users would be?
- Conclude the lesson, by showing a Primary Wall web page. Add a sticky note to the wall and ask: *What did you know about operating systems at the start of the topic?* Take a response from one of the children and post the note. Now, ask them about apps: *What did you know about apps at the start of the topic?* Write their reply and add the note.
- Ask them what they know about operating systems and apps now and add as many notes as possible.
- Explain that the Primary Wall tool can be used as collaboration tool to plan together or as an assessment tool, to see how their learning has progressed.

Curriculum objectives
- To understand computer networks and the opportunities they offer for communication and collaboration.

Lesson objectives
- To present to an audience to describe the sci-fi app.
- To describe the function of the sci-fi app.
- To explain how more than pupil can collaborate on one document.
- To demonstrate how to use a collaborative tool.
- To use a collaborative tool to demonstrate the class's progress of learning over the topic.

Expected outcomes
- Can present to an audience to describe an app and its function.
- Can explain how more than one pupil collaborated using an online tool.
- Can record progress of learning, using an online tool.

Resources
Photocopiable page 135 'Our app idea'; photocopiable page 'Voting time' from the CD-ROM; photocopiable page 'Our presentation' from the CD-ROM; photocopiable page 'Presentation evaluation' from the CD-ROM

Curriculum objectives
● To understand computer networks and the opportunities they offer for communication and collaboration.

● Lesson objectives
● To explain why different computers use different operating systems.
● To identify software on a computer.
● To describe how different software can have different functions.

Expected outcomes
● Can identify software on a computer.
● Can explain why different pieces of software may be used for different functions.

Resources
Interactive activity 'Space shuttle' on the CD-ROM; photocopiable page 'Space shuttle book' from the CD-ROM

Science fiction: Assess and review

In this assess and review lesson the children plan a science fiction story about the space shuttle.

Introduction
● Introduce the lesson by showing the space shuttle website (www.nasa.gov/mission_pages/shuttle/main/index.html) or the National Geographic website (http://video.nationalgeographic.com/video/kids/science-space-kids/space-shuttle-sci-kids/). Explain that this is not science fiction, but non-fiction and factual. However, they could write a story based on the space shuttle that could be fictional.
● Remind the children about operating systems. Can they name one and describe what it does?
● Ask the children to imagine that they are on the space shuttle. Can you describe what you would be doing? Would the operating software of the space shuttle need to help the parts communicate?

Whole-class work
● Use the interactive activity 'Space shuttle' on the CD-ROM, to describe how the operating system controls the parts of the space craft.
● Explain to the children that they have used many pieces of software. In Week 2, they thought about the software and its functions. They then took screenshots to record how they used the software.
● In this lesson, they will imagine they are going to create a children's science-fiction story about the space shuttle for younger children.

Paired work
● In pairs, the children plan a story about the space shuttle. Using photocopiable page 'Space shuttle book' from the CD-ROM, they sketch the pictures and write a few words under each one.
● In their planning, the children need to say how they would use software to design the different parts of the book. For example, they might use an internet browser to find pictures and save them, and they could use a paint program to design the front cover.
● Ask: *Can you identify different pieces of software on a computer?*

Differentiation
● Support: Less confident learners may need support to create the story and with the construction of sentences to create an engaging story.
● Challenge: More confident learners could name and describe the functions of different pieces of software.

Review
● Bring the class together and ask the children to take turns to read their stories. In each case, they need to identify the software they might use to create the parts of the story and describe why it is fit for purpose.
● Ask: *Can you explain why different pieces of software may be used for different functions?*
● Conclude the lesson by reminding the children that they have learned about the computer's hardware (the keyboard, the mouse, the CPU, the hard drive, for example), the operating system (the main software) and the other software (the programs for doing particular tasks). They also have an understanding of how computers are networked together, via wired, wireless and mobile networks.

Future robots

■ Draw your robot of the future in the box below.

[ ]

■ What does the operating system on your robot do?

_____

_____

_____

I can explain the function of an operating system.

How did you do?

What do I do?

■ Write in the table what you do on the computer in school.

For example, 'I draw pictures.'

■ Try to name the software you use to do that activity.

For example, 'I use the Paint software.'

What do I do on the computer in school?	Which software do I use?

■ Write in the table what you do on the computer at home or outside of school.

■ Which software do you use?

What do I do on the computers at home or outside of school?	Which software do I use?

I can recognise which software I use and for what purpose.

How did you do?

PHOTOCOPIABLE

■SCHOLASTIC
www.scholastic.co.uk

Inventions of the future

■ Design an invention for a school of the future.

For example: a sweet which helps children learn their times tables; a pencil that draws by itself or a computer that replaces the teacher.

■ Describe your invention.

_____

_____

_____

_____

I can imagine and design an invention for the future.

How did you do?

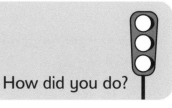

Communicating in the future

■ Design an invention to communicate in the future. Will it be a wristwatch phone or a device implanted in your body?

■ Describe your communication device.

_____

_____

_____

_____

I can imagine and design a communication device for the future.

How did you do?

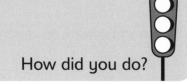

PHOTOCOPIABLE

■SCHOLASTIC
www.scholastic.co.uk

Name: _____   Date: _____

App of the future

■ Can you design a new app for the future? What would be the impact on your life? Will it help to keep you alive for longer? Will it make it easier to share information? What about a games app or a music app?

■ Draw your design here.

■ Describe your future app and how it will impact on people's lives.

_____

_____

_____

_____

I can imagine and design an app of the future and describe the impact it may have on people's lives.

How did you do?

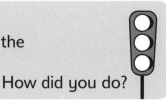

Sci-fi school story

- Design your sci-fi news story about your school.
- Use 'who, what, why, when and how' to structure the piece.
- Use headlines and direct speech.
- Use captions with any images you use.

I can plan a science fiction story in the style of a newspaper.

How did you do?

SCHOLASTIC
www.scholastic.co.uk

Name: _____   Date: _____

Our app idea

- Design a new sci-fi app.
- Think about a story you have read or a TV show or film you have watched, to design for a particular person.
- Sketch your app below. Add labels to describe what it does.

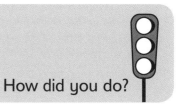

I can design an app and explain the main features.

How did you do?

Dragons

This chapter uses a dragons theme to build on the knowledge, skills and understanding of programming that children have developed in previous years. Using the graphical programming language Scratch, the children extend their understanding of creating an animation in Scratch, from evaluating existing animations through to planning, creating and evaluating their own short dragon animation.

Expected prior learning

● The children have already been introduced to programming using Scratch and have already covered some of the skills they will be developing further in this chapter, such as effective planning, creating sprites, backgrounds and sounds, and programming and debugging their animation.

Chapter at a glance

Subject area
• Algorithms and programming

National Curriculum objective
• To design, write and debug programs that accomplish specific goals, including controlling or simulating physical systems; solve problems by decomposing them into smaller parts; use sequence and repetition in programs; use logical reasoning to explain how some simple algorithms work and to detect and correct errors in algorithms and programs.

Week	Lesson objectives	Summary of activities	Expected outcomes
1	• To understand what an animation is. • To identify what makes an effective animation. • To establish their own criteria for effective animations. • To evaluate an animation, using their own criteria. • To identify what elements they can include in their own short animation to ensure it is effective.	• Children understand what makes an effective animation. • They evaluate animations based on the criteria they have established as a class.	• Can understand what makes a good animation. • Can evaluate an animated game based on given criteria.
2	• To understand why planning is important. • To brainstorm ideas for their own animation and develop one. • To give and receive feedback to their peers. • To understand what a storyboard is. • To plan a simple animation using a given paper storyboard template. • To check they have included identified elements to ensure their animation is effective and explain how they have done so.	• Children brainstorm ideas for a dragon-themed Scratch animation. • They give and receive feedback to decide on one idea for an animation. • They develop one idea and create a storyboard plan for their animation.	• Can plan a simple animation using a template. • Can explain why their animation will be effective.
3	• To identify the assets needed for their animation. • To use built-in sounds and sprites for their animation as appropriate. • To understand the importance of naming assets carefully within their animation. • To use basic drawing tools to create multiple sprites and backgrounds for their animation. • To record appropriate sounds for their animation.	• Children identify the assets needed for their animation on paper. • They create and collect their assets within Scratch.	• Can plan what assets to use within their animation. • Can use multimedia tools to create effective assets for their animations.

Week	Lesson objectives	Summary of activities	Expected outcomes
4	• To use logical thinking to plan appropriate algorithms for their animation. • To use decomposition to break down algorithms into smaller parts. • To identify and use selection and repetition as appropriate within their algorithms. • To explain their algorithms verbally to their peers. • To give and receive feedback. • To debug their algorithms as appropriate after feedback. • To start to implement their algorithms using the Scratch programming language.	• Children identify the actions that take place within their animation. • They plan algorithms to accomplish the actions, using selection and repetition where appropriate. • They work out the code needed within Scratch to execute their planned algorithms. • They work collaboratively to debug their code.	• Can plan algorithms to achieve predicted outcomes. • Can use repetition (loops) and selection where appropriate.
5	• To implement their algorithms using the Scratch programming language. • To use selection and repetition as appropriate within their program. • To work collaboratively with their peers to test and debug programs. • To give and receive constructive feedback.	• Children program their planned algorithms into Scratch. • They work collaboratively to test and debug their programs. • They give and receive feedback to improve their work.	• Can implement algorithms using a suitable program. • Can use repetition (loops) and selection where appropriate.
6	• To add simple comments to a program. • To explain why adding comments can help the programmer. • To explain how comments can help other people viewing a program. • To evaluate their own animation.	• Children understand how and why comments are used in programming. • They add comments to their work. • They evaluate their animations.	• Can work collaboratively to debug algorithms and programs to achieve specific goals. • Can evaluate their work in simple ways.
Assess and review	• Assess and review the half term's work.	• Children create an animation using a different programming tool.	• Assess and review.

Overview of progression

● The children build upon their knowledge and understanding of programming using Scratch. They consider what makes an effective animation and storyboard their own dragon-themed animation. They create and collect the assets for their animation before planning their algorithms and programming these into Scratch.
● The children apply and develop their knowledge and understanding of algorithms and programming by using their decomposition and problem-solving skills to achieve their planned outcomes and actions.
● The children are encouraged to work and think independently, although working collaboratively to debug their work is, by now, becoming the accepted norm.

Creative context

● The lessons link to the mathematics curriculum as children use logical thinking and problem solving to sequence and debug code. The computing lessons should also draw upon the children's learning in English as they type speech and record sounds for their sprites and also for planning and evaluation of animations.
● The lessons also link to the art curriculum as the children use paint tools to draw sprites and backgrounds.

Background knowledge

● From the work already completed, the children will know about sequencing, algorithms and programming. This chapter deepens their knowledge and understanding of how Scratch, and programming, works.
● From assessing the children's understanding in previous units, you will need to assess the children's capability in writing algorithms and translating these into code and provide additional support as necessary.
● It is important that you are a relatively able user of Scratch for this chapter. There are many tutorials on the Scratch website and by working through some of these you should feel comfortable with using Scratch.
● These lessons assume the use of Scratch 1.4 but other versions, including the online version, could be used.

Curriculum objectives
● To design, write and debug programs that accomplish specific goals, including controlling or simulating physical systems; solve problems by decomposing them into smaller parts; use sequence and repetition in programs; use logical reasoning to explain how some simple algorithms work and to detect and correct errors in algorithms and programs.

Lesson objectives
● To understand what an animation is.
● To identify what makes an effective animation.
● To establish their own criteria for effective animations.
● To evaluate an animation, using their own criteria.
● To identify what elements they can include in their own short animation to ensure it is effective.

Expected outcomes
● Can understand what makes a good animation.
● Can evaluate an animated game based on given criteria.

Resources
Photocopiable page 145 'What makes an effective animation?'; animated cartoons from your own resources or YouTube; animations from the 'featured projects' section of Scratch http://scratch.mit. edu/; photocopiable page 146 'Key learning point'

What makes an effective animation?

In this first lesson, children consider what animation is and what makes an effective animation. They also evaluate an animation based on criteria established by the class. Such work will help children to appreciate the importance of creating work that meets a given criteria.

Introduction
● Display the word *animation* on the whiteboard and invite the children to share what they think the word means and examples of animations.
● Depending on your class, the children should be able to share a wide variety of animations such as *Wallace and Gromit* (you can discuss that this is stop frame animation), *Toy Story*, *Shrek* films and *Tom and Jerry* cartoons.

Whole-class work
● Ask the children to consider what they think makes a good animation: *What makes Toy Story and Tom and Jerry so good to watch?* You could do this as a 'think, pair, share' activity.
● Discuss as a class what they share, drawing out the three areas of audio (sound effects, speech, music), characters (simple to look at, but with personalities), colours (simple yet effective), story (all animations, even if short, have an engaging story).

Group/paired work
● Give each group a copy of photocopiable page 145 'What makes an effective animation?'.
● Ask the children to watch your chosen animated cartoon and answer the questions on the sheet as they do so.

Whole-class work
● Discuss what the children have listed under colours, story, audio and characters on the sheet.
● Use this as an opportunity to address any misconceptions and emphasise how the different elements combine to create an effective animation.
● Hopefully they have established that colours should be simple and bold; that sounds should be clear and work with the animation whether they are character voices, sound effects or music; that there is a simple, funny story; the character design is simple yet effective and gives the characters personality.
● As a class, write the most important points you agree on on the board and explain that these are the class 'criteria' for an effective animation.

Independent/paired work
● Ask the children to log on to Scratch and watch between three and five animations from the 'featured projects' section.
● Ask the children to use the class criteria to evaluate the animations (they can use the back of their sheet to jot down notes).

> ### Differentiation
> ● Support: Less confident learners may benefit from mixed-ability groupings and can be encouraged to come up with one or two clear points for each of the evaluation categories.
> ● Challenge: Stretch more confident learners to evaluate the animations more critically; for example: *Why is the audio particularly effective? What else would you like to see in the animation?*

Review
● Ask volunteers to share their views on some of the Scratch animations.
● Ask the children to write on photocopiable page 146 'Key learning point' their key learning point from the lesson and what they will ensure they include in their own animation so it meets the criteria.

Curriculum objectives
● To design, write and debug programs that accomplish specific goals, including controlling or simulating physical systems; solve problems by decomposing them into smaller parts; use sequence and repetition in programs; use logical reasoning to explain how some simple algorithms work and to detect and correct errors in algorithms and programs.

Lesson objectives
● To understand why planning is important.
● To brainstorm ideas for their own animation and develop one.
● To give and receive feedback to their peers.
● To understand what a storyboard is.
● To plan a simple animation using a given paper storyboard template.
● To check they have included identified elements to ensure that their animation is effective and explain how they have done so.

Expected outcomes
● Can plan a simple animation using a template.
● Can explain why their animation will be effective.

Resources
Photocopiable page 147 'Storyboard'; media resource 'Example storyboard' on the CD-ROM

Planning an animation

This week, the children plan their own short, effective dragon-themed Scratch animation based on the criteria they established in Week 1. They brainstorm their ideas, discuss them with their peers and develop one idea in more depth, planning it using a storyboard template. This work gives children an understanding of the design process and helps to ensure that their animation will be more effective.

Introduction
● Remind the children that last week they considered what made an effective animation.
● Recap the key learning points from the last lesson and explain that they will be creating their own short animation using Scratch.

Whole-class work
● Discuss with the children why planning their work is important.
● Explain that they will create a short animation (under 30 seconds) about dragons and that they will decide on their characters and what happens.

Independent/paired work
● Give the children five minutes to brainstorm ideas for their animation.

Paired/group work
● Explain to the children that they will now share their ideas with another person and get the other person's feedback. This will help them come up with one idea to develop further for their animation.
● Pair the children up. Explain that they each have two minutes to explain their favourite two ideas then the other person has one minute to feed back.
● Hopefully, the children now have a clear idea that they can develop further.

Whole-class work
● Explain to them that the next task is to create a storyboard of their animation so they can develop their idea further.
● Show the media resource 'Example storyboard' on the CD-ROM, leaving this on the whiteboard as reference for the children during the next activity.
● Discuss how the storyboard has simple text and images.

Independent/paired work
● Give the children a copy of photocopiable page 147 'Storyboard' and ask them to draw their own simple storyboard for their chosen idea.
● Encourage them to remember the key learning points from the last lesson and to ensure that they consider these when planning their animation.
● Once they have finished, they should show and explain their work to you. Use this as an opportunity to stretch and challenge the children, or suggest that they simplify their animation, depending on the child.

Differentiation
● Support: Less confident learners may benefit from working in pairs, or from adult support when planning their animation. They can be encouraged to stick to a simple yet effective animation with a strong storyline rather than complex programming.
● Challenge: More confident learners will be able to create an animation, which features more complex actions, for example changing backgrounds.

Review
● Ask volunteers to share their storyboard and ideas with the class and explain how the planning process helped them to develop their idea.
● Review with the whole class the progress they have made with their animation. Ask: *How did sharing your ideas with your partner help you to decide on your idea? How did your ideas develop?*

Curriculum objectives
• To design, write and debug programs that accomplish specific goals, including controlling or simulating physical systems; solve problems by decomposing them into smaller parts; use sequence and repetition in programs; use logical reasoning to explain how some simple algorithms work and to detect and correct errors in algorithms and programs.

Lesson objectives
• To identify the assets needed for their animation.
• To use built-in sounds and sprites for their animation as appropriate.
• To understand the importance of naming assets carefully within their animation.
• To use basic drawing tools to create multiple sprites and backgrounds for their animation.
• To record appropriate sounds for their animation.

Expected outcomes
• Can plan what assets to use within their animation.
• Can use multimedia tools to create effective assets for their animations.

Resources
Photocopiable page 148 'My assets'; completed storyboards from last lesson

Collecting assets

This week, the children start to work on their dragon-themed animation using Scratch. They identify, collect and create the assets they will need for the animation they planned last time, including characters, backgrounds and sounds. This will ensure that they have everything in place ready to start programming in the following lessons.

Introduction
• Remind the children that last week they were planning their dragon Scratch animation and explain that in this lesson they will collect together everything that they need for their animation.
• Explain that before they can get started on creating their assets (the different parts that will create their animation), they need to make a list of everything they will need.

Independent/paired work
• Give out photocopiable page 148 'My assets' together with the storyboards from last week and ask the children to write down all the assets they will need for their animation.

Whole-class work
• Display the Scratch interface on the whiteboard.
• Using volunteers, recap with the children how they can create their own sprites, backgrounds and record their own sounds using Scratch.
• Ensure that you remind the children how to name their sprites and sounds and discuss why this is important (so they know which is which easily).
• Depending on your class's confidence, you may need to spend more time on this, or work with small groups who are less confident, while others can work independently.

Independent/paired work
• The children should now work through their asset list, using photocopiable page 148 'My assets' gathering their assets into their Scratch file. They tick off each asset from their list as they go.
• They should work as independently as possible, asking their peers if they can't remember how to do something before asking you (this is to encourage independent and collaborative thinking and problem solving and ensure that time is used as effectively as possible).
• Encourage the children to save their work regularly.
• Any children who finish can check their work. Encourage them to improve the standard of their assets, if appropriate, or begin to plan their algorithms as per the next lesson.

Differentiation
• Support: Less confident learners may benefit from working collaboratively in mixed-ability pairings and may need further support when creating their assets.
• Challenge: More confident learners will be able to create their assets to a high standard independently. Encourage them to help others in order to share their understanding and deepen their own learning.

Review
• Ask the children to review their list of assets and to check that they have completed them all. Some may require more time next lesson and should ensure that these are clearly marked on their sheet.
• As a class, come up with three top tips for anyone creating assets using Scratch.

Curriculum objectives
● To design, write and debug programs that accomplish specific goals, including controlling or simulating physical systems; solve problems by decomposing them into smaller parts; use sequence and repetition in programs; use logical reasoning to explain how some simple algorithms work and to detect and correct errors in algorithms and programs.

Lesson objectives
● To use logical thinking to plan appropriate algorithms for their animation.
● To use decomposition to break down algorithms into smaller parts.
● To identify and use selection and repetition as appropriate within their algorithms.
● To explain their algorithms verbally to their peers.
● To give and receive feedback.
● To debug their algorithms as appropriate after feedback.
● To start to implement their algorithms using the Scratch programming language.

Expected outcomes
● Can plan algorithms to achieve predicted outcomes.
● Can use repetition (loops) and selection where appropriate.

Resources
Completed photocopiable page 148 'My assets' from last week; photocopiable page 149 'My algorithms'; photocopiable page 'Hiding (and showing) your sprite' from the CD-ROM; Scratch 1.4 installed on the computers

Planning algorithms to use in Scratch

In this lesson the children plan the algorithms they need to use to create their dragon animations, decomposing their animation into smaller parts and then planning the algorithm for each part, using loops and selection. They work collaboratively to predict the outcome of their algorithms, debugging them as necessary and start to program their algorithms into Scratch.

Introduction
● Remind the children that they have been working in Scratch, creating their assets for their dragon animation.
● Explain that this week they will be creating the algorithms for their animation, firstly on paper and then using Scratch.

Independent/paired work
● Give out photocopiable page 149 'My algorithms' and display it on the whiteboard. Children should use this to plan their animation algorithms.
● Explain that they *only* need to focus on the first two columns for now.
● Emphasise that they need to work step-by-step through their animation, thinking of what action needs to happen first, then expanding it to create an algorithm, using repetition and selection as appropriate.
● They can use Scratch to help them to write their algorithms.
● Children may need to 'hide' those sprites they are not using immediately, so show them how to do this (when the green flag is clicked, hide, wait 10 seconds, show OR you can use 'broadcast' and 'when I receive'). Also use photocopiable page 'Hiding (and showing) your sprite' from the CD-ROM.

Whole-class work
● Display the Scratch interface on the whiteboard together with the photocopiable page 149 'My algorithms' and talk through how the example has been developed into code from the algorithm, programming it into Scratch. Program the code in as per the third column and discuss with the children why the debugging column is there and how the code has changed.
● Highlight how the repeat loop has become a forever loop and that the show position has been changed. Discuss with them what has happened (a mistake has been made and they have changed it – debugging).
● Explain to the children that they will write the Scratch code for their algorithms and then work in pairs to debug the code they write. If/when they finish, they can begin to start programming their sprites to create their actual animation.

Independent/paired work
● Ask the children to complete the next column 'code' on their sheet, working in Scratch to turn their algorithm into the correct code.
● Once they think they have finished, ask them to work in pairs to test and debug their code, working on one algorithm/script at a time.

Differentiation
● Support: Less confident learners may need support when moving from writing their actions to creating an algorithm and then working out the code needed. They may benefit from working in pairs or need additional adult support.
● Challenge: Encourage more confident learners to use more complex algorithms and efficient code, for example using repetition and selection.

Review
● Think of a number of actions and ask the children to write the algorithm and Scratch code for each action. Debug the code as a class until the action is completed. For example: Action: Get the knight to slay the dragon. Algorithm: When the knight touches the dragon, a triumphant sound plays. Code: When green flag clicked, forever if touching dragon, play sound trumpet1 until done.

Curriculum objectives
● To design, write and debug programs that accomplish specific goals, including controlling or simulating physical systems; solve problems by decomposing them into smaller parts; use sequence and repetition in programs; use logical reasoning to explain how some simple algorithms work and to detect and correct errors in algorithms and programs.

Lesson objectives
● To implement their algorithms using the Scratch programming language.
● To use selection and repetition as appropriate within their program.
● To work collaboratively with their peers to test and debug programs.
● To give and receive constructive feedback.

Expected outcomes
● Can implement algorithms using a suitable program.
● Can use repetition (loops) and selection where appropriate.

Resources
Completed photocopiable page 149 'My algorithms' from last week

Programming planned algorithms with Scratch

This lesson sees the children implement the algorithms and programming they planned in the previous lesson into Scratch. The planning they have undertaken so far should make this process relatively straightforward, and they will build up their animation quickly and effectively, although they will work collaboratively to debug any errors they find as they work.

Introduction
● Remind the children that last week they wrote algorithms and code for their Scratch dragon animation.
● Explain that in this lesson they will be programming the assets they have already created in Scratch using these to create their animation.

Whole-class work
● If you have access to a shared area featuring all the children's work, open a volunteer's Scratch file that has all the assets created. If you do not have access to a shared area, you will need to load the Scratch file prior to the lesson, or add in sample assets.
● Explain to the children that they should work though the actions and algorithms they planned last lesson in a logical way, thinking about what needs to happen next as they go.

Independent/paired work
● The children work to create their animation, logically, step-by-step, programming their sprites and working collaboratively to test and debug their programs.
● Collaborative debugging is a very helpful process here so encourage this as much as possible before you intervene.
● You may find there are common misunderstandings or issues that you can deal with in small groups, or you can encourage others who know how to do something to help someone who is struggling.
● When children finish, encourage them to share their work with a partner and give and receive feedback on each other's work in order to improve it.

Differentiation
● Support: Less confident learners may need additional adult or peer support when programming their animation and all progress, no matter how small, should be encouraged.
● Challenge: More confident learners could be encouraged to help others to debug their work and improve their own work by considering how they can make their animations more effective and their algorithms more efficient using selection and repetition.

Review
● Ask for a few volunteers to share their work with the class and as a class give constructive feedback.
● Review with the children their progress during the lesson and, if unfinished, ensure that they know what they need to do at the start of the next lesson.

Curriculum objectives

● To design, write and debug programs that accomplish specific goals, including controlling or simulating physical systems; solve problems by decomposing them into smaller parts; use sequence and repetition in programs; use logical reasoning to explain how some simple algorithms work and to detect and correct errors in algorithms and programs.

Lesson objectives

● To add simple comments to a program.
● To explain why adding comments can help the programmer.
● To explain how comments can help other people viewing a program.
● To evaluate their own animation.

Expected outcomes

● Can work collaboratively to debug algorithms and programs to achieve specific goals.
● Can evaluate their work in simple ways.

Resources

Scratch animation file with comments created prior to the lesson (using one of the children's files and adding comments would be helpful); photocopiable page 150 'Dragon animation evaluation'

Adding comments to and evaluating animations

In this lesson children complete their dragon animations, finishing off any final programming and debugging. They also learn how comments can be used in programming to help programmers and others keep track of what is happening with the program. Finally, the children also evaluate their final work using the criteria created in the first lesson of the chapter.

Introduction

● Recap with the children whether they have completed their animation or the steps they need to take to complete their animation at the start of this lesson.
● Explain that this week they will also be adding comments to their code and evaluating their completed animation.

Whole-class work

● Display the example file you have created showing comments and ask the class to share their ideas around why comments might be used in programming (to help the programmer keep track of what is happening, to help others to know what the programmer intended to do).
● Explain to the children that you would like them to create comments in their scripts and show them how to do this (right-click and add a suitable comment, such as 'knight makes happy sound when dragon disappears').
● If you wish, you could also show the children how to 'clean up' their code by right-clicking in the scripts area and also save pictures of their scripts if you wish to use this to help to assess their work.

Independent/paired work

● The children should add appropriate comments to their work and complete their animation as necessary.
● Once they think they have finished, give them photocopiable page 150 'Dragon animation evaluation' and ask them to work through this in order to evaluate their work.

Differentiation
● Support: Less confident learners may benefit from peer or adult support in finishing their animation, adding comments and evaluating their work.
● Challenge: Encourage more confident learners to make useful comments in their scripts and evaluate their work in detail. Also encourage them to help others.

Review

● Bring the children together and select some of the animations to show (saving their work in a shared area will be helpful for this as will noting which children have included aspects in their animation that will be interesting to show). Ask the children to talk through their animations as they are shown to explain how and why they have programmed their animation in that way.
● You may have time to show all the animations, if not, make sure that you discuss each child's animation, which will help with assessment of the chapter's work.
● Assess the children's understanding from their dragon animation, their scripts and comments (you can ask them to print this to help with assessment), their evaluation and their review discussion with you.

Curriculum objectives
● To design, write and debug programs that accomplish specific goals, including controlling or simulating physical systems; solve problems by decomposing them into smaller parts; use sequence and repetition in programs; use logical reasoning to explain how some simple algorithms work and to detect and correct errors in algorithms and programs.

Lesson objectives
● To apply their knowledge and understanding of programming to another programming tool.
● To plan and create a short animation using a different programming tool.
● To evaluate their work.
● To present their work to others.

Expected outcomes
● Can plan and create an effective animation.
● Can create and debug simple algorithms and programs that accomplish specific goals.
● Can use repetition and selection where appropriate in algorithms and programming.
● Can evaluate their work.

Resources
Interactive activity 'My animation' on the CD-ROM; photocopiable page 151 'Planning my animation'

Dragons: Assess and review

This lesson sees children apply the knowledge, skills and understanding they have developed using Scratch to a different programming tool. This will help consolidate their learning and provide an opportunity for children to demonstrate their understanding of programming and of implementing algorithms with different programs. Assessment and observation of the children's work will allow you to make adjustments to future learning of this topic, as you deem appropriate.

Introduction
● Discuss with the children what they have learned about animation during this chapter.
● Explain that for this assessment task they will be creating a short animation using a different programming tool.

Whole-class work
● Display the interactive activity 'My animation' on the CD-ROM on the whiteboard.
● Click the Themes tab and show that there are a number of backgrounds, turtles and objects available. Explain that the children will plan an animation using their choice of these assets.
● Point out the programming box and try out some commands. Clicking the help document icon positioned near the bottom left corner of the screen will bring up a list of commands. Demonstrate any commands the children haven't used in previous chapters. This may include *Jump, Flash, Spin, Speak* or *Repeat*.

Independent work
● Give each child photocopiable page 151 'Planning my animation' and ask them to complete it to plan their animation.
● Once they are sure their plan is complete they can access the interactive activity 'My animation' on the CD-ROM to create their animation.

Differentiation
● Support: Less confident learners may need support in using new commands.
● Challenge: More confident learners should be challenged to create a complex animation which uses a wide range of commands

Review
● The end of this chapter is an ideal opportunity to get the children to present the work they have created, whether this is their dragon animation or the animation they have created during this lesson.
● Videoing them explaining their work, for example, how the program is executing their algorithms, or how they debugged their code, could be used for assessment.
● Similarly, you could use screenshots of their work and printouts of their code for display purposes.
● Assess the children's work through the outcomes of their challenges and you should make adjustments to future algorithms and programming work based on these assessments.

What makes an effective animation?

■ Watch the animation. Write down how it makes use of the following:

Colours: _____

_____

_____

_____

_____

Story: _____

_____

_____

_____

_____

Audio (speech, sound effects, music): _____

_____

_____

_____

_____

Characters: _____

_____

_____

_____

_____

I can judge what makes an effective animation.

How did you do?

Key learning point

■ What is the key learning point you have discovered from your lesson today?

_____

_____

■ How will you make sure that you include this in your own animation?

_____

_____

_____

_____

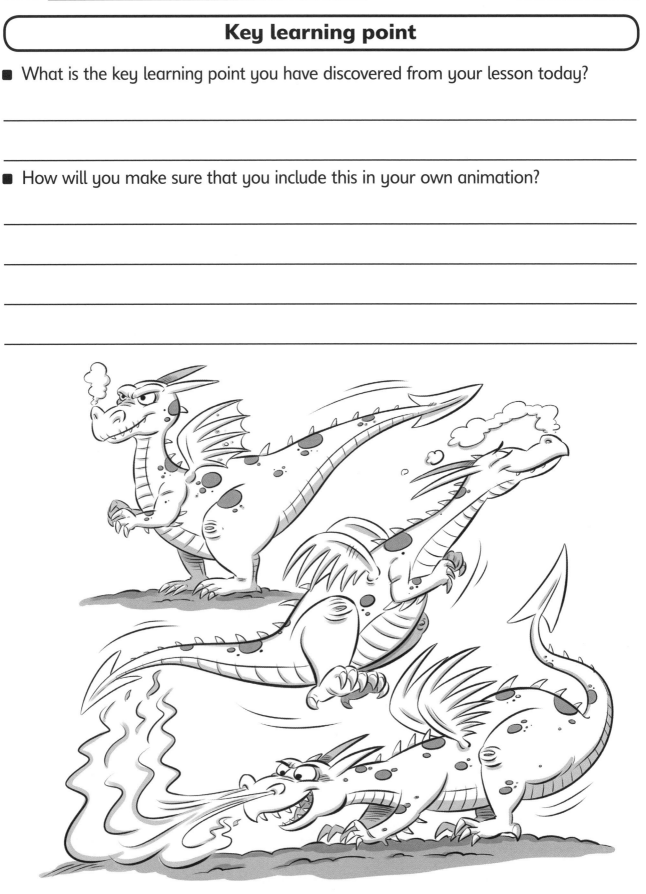

I can decide what the key learning point from a lesson is.

How did you do?

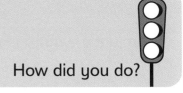

PHOTOCOPIABLE

SCHOLASTIC
www.scholastic.co.uk

Storyboard

■ Plan your Scratch dragon animation using the template below.

I can plan a Scratch animation.

How did you do?

My assets

■ Write down ALL the different parts that you need to create and collect for your animation.

Characters: _____

_____

_____

_____

Objects: _____

_____

_____

_____

Sounds: _____

_____

_____

_____

Text: _____

_____

_____

_____

Backgrounds: _____

_____

_____

_____

I can plan the assets needed for my Scratch animation.

How did you do?

PHOTOCOPIABLE   **SCHOLASTIC**
www.scholastic.co.uk

Name: _____   Date: _____

My algorithms

- Use another sheet of paper to draw a table like the one below. Write down the action, algorithm and code you will need for your animation.
- Leave the debugging column until you are asked to complete it.

Action	Algorithm	Code	Debugging
Dragon goes across bottom of screen continuously.	Dragon starts at the left of the stage and glides slowly across to the right of the stage. Dragon disappears and reappears at the left-hand side of the screen.	When green flag clicked In repeat loop: Go to X -182 Y -116 Glide 3 seconds to X 177 Y -116 Hide Wait 1 second Show	When green flag clicked In forever loop: Go to X -182 Y -116 Show Glide 3 seconds to X 177 Y -116 Hide Wait 1 second

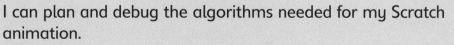

I can plan and debug the algorithms needed for my Scratch animation.

How did you do?

Dragon animation evaluation

■ Why is your animation effective?

_____

_____

_____

_____

■ What do you think is *most* effective about your animation?

_____

_____

_____

_____

■ *Why* do you think that is most effective?

_____

_____

_____

_____

■ How could you make your animation even more effective?

_____

_____

_____

_____

I can evaluate my own work.

How did you do?

PHOTOCOPIABLE

Name: _____ Date: _____

Planning my animation

■ Complete this plan before creating your animation. Although you only have a limited range of assets, can you make your animation interesting?

What sprite (turtle) will I use?

_____

What background will I use?

_____

What objects will I use?

_____

Now use another sheet of paper to add your action, algorithm, code and debugging.

Action	Algorithm	Code	Debugging

I can plan and debug an algorithm for an animation.

How did you do?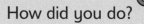

The Normans

This chapter engages the children in a Norman theme, focusing on the *Bayeux Tapestry* and *The Domesday Book*. Children look at the tapestry to see how it tells a story. Looking at timelines, they can see how that tells a story too. The children construct paper-based and digital timelines, thinking about their lives and what happens during a day, a week and a year. Focusing on *The Domesday Book*, the children look how the data is represented and how it was collected. They think about data representation and justify their decisions.

Expected prior learning

The children will have looked at data previously and focused on checking for errors. They use their prior learning when looking at timelines, questioning that the data is accurate. They will use their learning about pictograms and bar charts to consider which is the best representation of the data.

Chapter at a glance

Subject area
• Data and information

National Curriculum objective
• To select, use and combine a variety of software (including internet services) to create a range of content that accomplish given goals, including collecting and presenting data and information.

Week	Lesson objectives	Summary of activities	Expected outcomes
1	• To identify simple pictograms and graphs. • To interpret simple pictograms and graphs. • To explain that data tells a story. • To create paper-based pictograms and living graphs to describe well-known stories.	• Children are introduced to the *Bayeaux Tapestry*. They look at the scenes and attempt to work out what is happening. • They consider how the tapestry is telling a story and pretend to be detectives interpreting information. • They look at pictograms and graphs in newspapers, on TV and on the internet and begin to recognise that data tells a story.	• Can identify and interpret simple pictograms and graphs. • Can explain that data can tell a story.
2	• To identify a timeline. • To interpret simple timelines (for example, major historical events in their life times). • To create simple timelines using paper-based tools. • To explain what the *Bayeux Tapestry* is and why it is important.	• Children look at a timeline, read the scale and can identify when important events occurred. • They create timelines using paper-based tools. • They explain why the *Bayeux Tapestry* is important by finding information on the internet.	• Can identify a timeline. • Can interpret simple timelines. • Can create simple timelines using software.
3	• To create simple timelines (for example, of the children's own lives), using software or online tools. • To research online to locate historical information. • To check for errors in the created timelines.	• Children plan their own timelines using timeline software. • They check for errors in data building on their learning from Year 3.	• Can create a timeline for a specific purpose. • Can research online to locate historical information for a timeline. • Can check for errors in information.

Week	Lesson objectives	Summary of activities	Expected outcomes
4	• To research to collect different media for use in a timeline. • To evaluate the located media, using given criteria. • To describe the buttons and menus of the software and how they are adapted for the user. • To explain the importance of human–computer interface design.	• Children are encouraged to collect different media to use with their timeline to make it interesting and to add more information. • They evaluate the media they find using given criteria. • They consider the importance of human–computer interface design to enable them to understand the software.	• Can combine different media to create interactive timelines. • Can explain the importance of human–computer interface design.
5	• To present information, in the form of a timeline, to their peers. • To evaluate presentations, using given criteria. • To create new evaluation criteria, as a group or class.	• Children use a timeline to present a story of their lives to the class. • They evaluate each other's presentations using given criteria. • They consider whether the criteria they used can be improved.	• Can present information to their peers. • Can evaluate presentations, using given criteria.
6	• To describe different formats for presenting data. • To describe why certain formats are more suitable than others for particular data. • To justify the choice of format of presentation of data, for a specific purpose.	• Children are introduced to the *Domesday Book* as a survey of the kingdom in 1086. • They create questionnaires for a new *Domesday Book*. • They look at different formats of data presentation and justify which format most suits a specific purpose.	• Can describe different formats for presenting data. • Can justify the format of presentation for a specific purpose.
Assess and review	• To assess the half-term's work.	• Children create a modern-day Domesday Book for modern-day objects. • They decide on the most appropriate method of representing the data and justify their choices.	• Assess and review.

Overview of progression

● The children will progress their understanding of how information can be presented, by looking at the *Bayeux Tapestry* to see how a timeline can tell a story. They progress their understanding by constructing paper-based and digital timelines.
● Digital tools enable events and images to be added to the timeline and so they learn how they can add events and modify them.
● The children will progress their understanding of collecting, checking and representing data.

Creative context

● The lessons link closely to the English curriculum, where the children check that the text makes sense to them, discussing their understanding and explaining the meaning of words in context. They identify how language, structure and presentation contribute to meaning.
● Linking to maths, they interpret and present discrete data using bar charts.
● There are links to history, through the creation and interpretation of timelines and chronological data.

Background knowledge

● The children will have looked at data and how it can be represented as pictograms and bar charts. They have listened to and read stories, which follow a chronological order, for example, *The Very Hungry Caterpillar* follows a sequence of days. They will have also learned about autobiographies, following life stories.
● The children will have encountered simple timelines through their history lessons.

Curriculum objectives
● To select, use and combine a variety of software (including internet services) to create a range of content that accomplish given goals, including collecting and presenting data and information.

Objectives
● To identify simple pictograms and graphs.
● To interpret simple pictograms and graphs.
● To explain that data tells a story.
● To create paper-based pictograms and living graphs to describe well-known stories.

Expected outcomes
● Can identify and interpret simple pictograms and graphs.
● Can explain that data can tell a story.

Resources
Photocopiable page 161 'Bayeux Tapestry sketch'; photocopiable page 162 'Bayeux Tapestry tally chart'; interactive activity 'Bar chart' on the CD-ROM

The story of the Bayeux Tapestry

The children are introduced to the *Bayeux Tapestry*, showing how it tells a story and also how data tells a story too. The children look at examples of data, pictograms and charts. They create tally tables and represent information from the tapestry in charts.

Introduction
● Display to the class the first scene of the *Bayeux Tapestry* (http://hastings1066.com/bayeux1.shtml). Do any of the children recognise it? Do they know its name? Have they seen a tapestry before?
● Looking at the first scene, can they explain what is happening? Now look at the second scene (http://hastings1066.com/bayeux2.shtml). Can they explain what is happening?
● Tell the children that the tapestry is telling a story and that they are detectives interpreting the information.
● Using photocopiable page 161 'Bayeux Tapestry sketch', the children draw part of the first scene, to encourage them to look closely at the images.

Whole-class work
● To revise the learning about data in everyday life, the children think about pictograms and bar charts they have seen, for example, favourite meals.
● Prior to the lesson collect pictograms and graphs from newspapers or in the news on the internet, to show that the data is represented in different ways.
● Explain that they are going to use a tally chart to record how many different types of objects are in the first scene. Can they remember how to draw a chart and use tally marks?

Paired work
● In pairs, the children decide upon the objects in the first scene that they are going to count, for example, birds, dogs, horses, men and kings.
● They create a tally chart, using photocopiable page 162 'Bayeux Tapestry tally chart'.
● The children look at the data they collect to ensure that it is correct.
● They decide upon a format to represent the data and draw the charts.

Whole-class work
● Bring the class together for children to share their results and charts.
● Can they describe the data? For example, there are more men than kings, more horses than dogs. Can they add numbers to their descriptions? For example, there are five men on five horses. This will be a useful skill for future work, when they begin to describe trends.
● Demonstrate interactive activity 'Bar chart' on the CD-ROM to show how to add labels and increase the size of the columns to match the data.

Paired work
● In pairs, the children look at scene two of the tapestry and add the data straight into the interactive activity.

Differentiation
● Support: Less confident learners may need support to identify objects to collect the data. This group may need support to convert the tally chart into a bar chart.
● Challenge: More confident learners can decide on the data to collect.

Review
● Ask two pairs to share their findings from scene 2.
● Compare the processes of collecting data. In the first one, they created a tally chart, checked it and then drew a chart. In the second one, they put the data straight into the interactive chart. Highlight that the second method may have been much quicker, but there were more opportunities for errors to occur.

Curriculum objectives
● To select, use and combine a variety of software (including internet services) to create a range of content that accomplish given goals, including collecting and presenting data and information.

Lesson objectives
● To identify a timeline.
● To interpret simple timelines (for example, major historical events in their life times).
● To create simple timelines using paper-based tools.
● To explain what the *Bayeux Tapestry* is and why it is important.

Expected outcomes
● Can identify a timeline.
● Can interpret simple timelines.
● Can create simple timelines using software.

Resources
Washing line (or string) and clothes pegs; photocopiable page 163 'What do I do each day?'; photocopiable page 164 'My day'

Timelines

The children are introduced to timelines using the *Bayeux Tapestry* theme. They think about events from the day, collecting examples and adding them to the class timeline. The children extend their timescale to consider what are the significant events from that week and then the whole year.

Introduction
● Show the *Bayeux Tapestry* on the whiteboard and remind the children that it tells a story over time.
● Display the scenes in order and tell the children the story.
● Remind the children about storyboards.
● Ask the children whether they have seen a timeline before. Where might they see one? They may have seen one, for example, in articles from history or perhaps celebrities' lives may be portrayed as a timeline.

Whole-class work
● Display the BBC Timeline resource (www.bbc.co.uk/schools/primaryhistory/timeline/timeline.shtml). This shows important periods of history which the children will recognise; for example, the Romans, Vikings and the Second World War. Show how the timeline has a scale across the x-axis, progressing from the earliest date on the left to the most recent, on the right.
● Can the children identify the start and end dates of the different periods? Now select one of the periods and show how it zooms into a more detailed timeline. Can they read the dates more accurately now?
● Share photocopiable page 163 'What do I do each day?' and ask the children to think about their day or a regular week day, what sort of activities do they do and when?
● Talk about their day, for example, having lunch at school, what time does that occur? They can add the activity and time to the photocopiable sheet. They create one label for one event.
● Attach a washing line (or string) across the classroom and use clothes pegs to add the photocopiable sheets to it, in order from the morning, when they get up, to the night, when they go to sleep.
● Can they see how the timeline becomes more interesting and informative, as you put on more information?

Independent work
● Using photocopiable page 164 'My day', the children sketch a timeline for their typical week day.
● They can now talk about their week, do they do different things on different days? How is it different at the weekend? Using another copy of the photocopiable sheet, the children sketch a timeline for the week.
● Extending the time period, they discuss the events during a month and finally, they think about a full year.
● Using another copy of the sheet, the children think about the major events in the year. They might be birthdays, holidays or religious festivals.

Differentiation
● Support: Less confident learners may need support to think of significant events and to place them on the timeline correctly.
● Challenge: More confident learners could create a timeline for a month, in addition to the other timelines. They could explain verbally why certain events are significant.

Review
● Bring the class together and share three volunteers' timelines for the year. Did they have similar events for public holidays and celebrations? Did they have different types of events for more personal times in their lives?
● Returning to the *Bayeux Tapestry*, explain that it is important because it describes significant events in that period of history.

Curriculum objectives
• To select, use and combine a variety of software (including internet services) to create a range of content that accomplish given goals, including collecting and presenting data and information.

Objectives
• To create simple timelines (for example, of the children's own lives), using software or online tools.
• To research online to locate historical information.
• To check for errors in the created timelines.

Expected outcomes
• Can create a timeline for a specific purpose.
• Can research online to locate historical information for a timeline.
• Can check for errors in information.

Resources
Interactive activity 'My life timeline' on the CD-ROM; photocopiable page 165 'Significant events in your life'

Timeline of your life

Continuing to look at timelines, the children construct a timeline for their lives, using software. Linking to previous learning, they check for errors and consider the *Bayeux Tapestry*, will it be completely true?

Introduction
• Begin the lesson by displaying the 'History of flight timeline' (http://teacher. scholastic.com/activities/flight/timeline.htm.)
• Ask the children to describe the information it shows and to identify the corresponding times.

Whole-class work
• Display the washing line time line from the previous lesson. Remind the children how they selected significant events from their day and added them to the timeline. They could have added lots of detail, but should they include everything? For example, they may have 'Walk to school' as a significant event, but they may not have added 'Put left foot forward at 8.45 and 23 seconds, put right foot forward at 8.45 and 24 seconds'. Highlight that they had decided upon events that were significant to them.
• Ask the children to think about their own lives. What have been the significant events? If it helps, they can look at the 'My day' activity from the previous lesson. Make sure that you are sensitive to any children who have had upsetting incidents in their year, such as death or divorce.
• Explain that they are going to plan their own timelines about their own lives.

Paired work
• In pairs the children interview each other using photocopiable page 166 'Significant events in your life'. They take turns asking questions, using the prompts and recording the responses (again take care with any children who may have had difficult events to cope with).
• Using interactive activity 'My life timeline', they add the entries of the events in their lives.

> ### Differentiation
> • Support: Less confident learners may need support to identify the more important events and to place them chronologically on their timeline.
> • Challenge: More confident learners could create up to 20 significant events, verbally justifying why they chose those events and not others.

Review
• Bring the class together and ask ten children to stand in a line at the front of the class (you may want to ask for volunteers for this). Each child describes one event, when it happened and why it is significant. Once each child has spoken, they sort themselves into chronological order.
• Ask the children to compare making timelines on paper and digitally using the interactive activity.
• Ask them if they checked for errors in the data, building on their learning from Year 3. Highlight that, with all information, they need to check it is accurate.
• Demonstrate looking for significant events in local history, for example, when was a local castle built, a local famous person born or famous festival or concert.
• Returning to the *Bayeux Tapestry* theme, ask the children who made it. They should say it was the Normans. Explain that it may not be entirely accurate, as it was created by the winners of the battle. With all data and information, they need to know the source and make decisions about accuracy.

Curriculum objectives
● To select, use and combine a variety of software (including internet services) to create a range of content that accomplish given goals, including collecting and presenting data and information.

Lesson objectives
● To research to collect different media for use in a timeline.
● To evaluate the located media, using given criteria.
● To describe the buttons and menus of the software and how they are adapted for the user.
● To explain the importance of human–computer interface design.

Expected outcomes
● Can combine different media to create interactive timelines.
● Can explain the importance of human-computer interface design.

Resources
Interactive activity 'My Life timeline' on the CD-ROM; photocopiable page 166 'My timeline media'

Adding images to timelines

The children enhance their timelines by adding images to help the viewer to understand the content more easily. The children look at examples of timelines with images and then search online to find examples to add to their interactive timeline.

Introduction
● Display the history of LEGO timeline (from the LEGO website http://aboutus.lego.com/en-gb/lego-group/the_lego_history). Explain that this is a list of significant events in LEGO's history, though not displayed along a line, it still tells a story in chronological order.
● Display another LEGO timeline (http://lego.gizmodo.com/349509/lego-brick-timeline-50-years-of-building-frenzy-and-curiosities).
● Explain that this timeline shares information, but the images help the user to understand more clearly about the products as they evolved.
● Display another LEGO timeline (www.timetoast.com/timelines/the-story-of-lego). This timeline has images to support the text and this makes the timeline more interesting and easier to understand.
● With their permission, display an example of one of the children's timelines. What images could they add to make it more interesting and informative?

Independent work
● The children search online to find images related to their life events, for example, if the child mentioned the event, 'birth of my brother', they could search for an image of the hospital or a generic image of a hospital or a baby.
● Using photocopiable page 166 'My timeline media', the children search online for suitable images and record the type of image (for example, jpeg or gif) and the web address. They download the image onto the computer or network storage, for use with the timeline.
● Once located, they should evaluate the media they find, explaining why they are using them.

Paired work
● In pairs, review the images that their partner has found. Do they think they will help the user understand the information more easily? Even though the images may look attractive, a timeline needs to convey information clearly.

Whole-class work
● Do the children think a real image of themselves, that is a digital photograph, would be better than the images they have located?
● How could they transfer their own photographs from home to school? (They could upload images to a cloud-based images website, for example Flickr. They could transfer them with a cloud-based file storage, for example Dropbox. They could place the images on a DVD or USB drive.)

Differentiation
● Challenge: More confident learners could locate and evaluate images to add to their timelines. They can decide whether the images are suitable and write down their reasons. They will be able to verbally describe their reasons for selecting the images.
● Support: Less confident learners may need support to search for images and to then decide if they should be added.

Review
● Select two pairs of children to share one image they have chosen. Ask: *Why do you think the image is appropriate for your life event?*
● Bring their attention to the software they have been using (for example, the web browser). Human–computer interface design is important to enable the user to easily use the software. Ask the children to describe the menus and buttons. Do they think they are adapted for children to be able to use easily?

Curriculum objectives
● To select, use and combine a variety of software (including internet services) to create a range of content that accomplish given goals, including collecting and presenting data and information.

Lesson objectives
● To present information, in the form of a timeline, to their peers.
● To evaluate presentations, using given criteria.
● To create new evaluation criteria, as a group or class.

Expected outcomes
● Can present information to their peers.
● Can evaluate presentations, using given criteria.

Resources
Photocopiable page 167 'Presentation prompt cards'; photocopiable page 'Timeline talk evaluation' from the CD-ROM; interactive activity 'My life timeline' on the CD-ROM

Your life story

Using a timeline, the children present the story of their lives. They consider the *Bayeux Tapestry*, William the Conqueror, the Battle of Hastings and the *Domesday Book* and how these each tell a story. The children prepare their presentations and share them with the class.

Introduction
● Introduce the lesson by displaying the *Bayeux Tapestry* images. Ask: *Can you remember that the tapestry tells a story?*
● Display the dates in William the Conqueror's life (www.historyonthenet. com/Chronology/timelinewilliami.htm). Ask: *Does it tell a story?*
● Display the important dates from the Battle of Hastings (www. normaninvasion.info/timeline-battle-hastings.htm). Ask: *Does it tell a story?*

Whole-class work
● Display one of the children's timelines. Explain that a timeline could be used to present a story of their lives to their class.
● Explain that they are going to prepare a talk about themselves and that they will use prompt cards to help remind them what to say.

Paired work
● Looking at their timelines (using the interactive activity 'My life timeline' on the CD-ROM), the children select six events.
● In pairs, the children draft their talks, by reading through the six events in their timelines. They listen carefully to each other and give kind, specific and helpful advice about where they could add more detail.
● The children take turns and create a first draft of their notes, using photocopiable page 167 'Presentation prompt cards'. They write a sentence about each event on each of the six lines.
● They think about the facts for their events, look at the sentence they have written and then write three bullet points to remind themselves what to say. Emphasise that they should not read all of the words from the cards, they are there as a reminder.
● Cut up the cards, so they have six cards to hold in their hands.
● They practise again, reading slowly and clearly, to their partner.
● Taking turns again, they give kind, specific and helpful advice.

Differentiation
● Support: Less confident learners may need support to identify the six events in their timelines and to draft notes for each one. They could prepare notes for less events, if appropriate.
● Challenge: More confident learners could support less confident learners to improve their presentations. They could give kind, specific and helpful feedback and help them to draft their notes. For their own prompt cards, they should include at least three bullet points of information to remind them what to say, while presenting.

Review
● Bring the class together to listen to the talks. These could be heard over several lessons, if appropriate.
● Evaluation criteria for the talks can be found on photocopiable page 'Timeline talk evaluation' from the CD-ROM.
● As a class, can they think of one more evaluation criterion? For example, 'Should smile when presenting' or 'Should make sure everyone is quiet before they begin'.
● Once decided upon, the children write the extra criterion to their list on the photocopiable sheet.
● The children should display their timeline and refer to it as they present.
● Listen to the talks and evaluate using the criteria. Each child should select another child in the class, to give them kind, specific and helpful feedback.

The Domesday Book

Continuing the Norman theme, this week focuses on the *Domesday Book*. The children look at how the data is represented and how the original data was collected. To improve the process, they create questions, which the original officials may have asked. The children look at a modern census and see how the questions are not ambiguous. They remember that data tells a story.

Curriculum objectives
● To select, use and combine a variety of software (including internet services) to create a range of content that accomplish given goals, including collecting and presenting data and information.

Lesson objectives
● To describe different formats for presenting data.
● To describe why certain formats are more suitable than others for particular data.
● To justify the choice of format of presentation of data, for a specific purpose.

Expected outcomes
● Can describe different formats for presenting data.
● Can justify the format of presentation for a specific purpose.

Resources
Interactive activity 'Domesday Book' on the CD-ROM; photocopiable page 'Domesday questions' from the CD-ROM; photocopiable page 'Better Domesday questions' from the CD-ROM; photocopiable page 'Showing the data' from the CD-ROM; printable census from www.censusatschool.org.uk/take-part/questionnaires

Introduction
● Introduce the lesson by showing a page from the *Domesday Book* (www.nationalarchives.gov.uk/education/focuson/domesday/default.htm).
● Show the children the text the data held on the Essex page. Can they see that the data is laid out in sentences, for example, 'Then 4 horses, 13 cows, 25 pigs, 105 sheep; now 5 horses, 2 colts, 11 pigs, 80 sheep and 11 goats.'
● Explain that the *Domesday Book* was a big survey of the kingdom in 1086, commissioned by William the Conqueror, to find out all about the new country in order to collect taxes.

Whole-class work
● Explain that the information is not very easy to use, as it is all laid out in sentences. How could the children arrange it? Using interactive activity 'Domesday Book' on the CD-ROM, create a bar chart for the data.
● Watch the videos on the National Archives website about the collecting of data and questions (www.nationalarchives.gov.uk/education/focuson/domesday/how-was-it-made/collecting-the-information.htm).

Paired work
● Using photocopiable page 'Domesday questions' from the CD-ROM, the children imagine the questions that would have been asked.
● The children role play being Normans asking the Anglo Saxons questions.

Whole-class work
● Bring the class together and select three pairs to share their questions.
● Ask the class whether the questions are clear and unambiguous. For example, 'Are you a boy or a girl?' could be answered 'Yes'.
● Can the children refine their questions, so that they are clearer, for example, 'Are you a boy? (Yes or No).
● Using photocopiable page 'Better Domesday questions' from the CD-ROM, the children look at different styles of questions.
● Ask the children to look at the questions again. They should write down which ones they think are the most suitable.

Paired work
● Using photocopiable page 'Showing the data' from the CD-ROM, the children look at different formats of data presentation, and then justify which format most suits a specific purpose.

> ### Differentiation
> ● Support: Less confident learners may need support to refine their questions. A word bank may help their vocabulary to create questions.
> ● Challenge: More confident learners could review their questions to make them less ambiguous. They can create new questions for Domesday Book researchers.

Review
● Bring the class together and display photocopiable page 'Showing the data' from the CD-ROM. Ask children to explain which format is most suitable?
● Explain that there are still censuses that are carried out today. There is a project called CensusAtSchool, which happens each year. Access the current questionnaire (www.censusatschool.org.uk/take-part/questionnaires).
● Allow the children time to complete the questionnaire.

Curriculum objectives
• To select, use and combine a variety of software (including internet services) to create a range of content that accomplish given goals, including collecting and presenting data and information.

Lesson objectives
• To describe different formats for presenting data.
• To justify the choice of format of presentation of data, for a specific purpose.

Expected outcomes
• Can describe different formats for presenting data.
• Can justify the format of presentation for a specific purpose.

Resources
Photocopiable page 'Modern Domesday Book' on the CD-ROM; interactive activity 'Modern Domesday' from the CD-ROM

The Normans: Assess and review

This week, the children review their learning of the Normans and the *Domesday Book*. They create a modern Domesday Book, thinking about the possessions that the children own now. They create questions, collect data and represent it in a suitable format. Finally, they return to timelines and create a modern timeline for the previous ten years.

Introduction
• Introduce the lesson by reminding the children of the *Domesday Book*. Display a picture of the book (www.nationalarchives.gov.uk/education/focuson/domesday/default.htm).
• Can the children remember what the *Domesday Book* is and why it was important?
• Explain that they are going to create a modern-day Domesday Book for modern objects, for example electronic games devices or bikes.

Whole-class work
• For a modern Domesday Book for the class, ask what the objects of interest will be. The children choose five objects, for example, bike, TV, video game console, pet and book.

Paired work
• Using photocopiable page 'Modern Domesday Book' from the CD-ROM, the children construct their questions. In pairs, they try out the questions to see whether they are clear and unambiguous. Their partners give kind, specific and helpful feedback.
• Once the questions are refined and finalised, the children ask their class for responses. They record the data in a table.
• They can now discuss the different formats that they could use to display the data for the class.
• Ask: *Which formats could you use for presenting data, for example a timeline, bar chart, pictogram?*

Whole-class work
• Bring the class together and ask each pair in turn to report back.
• Each pair states their five objects that they collected data for and how many of each they counted.
• They then explain which format of data representation they chose and why.
• Ask: *Can you justify the format of data presentation that you have chosen?*

> **Differentiation**
> • Less confident learners may need support to identify which objects to collect data for and how to organise their table. They can represent the data as a pictogram.
> • More confident learners could identify the five objects for which they will collect data. They will be able to justify which method of data representation they select.

Review
• Display the 'Domesday timeline' (www.domesdaybook.co.uk/timeline.html). Can the children identify significant events and their date?
• Using interactive activity 'Modern Domesday' on the CD-ROM, they can suggest significant events that have occurred over the previous ten years (going back to a year before the children were born).
• On Wikipedia, the entry for '21st century' has an extensive list of events (http://en.wikipedia.org/wiki/21st_century).
• Select one event per year and ask the children to research online to find one fact about that event.
• To conclude the lesson, ask the children to describe different methods of displaying the data.

■SCHOLASTIC

Bayeux Tapestry sketch

■ Sketch the first scene from the *Bayeux Tapestry* in the box below.

■ Describe what is happening in your sketch.

_____

_____

_____

_____

I can draw in the style of a historical Tapestry.

How did you do?

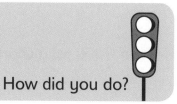

Bayeux Tapestry tally chart

■ Complete the tally chart for objects in the *Bayeux Tapestry*.

Object	Tally	Total

I can use a tally chart to count objects.

How did you do?

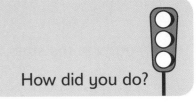

■SCHOLASTIC
www.scholastic.co.uk

What do I do each day?

■ Draw something you do everyday and write the time you do it below.

Time:

I can identify an event in my day and draw it.

How did you do?

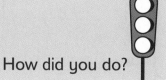

Name: _____

Date: _____

My day

■ Sketch a timeline for your typical week day.

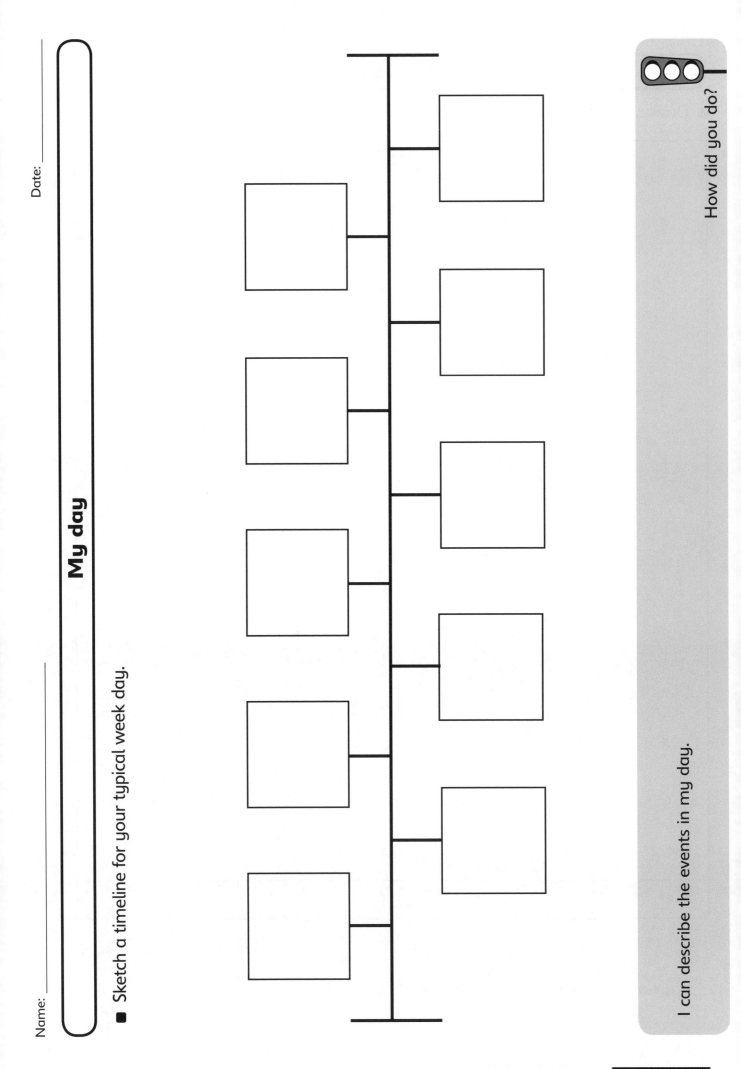

I can describe the events in my day.

How did you do?

PHOTOCOPIABLE

Significant events in your life

■ Interview your partner.
■ What have been the significant events in their life?

1. _____

2. _____

3. _____

4. _____

5. _____

6. _____

7. _____

8. _____

9. _____

10. _____

I can interview my partner about their life.

How did you do?

Name: _____   Date: _____

My timeline media

■ List the images you find for your timeline. Use the Evaluation column to add notes on why you think the image is worth adding to your timeline.

Image	Type of image (jpg, gif, etc.)	Web address	Evaluation

I can find images to add to my timeline.

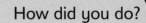

How did you do?

PHOTOCOPIABLE

Presentation prompt cards

- Read through your timeline.
- Make notes below about six events in your timeline.

1. _____

2. _____

3. _____

4. _____

5. _____

6. _____

- Now create notes for your talk. Write three points for each event.

1. ■ ■ ■	2. ■ ■ ■
3. ■ ■ ■	4. ■ ■ ■
5. ■ ■ ■	6. ■ ■ ■

I can make notes to prompt my presentation.

How did you do?

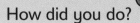

Jacqueline Wilson

Through a Jacqueline Wilson theme, the children learn about the author and her books. They continue to learn about online profiles and sharing information online. Using online web tools, the children develop their collaboration skills and are introduced to online voting tools. They create a class blog and they compare sharing in a diary and also in a blog post. To give feedback, they use comments to respond to their class peers, being kind, specific and helpful.

Expected prior learning

● The children will have created online profiles before and considered sharing information. They will have written about characters and their actions in English and written in the first person. Using an online collaborative tool, they will have written and shared information, though they may not have used a voting tool before.
● The children will have used a word processor, though may not have used the spellchecker tool.

Chapter at a glance

Subject area
• Data and information

National Curriculum objective
• To use technology safely, respectfully and responsibly. • To select, use and combine a variety of software (including internet services) on a range of digital devices to design and create a range of programs, systems and content that accomplish given goals, including collecting, analysing, evaluating and presenting data and information.

Week	Lesson objectives	Summary of activities	Expected outcomes
1	• To identify characters from fictional books (for example, Tracy Beaker). • To describe characters from fictional books; to begin to develop profiles. • To identify personalities from real life and locate information about them, using search tools. • To describe the validity of the information located.	• Children are introduced to the Jacqueline Wilson stories. • They find out which Jacqueline Wilson books they have read. • They research online to find out more information about the author and whether the information they find is valid.	• Can discuss online identities, including profiles. • Can describe how to search for information about personalities and discuss the validity of the information.
2	• To decide the type of information required in a profile of a person. • To create a profile for a fictional character in a book based on the information located.	• Children are introduced to the story *The Suitcase Kid*. • They profile the characters in the story. How do we know what they are like? What do they say and do? • Building on previous learning, the children create a profile of the main character. • They discuss how the cuddly toy the main character has helps her to cope with difficult situations. • They create an imaginary profile of a cuddly toy and a celebrity.	• Can create a profile for a character in a book, based on information located. • Can create a profile for a current celebrity, based on information located.
3	• To describe locating information and evaluating it, in the form of a user guide for their peers. • To proofread materials before sharing with others. • To use a given checklist to check information before sharing it. • To name different software used on different hardware. • To explain why different hardware may use different software.	• Continuing the theme of *The Suitcase Kid*, the children think about true and false questions. • They use an online questioning tool to vote true or false. • They write questions to ask about the story. • Using a checklist they proofread their work. • Linked to 'How computers work' they look at the different types of software.	• Can create a user guide for peers, for locating digital content and how to evaluate it. • Can use different software and understand different hardware may have different software (for example, tablet operating systems and apps).

Week	Lesson objectives	Summary of activities	Expected outcomes
4	• To collaborate to create a new story, in-person and face-to-face. • To collaborate using online tools to plan and create a new story. • To compare the writing processes of online and in-person collaboration and describe the advantages and disadvantages. • To correct errors using software tools, such as spell checking.	• Children plan a Jacqueline Wilson style story. • They look at the plot structure: opening, problem, the problem develops, resolution. • Comparing the processes of online and in-person collaboration, children think about when each would be appropriate. • They proofread and check for errors using software tools like spellchecker.	• Can collaborate face-to-face to plan a new story. • Can collaborate online to plan a new story. • Can compare the processes of collaborating face-to-face and online.
5	• To name different application software and describe its functions. • To explain why different application software is used for different purposes. • To explain the function of a blog. • To create a simple blog.	• Children write a review of *The Suitcase Kid* using the headings: plot, characters, my favourite part, my favourite language, why I would recommend it, and so on. • They compare blog posts and blogs and decide how much information to share.	• Can explain why there are different application software for different purposes. • Can create a simple blog using online tools.
6	• To read and review blog comments, using given criteria. • To respond to a blog post, giving positive and supportive comments. • To evaluate blogs for the quality of information shared, using given criteria.	• Children respond to a blog post using 'kind, specific and helpful' criteria. • They evaluate the blogs to look at the quality of the information shared.	• Can give positive and supportive comments, using a blog. • Can evaluate the information given within a blog.
Assess and review	• Assess and review the half-term's work.	• Children create a diary entry for Andy from *The Suitcase Kid* to review creating blog posts. • They evaluate comments to see whether they are kind, specific and helpful.	• Assess and review.

Overview of progression

● The children learn about Jacqueline Wilson, as an author and about her books. They consider the profiles of characters, building on the previous learning about online profiles and sharing information.
● They develop their questioning skills and learn about using online voting tools.
● To develop their writing and feedback skills, the children create simple blog posts and comment upon them. They learn that comments need to be kind, specific and helpful.

Creative context

● There are many links to the English curriculum, through the development of writing for different contexts, progressively building a varied and rich vocabulary and an increasing range of sentence structures.
● The children draw inferences, such as inferring characters' feelings, thoughts and motives from their actions. Also, they ask questions to improve their understanding of a text and participate in discussion about both books that are read to them and those they can read for themselves, taking turns and listening to what others say.
● They use speech marks, apostrophes, pronouns and connectives to describe characters, their feelings and actions.

Background knowledge

● The children will have created profiles for themselves and characters before. In these lessons, they begin to imagine what they might say in a diary entry or blog post.
● They have used some online collaborative tools, but they may not have used online voting.
● Their previous learning about e-safety will have taught them to be careful about what they share online. In addition, they know that they need to be kind, specific and helpful when giving feedback.

Curriculum objectives
● To use technology safely, respectfully and responsibly.
● To select, use and combine a variety of software (including internet services) on a range of digital devices to design and create a range of programs, systems and content that accomplish given goals, including collecting, analysing, evaluating and presenting data and information.

Lesson objectives
● To identify characters from fictional books (for example, Tracey Beaker).
● To describe characters from fictional books; to begin to develop profiles.
● To identify personalities from real life and locate information about them, using search tools.
● To describe the validity of the information located.

Expected outcomes
● Can discuss online identities, including profiles.
● Can describe how to search for information about personalities and discuss the validity of the information.

Resources
Photocopiable page 'Jacqueline Wilson's books' from the CD-ROM; photocopiable page 'Jacqueline Wilson facts' from the CD-ROM; interactive activity 'Book comparison' on the CD-ROM

Who is Jacqueline Wilson?

This week is an introduction to Jacqueline Wilson. The children will search for information about the author and think about the validity of different websites. The many books of Jacqueline Wilson will be located on an online website and the children will compare the list of books found with the official author's website. The children consider the validity of information and sources.

Introduction
● Introduce the lesson by asking whether the children know of Jacqueline Wilson. What does she do?
● Show them one of her books, for example, *The Story of Tracy Beaker* or *The Suitcase Kid*. Can they name other titles written by her? Make a list to display.
● Show a clip of an episode of the TV programme *Tracy Beaker* (found on BBC iPlayer).
● Show the video introduction from Jacqueline Wilson on her website (www. jacquelinewilson.co.uk/).

Paired work
● Using photocopiable page 'Jacqueline Wilson's books' from the CD-ROM, the children open a commercial reseller's website such as Amazon (www. amazon.co.uk/) and search for her books.
● Using the photocopiable sheet, the children attempt to find books which have not been listed by the class.

Whole-class work
● Bring the children together and ask for titles of books to add to the list.
● Display the library on the Jacqueline Wilson website (www.jacquelinewilson. co.uk/library.php). Does Amazon sell all of her books?
● Select three well-known titles and ask children who have read them to summarise the plot. Ask: Is there a common theme? (They tend to focus on families with relationship problems and are told from the child's point of view.)
● Use interactive activity 'Book comparison' on the CD-ROM to list the features of the books.

Paired work
● Using photocopiable page 'Jacqueline Wilson facts' from the CD-ROM, the children research the life of Jacqueline Wilson. They should use relevant search terms and narrow their searches, using the Advanced search feature, to find the most recent articles and web pages.
● Does her life story mirror the scenarios in the book?

> **Differentiation**
> ● Support: Less confident learners may need support to identify the main characters in a story and then the story plot.
> ● Challenge: More confident learners could identify the main features of the books and describe the similarities and differences between two or more books.

Review
● Bring the class together and ask children for a Jacqueline Wilson fact.
● How do they know that the information they have found is valid? On the photocopiable sheet, it had space to list the source of the information. Encourage the children to look at the name of the website.
● Information from the BBC or the Jacqueline Wilson website, will generally be reliable. However, would Jacqueline Wilson's website be biased?
● On Wikipedia, anyone can add to the information. It could be accurate, because people may have specific knowledge about something. However, it may also not be completely true, as it may be biased.
● They should always check information from more than one source. Wikipedia is a good starting point but they must check using other websites.

Curriculum objectives
● To use technology safely, respectfully and responsibly.
● To select, use and combine a variety of software (including internet services) on a range of digital devices to design and create a range of programs, systems and content that accomplish given goals, including collecting, analysing, evaluating and presenting data and information.

Lesson objectives
● To decide the type of information required in a profile of a person.
● To create a profile for a fictional character in a book based on the information located.

Expected outcomes
● Can create a profile for a character in a book, based on information located.
● Can create a profile for a current celebrity, based on information located.

Resources
Photocopiable page 177 'Character profiles'; photocopiable page 178 'Andy's diary'; *The Suitcase Kid* by Jacqueline Wilson

Character profiles

Returning to character profiles, the children focus on the Jacqueline Wilson book, *The Suitcase Kid*. They create profiles for the main character and her favourite toy. Thinking about sharing information, the children create a diary entry by the main character, about her situation.

Introduction
● Introduce the lesson theme of *The Suitcase Kid* by Jacqueline Wilson. Read the introduction to the book. Who are the main characters?
● From the introduction to the story, ask: *Can we know what the characters are like? From what they say, do and how they are described, what can we infer about what they think?*
● Explain that people can often write about their thoughts in a diary or, publicly, in a blog. Explain that in the coming lessons, the children will be learning about blogging and creating their own blog.

Whole-class work
● In the story, they have read about Andy – the main character. Can the children imagine a profile for her? What about her toy rabbit, Radish? What would Radish's profile be like?

Paired work
● Using photocopiable page 177 'Character profiles', the children create a profile for Andy.
● Look at the style of pictures by Nick Sharratt, the illustrator of the books. Can they use the same style to create an avatar for Andy?
● Create an imaginary profile for Radish, using the photocopiable sheet.

Whole-class work
● In the story, Andy's toy rabbit Radish acts as a confidante. How does having something to confide in help Andy cope with the situation and how does it help the story?
● Ask the children to imagine that they are Andy. She is going to write an entry into her diary about her situation.

Paired work
● Using photocopiable page 178 'Andy's diary', the children, in pairs, discuss what Andy might write in her diary. It is her most private thoughts, that she would not share on a blog or even tell another. However, she might tell her rabbit, Radish, what she is thinking.

Differentiation
● Support: Less confident learners may need support to imagine how a diary entry is written and also with their spelling and sentence structures.
● Challenge: More confident learners could improvise their own diary entry about Andy and her situation. They should use direct speech to record Andy talking to Radish.

Review
● Discuss what information can be shared and what is best not to be shared.
● Ask for volunteers to share their diary entries for Andy.
● Conclude the lesson by thinking of a celebrity or Jacqueline Wilson. What would their profile be like and what would they write in their diaries?

True or false?

Using true and false questioning, the children think about the story. Can they locate information and then create their questions? This leads to them using an online voting tool, to allow them to vote and collaborate together.

Introduction
● Continuing the theme of *The Suitcase Kid*, from the previous lesson, remind the children of the story. Ask individual children true or false questions about the story, for example: *Andy is a boy – true or false? The toy, Radish is a rabbit – true or false?* Further questions can be found on photocopiable page 'True or false' from the CD-ROM.
● Ask the whole class true or false questions. If they think the statement is true, they stand up, if they think it is false, they sit down.
● Label one end of the classroom true and the other end false. Ask true or false questions and children move to the appropriate end of the room.

Whole-class work
● Explain to the children that when they were answering the questions, they may have been copying their friends. How could they answer the questions without knowing what the others were thinking?
● The children will now use an online questioning tool, to vote true or false.
● Open the Socrative website (www.socrative.com/). Every time you log in, it will be the same room number.
● The children log in by selecting 'Student Log In'. They enter the teacher's room number and then they are ready.
● Ask a true or false question and then select True/False from the teacher's dashboard.
● The children vote on their computers and the results are displayed.

Paired work
● How many questions can the children ask about the story? Using photocopiable page 179 'Suitcase Kid questions'. the children collect their ideas. Once complete, they choose one question to share. They convert the question into a true or false question.
● Display or share photocopiable page 'Proofreading checklist' from the CD-ROM. Looking at their question, they proofread it, to ensure it makes sense.

Whole-class work
● Using the Socrative website, children take turns to ask the class questions.
● They see the results displayed on the teacher's screen.

Differentiation
● Support: Less confident learners may need support to form questions, which can be answered as true or false.
● Challenge: More confident learners could create their own proofreading checklist, which they could use with their English lessons.

Review
● Recap that the children have been looking at true and false questions. Could they create a 'User guide for locating and evaluating information' using true and false. For example, 'All information found on the web is reliable – true or false?' Ask them for further examples.
● The online voting tool, Socrative, is accessed through a web browser. Explain that the computer may use Internet Explorer, Safari, Chrome or Firefox web browsers, for example. There is even an app on the tablet computers.
● Relating to the 'How computers work' learning, they should notice that these different types of software can be used on the same computer.
● Also, different types of computer may use different operating systems and yet still be able to run the same Socrative tool, through a browser or app.

Curriculum objectives
● To use technology safely, respectfully and responsibly.
● To select, use and combine a variety of software (including internet services) on a range of digital devices to design and create a range of programs, systems and content that accomplish given goals, including collecting, analysing, evaluating and presenting data and information.

Lesson objectives
● To collaborate to create a new story, in-person and face-to-face.
● To collaborate using online tools to plan and create a new story.
● To compare the writing processes of online and in-person collaboration and describe the advantages and disadvantages.
● To correct errors using software tools, such as spellchecking.

Expected outcomes
● Can collaborate face-to-face to plan a new story.
● Can collaborate online to plan a new story.
● Can compare the processes of collaborating face-to-face and online.

Resources
Photocopiable page 180 'The new story'; Edublogs or similar class blog software set up before the lesson

Writing a new story

The children collaborate to create a new Jacqueline Wilson story. They work face-to-face initially and then online. They compare the two processes to discuss the advantages and challenges of them both. They use the spellchecking tool in a word processor to help with proofreading.

Introduction
● The children plan a new Jacqueline Wilson-style story.
● Explain that they will plan it by collaborating face-to-face and also online.
● Discuss the plot structure of some of the Jacqueline Wilson novels: Opening > problem > the problem develops > resolution.

Group work
● The children think of as many problems that their character could encounter, for example, *The Suitcase Kid* involves the parents separating and arguing. They list their ideas on photocopiable page 180 'The new story'.
● The children read out the problems and decide which one they want to develop. They are able to see each other's faces which gives them facial clues as to their partner's feelings and reasons for choosing the different problems.

Whole-class work
● Bring the class together and explain that they are now going to plan the next stage of the 'problem develops' using an online tool.
● Open the class blog set up before the lesson (such as Edublogs, for example, where a class blog and additional blogs can be created).
● Demonstrate to the children how to add a post to the blog (going to 'Site Admin' and 'Write new blog post').

Independent work
● The children write the next part of the story, to develop the problem. They can draft this using a word processor such as Microsoft Word, and then they are going to paste the text into a blog entry.
● Before they post their writing, draw their attention to the spellchecker. It might be that misspelled words are underlined in red.
● They could also select the spellchecker from the menu (in Word, this can be found in the Tools menu, then by selecting 'Spelling and Grammar').
● Once they have checked their story, they can paste it into the blog, by selecting 'Write new blog post'.
● The children then read each of the blog posts for their group, as they appear and decide which one they would like to progress.
● Under the one they like, they can select 'Reply' and say their name.

Differentiation
● Support: Less confident learners may need support in their writing and also to use the spellchecker tool.
● Challenge: More confident learners could consider how the problem in their story may be in conflict with what the character would like to happen (similar to *The Suitcase Kid*).

Review
● Explain that the children could continue to discuss their decisions about which way the problem develops using comments or an online voting tool. Ask: *How did you feel when someone disagreed with your decision?*
● Compare online and in-person collaboration. Ask: *Was it easier to discuss face-to-face, because you could read each other's emotions? Was it more difficult?*
● Explain that when we talk face-to-face, we can pick up on clues more easily than when typing words or even using video to communicate.
● Ask the children to think of a situation where online communication should be used, instead of face-to-face?

Curriculum objectives
● To use technology safely, respectfully and responsibly.
● To select, use and combine a variety of software (including internet services) on a range of digital devices to design and create a range of programs, systems and content that accomplish given goals, including collecting, analysing, evaluating and presenting data and information.

Lesson objectives
● To name different application software and describe its functions.
● To explain why different application software is used for different purposes.
● To explain the function of a blog.
● To create a simple blog.

Expected outcomes
● Can explain why there are different application software for different purposes.
● Can create a simple blog using online tools.

Resources
Photocopiable page 181 'The Suitcase Kid book review'

Book reviews and blogging

The children think about the purpose of blogs and create a simple one themselves. The subject chosen is a book review of *The Suitcase Kid*. They contribute reviews, considering the impact of the reviews on the author and book sales and then rate each other's reviews.

Introduction
● Reading *The Suitcase Kid* enables the children to write a review of the book.
● Ask three children if they would recommend the book? Why would they recommend it? It may be that they struggle to justify their decision and, if so, having a structure for a book review may help.
● Suggest that they use headings such as: The plot, The characters, My favourite part, My favourite language, Why I think another child my age would like it, for example.

Paired work
● In pairs, the children use photocopiable page 181 '*The Suitcase Kid* book review' to write their review of the story. They carry the process out as an interview; one child asks questions and takes notes, while the other answers.

Whole-class work
● A book review could be written as a blog. Ask one of the children to read out their review and demonstrate how to write a new blog post.

Paired work
● The children draft their book review entries into the class blog.
● Before posting their entries, they should proofread and use spellcheck.
● Once posted, the children should read each other's posts and consider whether they are positive or negative book reviews.

Whole-class work
● Bring the class together and explain that book reviews can encourage new readers to read or buy a book. However, if they are bad, then it can put people off reading it.
● Display the Amazon website for Jacqueline Wilson's books. Choose one book and read the review.
● Ask them about the book reviews they have written and the ones on Amazon. Highlight that the Amazon reviews have a star rating, do the children think that this is helpful? Could they give a star rating for the book?
● The children can return to their blog posts and under them select 'Reply'. They can add a star rating out of five and use the asterisk symbol as the star, for example, *****.

Differentiation
● Support: Less confident learners may need support to write their reviews, to reflect on the story and to construct their sentences to reflect their feelings about the book.
● Challenge: More confident learners could add further headings, for example, did the book meet their expectations or was it better than they expected?

Review
● Explain to the children that a blog is an online web log similar to a captain's log on a ship. It records information in an ordered way, by date.
● Recap that in earlier weeks, the children wrote diary entries (for Andy) and now they have considered how they can use a blog to record their thoughts.
● Ask whether they would share the same thoughts on a blog as they would in a diary? What information would they share?
● Highlight the software used. The blog is created using a web browser. Remind the children that they have used different software for different purposes; for example, pasting text into the word processor to check spelling.

Curriculum objectives
● To use technology safely, respectfully and responsibly.
● To select, use and combine a variety of software (including internet services) on a range of digital devices to design and create a range of programs, systems and content that accomplish given goals, including collecting, analysing, evaluating and presenting data and information.

Lesson objectives
● To read and review blog comments, using given criteria.
● To respond to a blog post, giving positive and supportive comments.
● To evaluate blogs for the quality of information shared, using given criteria.

Expected outcomes
● Can give positive and supportive comments, using a blog.
● Can evaluate the information given within a blog.

Resources
Photocopiable page 182 'The event blog post'

Adding comments to blogs

The children have written blog posts and begun to think about adding comments. They now need to consider about what they write when commenting. Whenever comments are made, they need to be kind, specific and helpful to them. They also consider that blog posts can be the opinions of different people, so they should think whether they agree or disagree with them. They should always be careful when posting information online.

Introduction
● Begin by sharing the blog posts from the previous lesson, where the children wrote book reviews and then added a star rating.
● Explain that where they selected 'Reply' and added the stars is called adding a 'comment'.
● You could stand up and say to the class, for example: *What do you think about my clothes?* Select three children to give comments.
● From the children's responses, say that they could make the person feel really good about themselves or be really hurtful if they took the criticism personally. Therefore, when it comes to commenting, the children must be kind, specific and helpful about their blog posts.

Whole-class work
● The children think about an event at school, for example, a special visitor or when they went to a particular place with school.
● They could use 'who, what, when, where, why and how?', using photocopiable page 182 'The event blog post'.

Paired work
● The children write a short blog post about the event and then post it onto the class blog, ensuring that they proofread it first. If they have suitable photographs, they could add them to the post.
● In pairs, they review their partner's blog post and leave a comment about the quality of the post. For example, a star rating followed by a comment about how well it is written.
● The children then read the comments written by their partners.

Whole-class work
● The children look at the comment left by their partners. Do they think that the comments are kind, specific (addressing a particular part of the post) and helpful (suggesting a way of improving their writing)?
● The children tell their partner whether they think their comment helped.
● Returning to the class blog, choose one example and add a comment under another comment – to review whether it was kind, specific and helpful.

Differentiation
● Support: Less confident learners may need to use the 'two stars and a wish' criteria to help them leave a comment for their partner.
● Challenge: More confident learners could respond independently to the blog posts, using the kind, specific and helpful criteria, to make a concise comment.

Review
● The children need to evaluate blogs to look at the quality of information shared and if they think this is true and factual or biased. Explain that this is a difficult skill to develop and as they look at more blogs, they can decide whether they agree with the author or not.
● Finally, explain that the comments that are added to blog posts are also people's opinions about the writing. However, everything written online can be recorded (even if a blog entry or comment is deleted), so the children need to always be careful what they write and to be kind, specific and helpful in their comments.

Curriculum objectives
● To use technology safely, respectfully and responsibly.
● To select, use and combine a variety of software (including internet services) on a range of digital devices to design and create a range of programs, systems and content that accomplish given goals, including collecting, analysing, evaluating and presenting data and information.

Lesson objectives
● To create a simple blog.
● To read and review blog comments, using given criteria.
● To respond to a blog post, giving positive and supportive comments.

Expected outcomes
● Can create a simple blog using online tools.
● Can give positive and supportive comments, using a blog.

Resources
Photocopiable page 183 'Our class blog'

Jacqueline Wilson: Assess and review

To review the learning from this half term, the children use the class blog to write an entry as the character, Andy, from *The Suitcase Kid*. They will then review a partner's post and add a comment. They will then decide whether their partner's comments are kind, specific and helpful.

Introduction
● Introduce the lesson by asking the children: *What is a blog?*
● Remind the children that they have written blog posts using a web browser: *Can you name the browser you used? Can you name another web browser?*
● In this lesson, the children return to *The Suitcase Kid* story. They have written diary entries for the main characters, so they will now create a blog post diary entry for Andy.

Whole-class work
● Read the introduction to the story and ask the children to think about what Andy might be thinking and feeling.
● Using today's date, they can begin to plan their diary entry. It needs to be written in the first person and describe an event from the story.
● Ask: *Can you create a simple blog using online tools?*

Paired work
● The children write their individual blog posts for Andy. If it helps, they can use 'who, where, why, when, what and how' to structure the post.
● Once complete, they proofread their words to ensure that it makes sense.
● They could use the word processor to spellcheck their post, by pasting the text into the software and seeing if misspelled words are underlined in red (using Microsoft Word).
● Now, the children's partner reads their post and responds by adding a comment.
● The comment must be kind, specific and helpful. Before children post their reply, they must proofread it and they should also check the spelling.
● Finally, the original blog post author reads the comment. They need to think about their partner's comment. Do they agree it is kind, specific and helpful?
● They now write a response to the comment.

Differentiation
● Support: Less confident learners may need support to identify ways forward. They could use 'two stars and a wish' if that helps structure their response.
● Challenge: More confident learners could write comments for their partner, which are spelled correctly, are concise and offer specific guidance on how they could improve their blog post.

Review
● Bring the class together and ask the children to feedback on the experience. Choose one pair and ask them to read their blog post, comment and comment responses out to the class.
● Ask: *Can you give positive and supportive comments, using a blog?*
● Ask the children whether they think it is helpful to use the word processor to check the spelling or is it easier to use a dictionary?
● Ask them if they think a regular class blog would be a good idea. Would they like to write regularly about their interesting events?
● What information do they think should be included in the blog (considering their previous learning on safety)?
● Use photocopiable page 183 'Our class blog' to plan the future month and the blog posts that could be written.
● Conclude by highlighting that blogs can be very useful for sharing information about their lives, but they need to always be careful about the information they share.

Character profiles

- Create a profile for Andy.
- Look at the style of pictures by Nick Sharratt, the illustrator of the books.
- Can you use the same style to create an avatar for Andy?

Name:	Avatar:
Age:	
Address:	
Interests:	

- Create an imaginary profile for Radish.

Name:	Avatar:
Age:	
Address:	
Interests:	

I can create a profile for a character.

How did you do?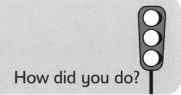

Andy's diary

■ What would Andy write in her diary?

Date:	
What she is thinking:	What she might write:

I can create a diary entry, inferring the feelings of a character.

How did you do?

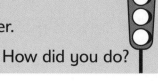

PHOTOCOPIABLE

SCHOLASTIC
www.scholastic.co.uk

Suitcase Kid questions

■ Create as many questions as you can about the story *The Suitcase Kid.*

■ Choose one question to make into a true or false question.

_____

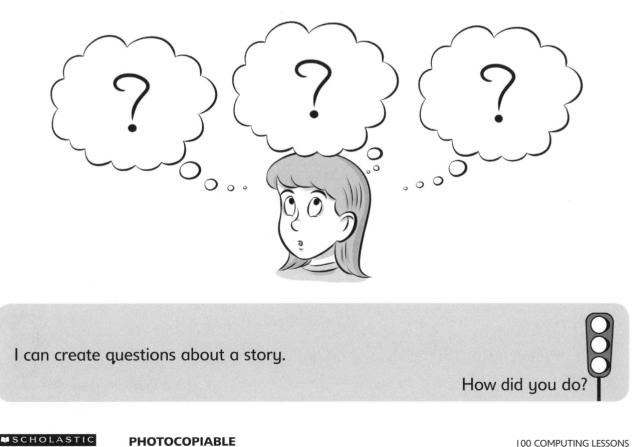

I can create questions about a story.

How did you do?

The new story

- Write down the details of the story featuring your new character.

- Describe the opening.

_____

_____

_____

_____

- What is the problem?

_____

_____

_____

_____

- How does the problem develop?

_____

_____

_____

_____

- What is the resolution?

_____

_____

_____

_____

I can develop a story in the style of an author.

How did you do?

The Suitcase Kid book review

■ Write a review of the story *The Suitcase Kid*.

The plot:

_____

_____

_____

The characters:

_____

_____

_____

My favourite part:

_____

_____

_____

My favourite language:

_____

_____

_____

Why I think another child my age would like it:

_____

_____

_____

I can write a book review using prompts.

How did you do?

The event blog post

- Write a blog post about a special event.
- Use 'who, what, when, where, why and how' in your blog.

BLOGFUN

_____

_____

_____

_____

_____

_____

_____

_____

_____

_____

_____

_____

I can write a factual report.

How did you do?

PHOTOCOPIABLE

SCHOLASTIC
www.scholastic.co.uk

Name: _____

Date: _____

Our class blog

■ Plan the events you could share on the class blog.

Day	Mon	Tues	Wed	Thurs	Fri	Sat	Sun
Date							
Content							
Who will do it?							

I can plan entries for a class blog.

How did you do?

Rainforest

This chapter uses a rainforest theme and builds on the combination of knowledge, skills and understanding of effective internet searching and programming that the children have developed in previous years. The children will use search engines to find accurate information on the rainforest to use in their quiz and then plan and create their quiz using Scratch. They develop their understanding of using selection and repetition and are introduced to the use of variables for the first time.

Expected prior learning

● The children have already been introduced to searching effectively in YEAR 4 Spring 1 and Year 4 Autumn 1 and have been gradually improving their confidence in programming using Scratch. They therefore have already covered some of the skills they will be developing further in this chapter, such as searching for information efficiently and accurately, planning effectively, using selection and repetition in their programming and debugging their animation.

Chapter at a glance

Subject area
• Algorithms and programming

National Curriculum objective

• To design, write and debug programs that accomplish specific goals, including controlling or simulating physical systems; solve problems by decomposing them into smaller parts; use sequence and repetition in programs; use logical reasoning to explain how some simple algorithms work and to detect and correct errors in algorithms and programs.
• To use search technologies effectively.

Week	Lesson objectives	Summary of activities	Expected outcomes
1	• To use a search engine to locate basic information. • To know there are many different search engines. • To use at least two search engines. • To evaluate located information using given simple criteria. • To know that websites may not contain truthful information.	• Children searching for informative and easy to use websites about the rainforest using two different search engines. • They evaluate a chosen website for reliability.	• Can use search technologies to locate and evaluate information. • Can explain that websites may not contain truthful information.
2	• To understand how a quiz can be created using Scratch programming software. • To evaluate existing Scratch quizzes in order to identify their favoured approach. • To use search engines to locate appropriate material for their quiz as necessary using appropriate search terms. • To plan a simple quiz based on the rainforest using a paper-based template.	• Children evaluate two different types of Scratch quiz. • They search for questions for their quiz. • They plan their quiz on paper.	• Can plan a simple quiz based on a given topic. • Can search for images and content using appropriate search words and determine the trustworthiness of content.
3	• To understand how selection can be used within a Scratch quiz to achieve different outcomes. • To understand how inputs and outputs can be used within a Scratch quiz. • To plan their own algorithms including inputs, outputs and selection. • To work collaboratively to debug their algorithms.	• Children identify and understand how inputs, outputs and selection can be used in a Scratch quiz. • They experiment with using inputs, outputs and selection. • They plan actions, algorithms and code for their quiz.	• Can create a simple quiz using a visual programming language. • Can solve problems by decomposing them into smaller parts.

■ SCHOLASTIC

Week	Lesson objectives	Summary of activities	Expected outcomes
4	• To implement their algorithms using Scratch. • To use selection and repetition as appropriate within their program. • To work collaboratively with their peers to test and debug programs.	• Children collate and create assets for their quiz. • They program their algorithms into their quiz. • They test and debug their quiz.	• Can use selection and repetition within a program. • Can debug a program.
5	• To understand what variables are and how to declare and assign variables within Scratch. • To know how variables can be used in a simple Scratch quiz. • To plan, implement and test simple scoring variables. • To explain how they have used variables in their quiz.	• Children understand what variables are and how they are used in Scratch. • They make and use score variables in their quiz. • They test and debug variables. • They add comments to their code to explain how they have used variables and other blocks. • They demonstrate their understanding of a variable.	• Can understand the use of variables. • Can declare and assign variables within a program.
6	• To work collaboratively with their peers to take and evaluate their quizzes. • To give and receive feedback. • To explain how they have implemented their algorithms using the Scratch program. • To explain verbally how they have used selection, repetition and variables within their work.	• Children evaluate their own and other's quizzes. • They share their quiz with others and explain their use of code.	• Can evaluate their own and other's work using given criteria. • Can explain how they have used selection, repetition and variables in their work.
Assess and review	• To assess the half-term's work.	• Children undertake a series of challenges within Scratch to demonstrate their knowledge, skills and understanding. • They use comments to explain how they have used repetition, selection, inputs, outputs and variables in their Scratch code.	• Assess and review.

Overview of progression
• The children build upon their prior knowledge and understanding of programming using Scratch. They begin by using different search engines to locate information about the rainforest and learn that information given in websites can be inaccurate. The children then plan and create their quiz using Scratch and their research skills, deepening their knowledge of the creative programming process and being introduced to the use of variables.
• They use their decomposition, problem-solving and debugging skills to achieve the desired outcomes in their quiz and use their developing planning and evaluative skills to ensure that their quiz is suitable.

Creative context
• The lessons have links to the mathematics curriculum as children use logical thinking and problem solving to sequence and debug their quiz. The computing lessons should also draw upon the children's learning in English as they type accurate search queries, create questions for their quiz and plan and evaluate their work.
• The lessons also have links to the geography curriculum as the children research the topic of rainforests, and also the art curriculum if they choose to create their own sprites and backgrounds in Scratch.

Background knowledge
• From the work they have already completed, the children will know about including selection and repetition when programming using Scratch, how to plan and evaluate their work and how to conduct internet searches.
• From assessing the children's understanding in previous units, you will need to assess their capability in writing algorithms and translating these into programming code within Scratch.
• It is important that you are a relatively able user of Scratch. There are tutorials on the Scratch website and by working through these, and by undertaking the lesson activities prior to the lesson, you should feel comfortable with Scratch. The children can also be encouraged to share their learning.
• The lessons in this chapter assume the use of Scratch 1.4, but other versions can also be used.

Curriculum objectives
- To use search technologies effectively and be discerning in evaluating digital content.

Lesson objectives
- To use a search engine to locate basic information.
- To know there are many different search engines.
- To use at least two search engines.
- To evaluate located information using given simple criteria.
- To know that websites may not contain truthful information.

Expected outcomes
- Can use search technologies to locate and evaluate information.
- Can explain that websites may not contain truthful information.

Resources
Two different search engines downloaded onto the classroom computers; photocopiable page 193 'Rainforest website evaluation'; selection of websites about the rainforest located prior to the lesson, if required

Using search engines effectively and discerningly

In this first lesson, the children are reminded of basic Boolean search techniques and how to use advanced searching. They are asked to use two different search engines to search for basic information and are challenged to evaluate whether the information contained in websites is up to date, accurate and unbiased.

Introduction
- Display the phrase 'search engines' on the whiteboard and ask the children to explain what it means.
- Recap the search engines they know (Google, Firefox, Bing and so on).
- You could ask for a quick hands-up poll to see who uses which search engine most and discuss why they like it best.

Whole-class work
- Explain that in this lesson they will be locating information about rainforests using two different search engines and that they will then be picking one website to evaluate.
- Using volunteers, demonstrate how they can access the two different search engines you have identified for the purposes of the lesson and discuss what search terms might help them to find out information about the rainforest.
- This is an ideal opportunity to recap the basic use of Boolean searches and advanced searches covered earlier in Years 3 and 4.

Paired work
- Ask the children to access the two different search engines you have chosen and find their favourite website about the rainforest – that is the website that they think is most informative, has the best design and is easy to use.

Whole-class work
- As a class show and discuss the websites they have found. Were the same websites displayed on both search engines? Why is that website their favourite?
- Give the children a copy of photocopiable page 193 'Rainforest website evaluation' and explain that they will be using the questions on the sheet to evaluate the website they have located. (Depending on your class and their level of confidence, you may wish to assign websites to them that you have found prior to the lesson.)

Paired work
- Ask the children to work through the questions, answering them as best they can and leaving out any questions that are irrelevant to their website.

Differentiation
- Support: Less confident learners may benefit from mixed-ability pairings. They explain their thoughts simply in the evaluation of their website.
- Challenge: More confident learners could explain their thoughts about their website in detail and be encouraged to make more sophisticated evaluations of it. For example, Why is that website their favourite? What else would they like to see in the website?

Review
- As a class, discuss the answers to the questions, displaying and discussing any interesting points the children raise about their chosen website.
- As a class, come up with the top five tips to use to evaluate a website's reliability. Remind them that websites may not always contain reliable information.

Curriculum objectives

● To design, write and debug programs that accomplish specific goals, including controlling or simulating physical systems; solve problems by decomposing them into smaller parts; use sequence and repetition in programs; use logical reasoning to explain how some simple algorithms work and to detect and correct errors in algorithms and programs.

Lesson objectives

● To understand how a quiz can be created using Scratch programming software.
● To evaluate existing Scratch quizzes in order to identify their favoured approach.
● To use search engines to locate appropriate material for their quiz as necessary using appropriate search terms.
● To plan a simple quiz based on the rainforest using a paper-based template.

Expected outcomes

● Can plan a simple quiz based on a given topic.
● Can search for images and content using appropriate search words and determine the trustworthiness of content.

Resources

Photocopiable page 194 'Rainforest quiz questions'; photocopiable page 195 'Rainforest quiz planning'; Scratch file 'Rainforest animals quiz'; Scratch file 'Rainforest quiz'; Scratch 1.4 installed on the class computers

Quiz planning

In this lesson, the children learn that Scratch can be used to create quizzes and evaluate examples of existing Scratch quizzes in order to determine which type of quiz they want to create. They plan their own quiz, conducting question research on the internet and planning the flow of their quiz using a template.

Introduction

● Remind the children that last week they were looking at researching information available on the internet and determining whether the information was reliable, up to date and accurate.
● Explain that today they will be using the internet to research questions for a quiz they will be creating using Scratch about the rainforest.

Whole-class work

● Show the children the Scratch file 'Rainforest animals quiz' (opened from the Quick links section on the CD-ROM) on the whiteboard and work though it.
● Using a 'think, pair, share' technique, discuss what is good about it (for example, it's simple), what's not so good (for example, answers need to be typed in carefully) and what they would like to improve (for example, adding sound, better questions).
● Talk through how the quiz is working by going through the script step by step, discussing how the children see the different costumes and how they are changing, and how the 'broadcast' and 'when I receive' messages are working.
● Show the children the Scratch file 'Rainforest quiz' (opened from the Quick links section on the CD-ROM) on the whiteboard, explain that this is a different type of quiz, and work though it as a class.
● Again, using 'think, pair, share', discuss what is good about it (for example, it's easier to click on the answers rather than typing them), what's not so good (for example, it could have some instructions) and what they would like to improve (for example, more questions, better background, sounds).
● Explain that they are going to be creating their own quiz for the rest of the class to do and that their first step is to focus on a topic and identify the questions they wish to include in their quiz.
● Depending on your class and the children, you may wish to allocate topics, quiz types and numbers of questions (five questions is fine, with less confident children focusing on fewer questions and the first, simpler type of quiz). It may also be helpful for children to work in pairs.
● As a class, discuss possible areas of focus (rainforest plants, rainforest foods, rainforest tribes, and so on).

Paired work

● The children use the internet to search for suitable questions and answers.
● Give out photocopiable page 194 'Rainforest quiz questions' and ask the children to complete this as they go.
● You may need to remind the children that they should keep the answers to their questions short if the user is going to be typing them.
● Once they have finished and you have checked their questions, give out photocopiable page 195 'Rainforest quiz planning' and, using the example as a guide, ask the children to plan the flow of their quiz.

Differentiation
● Support: Less confident learners may benefit from working in pairs and should focus on a simple quiz with a few questions.
● Challenge: More confident learners will be able to plan a more complex quiz with greater numbers of questions. They should be encouraged to add sounds and instruction screens.

Review

● Ask volunteers to share their quiz ideas with the class and ask the class how evaluating other quizzes helped them to plan their own quiz.

Curriculum objectives
● To design, write and debug programs that accomplish specific goals, including controlling or simulating physical systems; solve problems by decomposing them into smaller parts; use sequence and repetition in programs; use logical reasoning to explain how some simple algorithms work and to detect and correct errors in algorithms and programs.

Lesson objectives
● To understand how selection can be used within a Scratch quiz to achieve different outcomes.
● To understand how inputs and outputs can be used within a Scratch quiz.
● To plan their own algorithms including inputs, outputs and selection.
● To work collaboratively to debug their algorithms.

Expected outcomes
● Can create a simple quiz using a visual programming language.
● Can solve problems by decomposing them into smaller parts.

Resources
Photocopiable page 196 'Rainforest quiz algorithms'; completed photocopiable page 195 'Rainforest quiz planning' sheets from last lesson; Scratch file 'Rainforest animals quiz'

Planning algorithms and programming a quiz

In this lesson, the children will begin the process of creating their quiz. First, they examine how selection and inputs and outputs are used in a Scratch quiz and then using this knowledge they plan their own algorithms and Scratch code.

Introduction
● Remind the children that they have been planning their rainforest quiz.
● This week they will be creating the algorithms for their quiz, firstly on paper and then using Scratch.

Whole-class work
● Explain that you are first going to be focusing on *inputs and outputs* and *selection*.
● Display the Scratch file 'Rainforest animals quiz' (opened from the Quick links section on the CD-ROM) on the whiteboard and ask the children to identify where the first input box is ('ask what is your name?' – *name* being the input).
● Ask them to identify the output ('hello name' – *name* being the output).
● Explain that this is the Scratch programming language making use of inputs and outputs and that they may choose to use this in their quiz. Ask: *Can you identify any other inputs in the sample quiz? Where could other outputs go?* (For example, an output could repeat the answer you typed.)

Paired work
● Ask the children to open Scratch and experiment with input and output scripts, getting a sprite to ask for an input and then giving an output (asking to input the name, then saying 'hello name' is an easy start).

Whole-class work
● Displaying the Scratch file 'Rainforest animals quiz' on the whiteboard, ask the children to identify the first selection script (where the program has to make a selection or decision – an *if* statement is a good sign, for example *If the answer is monkey, say 'well done', else say 'sorry, I'm a monkey'*).
● Explain that children will need to use selection in their quiz to identify the correct and incorrect answers and talk through how the quiz does this.
● You may also wish to recap the use of 'broadcast' and 'when I receive'.

Paired work
● Give out photocopiable page 196 'Rainforest quiz algorithms' and explain to the children that they should use this to plan the algorithms for their quiz.
● Emphasise that they need to work step by step through their quiz, thinking of what action needs to happen first, then expanding it to create an algorithm and then the code. They may need more space to write their algorithms, and they can continue on the back of their sheet.
● They can use Scratch and the sample files to help them if they wish. Working collaboratively will help them to debug their algorithms and code.

Differentiation
● Support: Less confident learners may need further support and to work through further simple examples of how to use selection before going on to plan their algorithms.
● Challenge: More confident learners will be able to understand the concepts of selection more easily and will be able to plan their algorithms with ease. They should be encouraged to use multiple selection.

Review
● Display a new Scratch file on the board and, using volunteers, as a class come up with a start to a quiz that uses inputs, outputs and selection.
● Assess the children's progress through their algorithms planning sheet.

Curriculum objectives

● To design, write and debug programs that accomplish specific goals, including controlling or simulating physical systems; solve problems by decomposing them into smaller parts; use sequence and repetition in programs; use logical reasoning to explain how some simple algorithms work and to detect and correct errors in algorithms and programs.

Lesson objectives

● To implement their algorithms using Scratch.
● To use selection and repetition as appropriate within their program.
● To work collaboratively with their peers to test and debug programs.

Expected outcomes

● Can use selection and repetition within a program.
● Can debug a program.

Resources

Completed photocopiable page 196 'Rainforest quiz algorithms'; completed photocopiable page 195 'Rainforest quiz planning'

Quiz creation

In this lesson, the children will undertake the majority of the work for their quiz, creating the assets needed for their questions, programming their algorithms using Scratch and working collaboratively to test and debug as they create their quiz.

Introduction

● Remind the children that they have been planning their rainforest quiz and explain that in this lesson they will be creating their quiz, collecting and creating the assets they need, programming their algorithms into Scratch and testing and debugging their quiz.
● Explain that how to program the score for their quiz will be dealt with in the next lesson, so they should not worry about this for now.

Whole-class work

● Explain to the children that using their completed 'Rainforest quiz algorithms' and 'Rainforest quiz planning' sheets, they should work through their quiz in a logical way, thinking *What needs to happen next?* as they go.
● Remind them that they will need to use 'if/else' scripts and 'broadcast' and go through the use of these again if needed (although it may be more beneficial to go through this with any pairs who are still struggling with the concepts).

Independent/paired work

● The children should work to create their quiz, logically, step by step, creating or importing their sprites and programming them as they go to create their quiz.
● Working in their pairs they should test and debug their quiz as they go, and they can ask other pairs to look at their work as they progress to improve it and to help with the debugging process.
● You may find that there are common misunderstandings or issues that you can deal with in small groups, or you can encourage others who know how to do something to help someone who is struggling.
● When they feel they have finished, they should get someone else to check their work, ensuring that spelling is correct, the flow of the quiz is as it should be and giving some suggestions for improvement (you could use a 'two stars and a wish' feedback activity here if you want to make it more formal, with the reviewer noting down their feedback on paper).

Differentiation
● Support: Less confident learners may need additional support when programming their quiz and may benefit from talking about what they wish to achieve step by step with a peer or adult. Again, encourage them to focus on a smaller number of questions and creating an accurate quiz.
● Challenge: Encourage more confident learners to help others to debug their work and improve their own work by considering how they can make their quiz more effective, for example, adding sound, instructions and an ending to their quiz. You could also challenge them to work out how the scoring works, which will be covered in the next lesson.

Review

● Ask for a few volunteers to share their work with the class and then together as a class give constructive feedback.
● Review with the children their progress during the lesson. While hopefully most have finished, some may need further time in the next lesson and should be clear about what they have to do to complete their quiz.

Curriculum objectives
● To design, write and debug programs that accomplish specific goals, including controlling or simulating physical systems; solve problems by decomposing them into smaller parts; use sequence and repetition in programs; use logical reasoning to explain how some simple algorithms work and to detect and correct errors in algorithms and programs.

Lesson objectives
● To understand what variables are and how to declare and assign variables within Scratch.
● To know how variables can be used in a simple Scratch quiz.
● To plan, implement and test simple scoring variables.
● To explain how they have used variables in their quiz.

Expected outcomes
● Can understand the use of variables.
● Can declare and assign variables within a program.

Resources
An example of a Scratch quiz from the class pre-loaded onto the teacher's computer; sticky notes

Scoring using variables

This week the children are introduced to variables for the first time. They learn what is meant by the term and understand how to declare and assign variables within the Scratch programming language. They then add variables to their work and explain to their peers how they have used variables in their quiz.

Introduction
● Ask for volunteers to play quick games of noughts and crosses (or similar), against you, on the board. Ask for one volunteer to keep score. As the players play the game, the scorer should write the score on the board, erasing the previous score and adding one to it each time and writing in the new score.
● Explain that the scoring completed on the board by the volunteer is the same as the scoring that they will program Scratch to do for their quiz; the computer stores the previous score, then adds one to the score when required. Explain that the score is a variable (you could write this on the board) and that a variable is a changeable value and can be anything that the computer needs to remember and change; in this case, the score.

Whole-class work
● If you have access to a shared area featuring all the children's work, open a volunteer's Scratch file that is completed, yet needs to have the scoring added. If you do not have access to a shared area, you will need to load this file prior to the lesson, or add in sample assets.
● Ask the children to identify where there needs to be a score (after a question is answered correctly).
● Show the children how to make a score variable in Scratch (in variables > make a variable > variable name 'score'). Make sure that they leave 'for all sprites' selected.
● As a class, discuss that they need to set the score to 0 at the beginning of their quiz and that after every correct answer is given the score should change by 1.
● Demonstrate how they can show or not show the score variable by ticking or unticking the box next to 'score'.

Paired work
● The children should work to make their own scoring variables and add them to their quiz.
● They should test and debug their variables as they go, working collaboratively as appropriate.
● When they finish, they add comments to their code to highlight their use of variables, selection and broadcast messages.

Differentiation
● Less confident learners may need additional support with understanding how variables work and implementing them into their quiz.
● More confident learners will be able to declare and assign variables confidently and can be encouraged to share their understanding with others to help them with their work. They can also add detailed comments to their code.

Review
● Ask all pairs to come up with a definition for a variable. They could write this on a sticky note if you like. Ask three to five pairs to share their definition with the class, correcting any misunderstandings as they do so.
● Assess the children's progress through their inclusion of variables in their quiz and the understanding they demonstrate during class discussion and the review activity.

Curriculum objectives
● To design, write and debug programs that accomplish specific goals, including controlling or simulating physical systems; solve problems by decomposing them into smaller parts; use sequence and repetition in programs; use logical reasoning to explain how some simple algorithms work and to detect and correct errors in algorithms and programs.

Objectives
● To work collaboratively with their peers to take and evaluate their quizzes.
● To give and receive feedback.
● To explain how they have implemented their algorithms using the Scratch program.
● To explain verbally how they have used selection, repetition and variables within their work.

Expected outcomes
● Can evaluate their own and other's work using given criteria.
● Can explain how they have used selection, repetition and variables in their work.

Resources
Photocopiable page 197 'My rainforest quiz evaluation'; Photocopiable page 198 'Classmates' rainforest quiz evaluation'

Evaluating the rainforest quizzes

This week, the children undertake evaluation of their own quiz and are asked to present their quiz to the class, explaining their code and receiving feedback on their work. They are also given the opportunity to take each other's quizzes and give constructive feedback to their peers.

Introduction
● Remind the children that they should have finished their quiz last lesson.
● Ask them to describe how they have used variables, selection and repetition in their work (you could display an example Scratch file on the whiteboard to help if you wish).

Whole-class work
● Show the children photocopiable page 197 'My rainforest quiz evaluation' on the whiteboard and explain that in this lesson they will be evaluating their own quiz and then taking and evaluating quizzes created by others in the class.

Independent/paired work
● Give out photocopiable page 197 'My rainforest quiz evaluation' and ask them to work through this in order to evaluate their work, giving as much detail as possible.
● Once they have finished, give them photocopiable page 198 'Classmates' rainforest quiz evaluation' and ask them to swap with another pair, taking each other's quizzes and evaluating them using the photocopiable sheet.
● Once they have evaluated the other quiz, they should share their feedback with each other.

Differentiation
● Support: Less confident learners may benefit from support when evaluating their work as such higher-order thinking can be challenging. Encourage them to focus on one or two aspects of their quiz.
● Challenge: More confident learners should be able to evaluate their work in detail and explain with confidence how they have used selection, repetition and variables in their work. They should also be able to provide useful feedback to others.

Review
● Bring the children together and select some of the quizzes to take as a class (saving their work in a shared area will be helpful for this as will be noting which children have included aspects in their quiz that will be interesting to show). Ask the children to talk through their quizzes as they are shown to explain how they have made use of selection, repetition, variables and other programming elements.
● You may have time to show all the quizzes. If not, make sure that you discuss their quiz with each pair, which will help with assessment of the chapter's work.
● Assess the children's understanding from their rainforest quiz, evaluations of their work and explanations of their code.

Curriculum objectives
● To design, write and debug programs that accomplish specific goals, including controlling or simulating physical systems; solve problems by decomposing them into smaller parts; use sequence and repetition in programs; use logical reasoning to explain how some simple algorithms work and to detect and correct errors in algorithms and programs.

Objectives
● To understand and explain how repetition can be used within Scratch.
● To understand and explain what inputs and outputs are and how they can be used in the Scratch programming language.
● To understand and explain how selection can be used within Scratch.
● To understand and explain what variables are and how they can be used within Scratch.

Expected outcomes
● Can understand and explain the use of repetition, selection, inputs, outputs and variables.
● Can use selection inputs, outputs, variables and repetition in a graphical programming language.

Resources
Photocopiable page 199 'Scratch challenges'

Rainforest: Assess and review

This week, the children undertake a number of challenges using Scratch and are asked to explain their approach to each challenge. In this way, they consolidate their learning and demonstrate their knowledge, skills and understanding of the main learning points of the chapter. The challenges do not directly relate to the quiz, and the children are asked to apply their knowledge and understanding to different scenarios. This may be tricky for some and you could adapt the challenges accordingly. The outcomes of the children's work will help with assessment of their work and allow you to adjust future learning of these topics as necessary.

Introduction
● Discuss with the children what they have learned during this chapter and review that they have used selection, repetition, inputs and outputs, and variables.
● You may wish to spend a little time going through each of the above, depending on your class.
● Explain that this week they will be undertaking a series of challenges using Scratch.
● Explain that they will be asked to apply the knowledge, skills and understanding that they have developed when creating their quiz to other scenarios.

Whole-class work
● Give the children a copy of photocopiable page 199 'Scratch challenges' and explain what they are asked to do, ensuring they understand.
● You may wish to work through the first challenge as a class.
● Ensure that they understand that there is more than one way to approach each challenge and they should be as creative as they like.

Independent work
● Ask the children to work through the challenge, using comments to explain how they have approached each challenge.
● To help with assessment, you could ask the children to print their Scratch code (right-click to save picture of a script and add to a Word document, or print directly).

Differentiation
● Support: Less confident learners may benefit from working in pairs or may need further support in understanding how to apply their learning. They could alternatively be asked to complete a short quiz (say three questions) on a topic of their choosing.
● Challenge: More confident learners should be able to apply their knowledge to the challenges and explain their approach in detail. They could also come up with their own challenges/ways to show their knowledge, skills and understanding.

Review
● As a class and using volunteers, go through the challenges with the children, asking them to share their solutions.
● Assess the children's work through the outcomes of their challenges and make adjustments to future algorithms and programming work based on these assessments.

Name: _____ Date: _____

Rainforest website evaluation

■ Evaluate a website about rainforests.

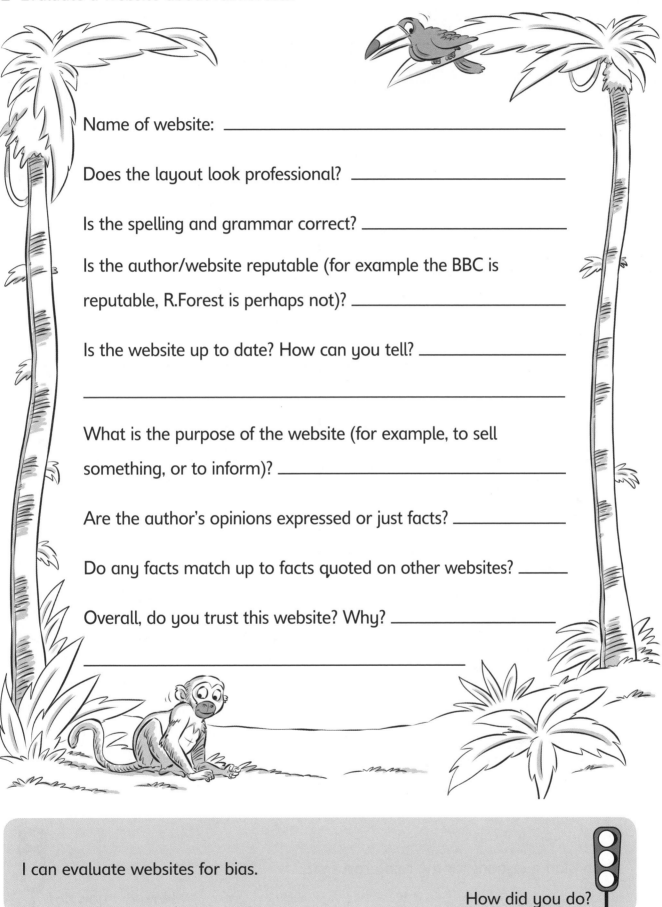

Name of website: _____

Does the layout look professional? _____

Is the spelling and grammar correct? _____

Is the author/website reputable (for example the BBC is reputable, R.Forest is perhaps not)? _____

Is the website up to date? How can you tell? _____

_____

What is the purpose of the website (for example, to sell something, or to inform)? _____

Are the author's opinions expressed or just facts? _____

Do any facts match up to facts quoted on other websites? _____

Overall, do you trust this website? Why? _____

_____

I can evaluate websites for bias.

How did you do?

Name: _____ Date: _____

Rainforest quiz questions

■ Use the space below to plan the questions you will ask for your quiz. Remember to note down the answers too.

Question	Answer

I can plan questions for my rainforest quiz.

How did you do?

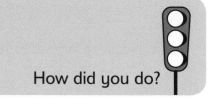

PHOTOCOPIABLE

Name: _____   Date: _____

Rainforest quiz planning

■ Use the space below to plan how the flow of your quiz will work.

Example

Question 1:

- Show picture of monkey.
- Ask 'what am I?'
- User types in answer.
- If answer is correct, say 'well done', play sound 'correct', move to next question.
- If answer is wrong, say 'sorry, that's wrong', play sound 'wrong', move to next question.

I can plan the flow of my quiz.

How did you do?

Name: _____ Date: _____

Rainforest quiz algorithms

- Write down the action, algorithm and code you will need for your rainforest quiz. Continue the table below on another sheet of paper.
- Leave the debugging column until you are asked to complete it.

Action	Algorithm	Code	Debugging
Instructions appear at start.	When quiz started, instructions appear in centre of screen. Everything else hides.	*Instructions:* When green flag clicked Show *All other sprites:* When green flag clicked Hide	

I can plan and debug the algorithms needed for my Scratch rainforest quiz.

How did you do?

Name: _____   Date: _____

My rainforest quiz evaluation

■ Why is your quiz effective?

_____

_____

_____

_____

■ What do you like about your quiz and why?

_____

_____

_____

_____

■ How could you make your quiz even more effective?

_____

_____

_____

_____

■ Explain how you used different Scratch blocks to make things happen in your quiz.

You might want to explain how you used the 'if' block and the score variable.

_____

_____

_____

_____

I can evaluate my own work.
I can explain how I have used selection and variables in my Scratch code.

How did you do?

Classmates' rainforest quiz evaluation

■ Does the quiz make sense?

_____

_____

■ Is it easy to understand what you need to do?

_____

_____

■ Are the questions too easy, too hard or just right?

_____

_____

■ Do the sprites and backgrounds work well with the quiz?

_____

_____

■ Do the sounds work well with the quiz?

_____

_____

■ Does selecting the right or wrong answers give you the correct response?

_____

_____

■ What do you like most about the quiz?

_____

_____

■ What do you think could be improved?

_____

_____

I can evaluate the work of others.

How did you do?

Name: _____ Date: _____

Scratch challenges

- For each challenge, add the correct code to Scratch.
- Add a comment to explain how you have used the blocks to meet the challenge.

Challenge 1: Repetition:
- Can you make a sound repeat every time an action happens? For example, when a sprite touches another sprite.

Challenge 2: Inputs and outputs:
- Can you ask a user to input text into Scratch and repeat this to them?

Challenge 3: Selection:
- Can you make something happen *if* an event happens? For example, if a sprite touches the edge.
- Can you make one thing happen *if* an event happens, and otherwise, something else happens? For example, if a sprite touches the edge it says one thing, but if it touches another sprite, it says something else.

Challenge 4: Variables:
- Can you make a score variable so that when something happens a point is given? For example, if a sprite touches another sprite, 1 point is given.

I can use repetition, inputs and outputs, selection and variables in Scratch.
I can use comments to explain my code.

How did you do?

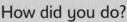

Year 3 Autumn 1: Roald Dahl

Overview

● In the lessons, the children have been learning about networks and communication. Using video communication tools, such as 'Skype' and 'FaceTime', people can talk over huge distances and time zones, in real time. The children may have experienced using these tools and it can be seen that they will become more important, as they grow up.
● Similar to having a penfriend, the children could even link to another school. The 'Skype in the classroom' initiative aims to connect schools around the globe, to learn from each other (https://education.skype.com/).

Resources

● 'Skype', 'FaceTime' or a video communication app.

Lesson activities

● Using a *Fantastic Mr Fox* theme, the children could use video communication tools to have a conversation from Mr Fox to Mrs Fox. This could be organised between children in the same room or between children in different classrooms.

● Set up the call between the two devices and check the connection prior to the lesson.
● Set the scene, Mr Fox has travelled along the tunnels to the store houses of the evil farmers. Instead of taking a shopping list from Mrs Fox, he says he will simply describe or show what is there (using his tablet computer).

Using 'Skype' on the iPad

● Prior to the lesson, you need to set up two 'Skype' accounts (https://login.skype.com/account/signup-form), one for each device being used to communicate. (The accounts could be named Mr Fox and Mrs Fox and fox avatars could be used.)
1. Open the Skype app and add the new contact names, by selecting the '+' at the top right-hand side.
2. Using the first iPad (Mrs Fox), call the second iPad (Mr Fox).
3. The children can role play being Mr Fox describing the contents of Mr Bunce's store house and Mrs Fox could decide which items to collect.

Year 3 Autumn 2: Robots (1)

Overview

● The children are learning about algorithms and programming. They have been introduced to moving an object by using simple commands, such as forwards, backwards, turn left, turn right. There are a number of apps that are based on the LOGO programming language, which uses these commands. In Year 2, the children used the 'Bee-Bot' app. In this example, the children will move a screen turtle around to complete challenges.

Resources

● 'Move the Turtle' app or screen turtle-style programming game.

Lesson activities

● The children have been 'human robots' before, where they moved around following simple instructions such as forwards and backwards. This could be a good starter activity for the lesson, navigating the obstacles in the room, while following another child's instructions.
● Using a screen turtle app, the children reinforce these skills in a game. The 'Move the Turtle' app leads the children through a tutorial, to learn the commands and teach them to break a larger problem into smaller parts (decomposition).

Using the 'Move the Turtle' app on the iPad

1. Open the 'Move the Turtle' app.
2. The menu offers:
   ● 'Play' – where the children work through a tutorial to teach them how to use the app
   ● 'Compose' – where they can simply program any movements, without an objective
   ● 'Projects' – where there are example projects to view and copy into their own library of projects.
3. Select 'Play'. This is divided into three chapters. Select 'Let's move'.
4. Within chapters 1 and 2 are nine activities for the children to work through. This can structure their learning, by keeping them challenged and at the same time supporting their learning.

Year 3 Autumn 2: Robots (2)

Overview

● Following on from the previous lesson, the children continue their learning about algorithms and programming.

● Using a different tool, which aims to teach the LOGO-style command, enables the children to transfer their learning from one context to another. The example of the 'Cato's Hike Lite' app, shows that many apps will offer a basic introduction and then an in-app purchase to unlock the complete app or there are often free 'lite' versions and then 'full' versions available to purchase.

Resources

● 'Cato's Hike Lite' app (free) or screen turtle-style programming game.

Lesson activities

● The children can use the app to step up from simple commands to handling more complex problems.

● Demonstrate on the display how to complete the first level.

● Highlight that they are breaking a larger problem into smaller parts and use the term 'decomposing the problem'.

● At the end of the lesson, ask a few children to demonstrate how they solved the problems, while getting them to talk through their actions.

Using 'Cato's Hike Lite' app on the iPad

1. Open 'Cato's Hike Lite' app.

2. Select 'Play' and 'Tutorial'. From the ten levels, select 'First step'.

3. This app has more text than the 'Move the Turtle' app, though it follows as similar pattern of introducing the commands.

Year 3 Spring 1: Kings, queens and castles

Overview

● The children have been learning about kings, queens and castles and have been searching for information and images. They have also been presenting their findings to the class.

● Using an avatar-type app, the children can prepare a speech to describe how they have located information and narrowed their searches.

● The background images for the avatar need to be researched and selected using key search terms.

Resources

● 'Tellagami' app (free) or an avatar-type app.

Lesson activities

● The children use the tablet devices to search for appropriate images, using the web browser search engine.

● They use '+' and '−' to narrow the search, for example, if they searched for castles, but did not want to include Windsor Castle, they could use 'castle–windsor'.

● Once an image has been selected, they can add it to the avatar-style app as the background.

● Using the avatar to talk for the children, they need to plan the words to say, so they write a short script to explain how they located the image and also interesting facts about the castle.

● Recording their voices directly into the app, they practise and re-record their speeches, until they are happy with them.

● Play back the completed avatar presentations to the class, who can review them using 'two stars and a wish'.

Using the 'Tellagami' app on the iPad

1. Using the search tool on the Safari web browser (typing directly into the address box at the top), the children search for images of castles.

2. Once one image has been selected, press and hold on the image to 'Save image' to the camera roll.

3. Open the 'Tellagami' app.

4. There is a tutorial to help understand the app, which can be watched by selecting 'How to'.

5. Select 'Create'.

6. From the menu on the left-hand side, select 'Character' – here the children can change the appearance of the avatar.

7. From the menu, select 'Emotion' – here the children can add emotion to the face, for example 'surprised'.

8. From the menu, select, 'Background' – here the children can add a castle picture they have found.

9. Select 'Library' and choose the castle image (saved earlier) from the camera roll. Pinch to resize.

10. Select 'Back' and then 'Record'. Then, on the new menu, on the right, select 'Record'.

11. The app will record 30 seconds of speech. Play it back by selecting 'Preview'.

12. Select 'Back' and then 'Record'. Then, on the new menu, on the right, select 'Record'.

13. The app will record 30 seconds of speech. Play it back by selecting 'Preview'.

14. Select 'Share' then 'Save' to place the video in the camera roll.

Year 3 Spring 2: Aliens

Overview

● The children have been introduced to programming using Scratch. The online version 'Scratch 2.0' (http://wiki.scratch.mit.edu/wiki/Scratch_2.0) is available via a web browser, though not all tablets are able to use it. There are similar programming tools available on the tablet, such as 'Hopscotch' on the iPad. They use a similar style of 'blocks' for the instructions.

Resources

● 'Hopscotch' app (free).

Lesson activities

● The children think about the example from the Scratch lessons. They can program a sprite to move around the screen. With the alien theme, the children can choose a character to move around the screen and ask it to respond to the sensors on the tablet.

● A tablet has a microphone which can be used to detect noise. It also has a gyroscope, so as the tablet is tilted, it can detect movement in a certain direction. Therefore, tablets can offer new opportunities for controlling the onscreen characters.

Using the 'Hopscotch' app on the iPad

1. Open the 'Hopscotch' app.

2. Select 'New project', then add a character (sprite) from the 'Add an object' window, then 'Start'.

3. At the top, where it says 'Untitled', press on the word and select 'Rename'. Give the project a title 'Alien rocket' and add a name in the 'Hopscotch nickname' box, then 'Update'.

4. From the drop-down menu, select 'When iPad is tilted up' and drag the 'change y by' block on to the page. It automatically suggests '300' units.

5. Press 'Play' and tilt the iPad upwards – the character should move up the screen. Now change the drop-down menu to say 'When iPad detects a loud noise' and change the distance to '600'. Press 'Play'.

6. Now the children can do a quiet countdown and then a loud 'BLAST OFF' – the character should move on the loud noise.

Year 3 Summer 1: Chocolate

Overview

● In the chocolate-themed lessons, the children have been thinking about collecting, checking, manipulating and presenting data. They have carried out class surveys to find out which types of chocolate bar are most popular.

● They have looked at data to identify errors, then presented their findings. In this lesson, the children can develop their experience of using another presentation tool.

Resources

● 'Haiku Deck' app (free).

Lesson activities

● The children carry out a survey into Easter eggs. What would they like to find inside an Easter egg, if money was no object? In pairs, they think of four items to go inside the eggs. Using 'Haiku Deck' or another presentation app, they are able to create a bar graph, directly in the app.

● As they ask the other children which item they would like in their egg, they can move the columns of the bar charts up.

● Finally, they can add a summary slide to explain their findings; for example, 'The most votes were to find an iPad inside an Easter egg'.

Using the 'Haiku Deck' app on the iPad

1. Open the 'Haiku Deck' app. (There is a tutorial, which can be viewed.)

2. Select the '+' at the bottom of the screen, to begin a new presentation. Type in a title.

3. On the left of the slide, there are four icons. Select the blue icon, second from the top. Type into the search box 'Easter egg'. Select an image and 'Done'.

4. Give the slide a title, such as 'My Easter egg survey'.

5. Select the '+' on the right-hand side, to add a new slide.

6. Again, select the blue icon, but this time select the blue 'Chart icon' near the middle of the screen. Select the bar chart icon, then 'Done'.

7. Add a title, then add two more columns by selecting the '+' on the chart. Select 'Edit label' to add the name of the item.

8. The scale can be adjusted to be a maximum of ten, if ten children are going to be in the survey.

9. Now, as the children ask each other the questions, they can move the bars up, as they receive a vote.

10. Finally, they can add a text slide to present their findings.

Year 3 Summer 2: Superheroes (1)

Overview
- The children have been learning about superheroes and especially about their characteristics.
- Using a finger puppet app such as 'Puppet Pals HD', the children can act out the roles of a superhero, their sidekick and their villain.
- The focus of the lessons is e-safety and thinking around online profiles on social media. By acting out the play of the superheroes, they think more about their characters and the type of information they might add to the profiles.

Resources
- 'Puppet Pals HD' (free for basic characters – the Director's pass version enables the children's own pictures to be added).

Lesson activities
- In the lesson, the children can work in pairs to act out the plays. They use a finger puppet app to represent their superhero and sidekick.
- They think about a day in the life of the superhero and act it out.
- As the children act it out, they think about the profile of the superhero and their characteristics, their hobbies and interests.
- Once they have completed their plays, they create a profile for their superhero and sidekick.

Using the 'Puppet Pals HD' app on the iPad
1. Open the 'Puppet Pals HD' app. Select 'Press to start' and choose two actors, then select 'Next'.

2. If using the Director's pass paid version, the children can 'Add actor from photo'. By adding their own characters and backgrounds, the children can then collect an image from the web and cut out their superhero from it. Alternatively, they could draw their own superhero, take a photograph and then cut it out, to add to the play.

3. Then they add backgrounds; they can select up to five backdrops.

4. To begin the play, the children act out the day in the life of the superhero. Press the red button at the top to begin recording.

5. In between scenes, press the 'Pause' button, then pull one of the pull ropes to change the backdrop. Take off the pause and continue. To complete the recording, press 'Stop' (square button).

6. To save the show, select the 'Save' icon. Give the play a title, then view the saved shows.

7. Finally, select 'Export' to save the video to the camera roll.

Year 3 Summer 2: Superheroes (2)

Overview
- The children have been learning about superheroes and reading comics. They have discussed the characteristics of the superheroes, such as their costumes, special powers and their strong moral code.
- Comics are a great way to engage the children in reading and thinking about direct speech. The computing curriculum focus for the lessons is e-safety and, especially, social media.
- The children can create a comic about a superhero who shares too much information.

Resources
- 'Comic Maker HD' app (free).

Lesson activities
- Using a comic creation app on a tablet, for example 'Comic Maker HD' on the iPad, the children can draft out their comic. The story could feature the superhero, who is sharing information on their social media page.
- In the comic story, the superhero realises they have given away the address of secret hideout and details of their daily routine. The sidekick could then appear to give good advice about sharing online.

Using the 'Comic Maker HD' app on the iPad
1. Open the 'Comic Maker HD' app. View the example comics to see the layouts that are possible.

2. Select 'Create comic' at the top left-hand side of the screen.

3. The children can select a layout, ideally one with only a few panels.

4. Using the grey menu on the right-hand side, select the photo image icon (two rectangles with a sun image), then navigate to the camera roll.

5. The image appears on the page and can be dragged and pinched into place.

6. From the 'Library' icon (two photographs on top of each other), navigate to the 'Photo assets > Library > Character > Heroes' to add an example hero.

7. The children create the story of the superhero giving away too much information online. Then the sidekick can give them advice about how they should behave online.

8. Finally, the comic can be exported to the camera roll, using the 'Share' icon, on the top right-hand side of the screen.

Year 4 Autumn 1: Myths and legends

Overview

● In the lessons, the children have been using a Myths and legends theme, based around the story of Robin Hood. They have been thinking about being discerning in evaluating digital content. They have considered spam messages, biased information and fake websites.

● Continuing the Robin Hood theme, the children create a TV news interview with the Sheriff of Nottingham, who can give false and biased information about Robin Hood.

Resources

● 'News Booth' app (by Rodskagg).

Lesson activities

● Using the Robin Hood theme, the children imagine that they are going to do a TV interview with the Sheriff of Nottingham.

● The roles are camera person, interviewer and the Sheriff.

● Display example TV news interviews, from websites such as BBC News, where they interview a person on location and also in the TV studio.

● The children can plan their script. First, is it going to take place on location or in the TV studio? How are the styles of interviews different?

● For the dialogue, what is the reason for the interview? What are the questions? How will the Sheriff give a biased or false response to the questions?

Using 'News Booth' app on the iPad

1. Open the 'News Booth' app.

2. On the screen it states 'Start by selecting a photo or video'. Press the 'Media' button.

3. Select 'Use camera', then swipe to select the video recorder.

4. The children can act out their play with the interviewer asking the Sheriff questions.

5. Once complete, select 'Theme' and swipe to choose the style of the screen titles, then 'OK'.

6. Select 'Texts' and change the words to say 'Interview with the Sheriff' and 'Evil Robin Hood', then 'OK'.

7. Select 'Save' then either 'Share video' to move it or 'OK' and access the video from the camera roll.

Year 4 Autumn 2: Science fiction (1)

Overview

● In the lessons, the children have been engaged in a science-fiction theme to think about 'How computers work'. They have learned about the operating system – the main software on the computer that enables the different parts to communicate with each other.

● The children have considered how they use software for different purposes. They then focused on apps on mobile phones and tablets. Using the science-fiction theme, the children design an 'app of the future' and present it to their class.

Resources

● 'POP' app – Prototyping on paper (by Woomoo).

Lesson activities

● In the lessons, the children have designed an app for the future. They have thought about the features and how they meet the needs of the users.

● In order to test out their ideas, the 'POP' app enables them to take photographs of their designs (called the 'wireframes').

● Look at the sample app included in the 'POP' app. Now, the children photograph their designs and add the interactivity of buttons to change screens.

● Test the app with other children to gain feedback, before revising and improving the design.

Using the 'POP' app on the iPad

1. Open the POP app and select 'Sample'. Let the children explore the example to see how it works.

2. Select the '+' from the bottom left-hand side, to begin a new project. Name the project.

3. Without an account, only two projects in total are allowed. By signing up with an email address, you can increase the number available.

4. Taking pictures of your wireframe enables the children to photograph their paper plans for their app.

5. They can choose black and white photos with 'B&W'. Take photos of each page.

6. Now select a page and the '+' to add a hotspot. Drag into place and adjust the size to fit.

7. Select 'Link to', then select the page, then 'Done'.

8. Press the play arrow to test it out.

Year 4 Autumn 2: Science fiction (2)

Overview

- In the lessons, the children have been learning about different types of software, through a science-fiction theme. They have been looking at apps and how these meet the needs of the user.
- Using a 'game creation' app, the children consider how intuitive it is to use and then evaluate the quality of the product, once complete.

Resources

- 'Sketch Nation Studio' app (by Sketch Nation).

Lesson activities

- Using a game creation app, the children can experience making their own games. Before they can do this, they need to play games to identify what they like about the games and why? This is a difficult skill, as they may not know why they like or become engrossed in one, other than it's 'fun'.
- An example game could be within the 'Sketch Nation Studio' app, playing a game called 'Draakon'. This style of game involves tapping the screen to make a dragon fly higher. It must avoid the objects and not drop off the bottom of the screen. The background scrolls from right to left, to give an impression of movement.

- By analysing other games, the children judge whether the difficulty is at the correct level, what sort of graphics are appropriate and whether there is a back story to the game.
- Using a game creation app, the children make their own side-scrolling game and then play their partner's game to assess it. They then evaluate the process of making the game. Were the instructions clear? Were the buttons and tools accessible for the users?

Using the 'Sketch Nation Studio' app on the iPad

1. Open the 'Sketch Nation Studio' app and select 'Play'.

2. Select 'Draakon' to play the game. Allow the children to enjoy the game and learn about its mechanics.

3. Then select 'Touch to create'. The children could begin with 'Simple mode' and the 'Advanced mode' later.

4. Choose the style of game. The 'Draakon' game is a 'Side flying' game.

5. Name the game, draw the characters or upload from the camera roll.

6. Once each part is complete, play the game.

7. Swap iPads with a partner and play their game.

Year 4 Spring 1: Dragons

Overview

- The lessons have used a dragons theme to build on the knowledge, skills and understanding of programming that children have developed in previous years. The children have been using the graphical programming language, Scratch. They have developed their understanding of logic and following instructions in their programs. They can reinforce the learning of using instructions, using a LOGO-based app. In addition, an augmented reality app, such as, 'Dragon Detector' can inspire their writing about 'dragons in the classroom'.

Resources

- 'Daisy the Dinosaur app' (by Hopscotch Technologies); 'Dragon Detector' app (by Useless Creations Pty Ltd).

Lesson activities

- Using the dragon theme, you could introduce the lesson using the 'Dragon Detector' app. As the iPad is moved around, animated dragons appear to be flying around the room. This could be a stimulus for writing and for making a game. For example you could say: *Dragons have invaded the country, can you create a game to show how to escape or capture the dragons?*

- In order to create games, the children need to develop their logical programming skills and Daisy the Dinosaur can step them through learning the commands. There is also a 'free play' mode, which lets them create their own programs.

Using the 'Dragon Detector' app on the iPad

1. Open the 'Dragon Detector' app. Select mode 'Dragon detector!'

2. Hold up the iPad and the camera shows the room. The animated dragons fly across the screen.

Using the 'Daisy the Dinosaur' app on the iPad

1. Open the 'Daisy the Dinosaur' app. Select 'challenge mode'. This takes the children through the stages of learning about the commands. Allow the children time to learn and experiment.

2. Returning to the menu, select 'Free-play mode'.

3. The children can create a program to control Daisy, by selecting any commands they would like to use.

Year 4 Spring 2: The Normans

Overview

● Using a Norman theme, the children have been focusing on the *Bayeux Tapestry* and the *Doomsday Book*.

● They have looked at the tapestry to see how it tells a story. Then they see how timelines tell a story too. The children construct a timeline of their lives and prepare a presentation for the class. Using the timeline, they present and their peers evaluate.

● There are apps which can show timelines. The 'Coca-Cola Heritage Timeline' app tells the story of the drink, in a very visual way. To create a timeline, the 'RWT Timeline' app, enables significant events to be added.

Resources

● 'Coca-Cola Heritage Timeline' app (by Coca-Cola); RWT Timeline app (by ReadWriteThink).

Lesson activities

● Remind the children about the timeline theme. Open a timeline example, such as, the Coca-Cola app and show how the product has changed over time. Ask the children to select images that interest them. Can they read the scale of time in years?

● Display a timeline app. Remind the children of their learning about the Norman *Bayeux Tapestry* and how it portrays the battle over time.

● The children have been preparing timelines. Allow time for them to add events into the app.

● Display their timelines and ask the children to identify how the timeline may be similar or dissimilar to their timelines.

Using the 'Coca-Cola Heritage Timeline' app on the iPad

1. Open the Coca-Cola Heritage app and select 'Enter the timeline'.

2. Swiping through the timeline, the children can view the images through time. Tap on an image to find out more information.

Using the 'RWT Timeline' app on the iPad

1. Open the 'RWT Timeline' app and select '+ New user' then 'Enter your name'. Choose an avatar and confirm.

2. Enter a 'Project title' and 'Start'.

3. Touch the timeline to add an event label. Complete the boxes.

4. Add more labels and the 'Finish' to view the timeline.

5. The final timeline can be viewed and saved into the camera roll.

Year 4 Summer 1: Jacqueline Wilson

Overview

● The children have been learning about Jacqueline Wilson and her books. They continue to learn about online profiles and sharing information online. A class blog is created and could be edited using the tablets. They compare sharing in a diary and in a blog post.

● A Jacqueline Wilson augmented reality app enables the children to hold an iPad over the front cover of the book and a short video introducing the story appears. Also, the children can use a word-processing app or collage app to create a profile page for the characters in the stories.

Resources

● 'Emerald Star' augmented reality app; 'Pages' (by Apple).

Lesson activities

● Using the Jacqueline Wilson theme, remind the children about the book titles and covers. Show the books, including *Emerald Star*. Using an augmented reality app, the children can view a short video, introducing the story. What would they record in a video about a story, such as *The Suitcase Kid*?

● Using a word-processing app, the children create a profile page for one of the characters in a story or even a profile of Jacqueline Wilson herself.

Using the 'Emerald Star' app on the iPad

1. Open the 'Emerald Star' app. Hold the iPad over the cover of the book to start the video.

2. Alternatively, on another computer or iPad, search online for an image of the front cover of the book. Point the first iPad at the device with the book cover image on it and the video should appear.

Using the 'Pages' app on the iPad

1. Open the Pages app and create a new document.

2. The basic outline of the profile can be created using basic shapes. Using the '+' button, then from the column on the right (the square icon), select a shape. Add text to the boxes.

3. To add a profile picture, search online for an image of Jacqueline Wilson or a character from the books. Save it into the camera roll. Return to 'Pages' and select '+' and choose the camera roll button. Add the picture of the character. A video of a character could also be recorded and added.

Year 4 Summer 2: Rainforests (1)

Overview
• Using a rainforest theme, the children have been using search engines to find accurate information to use in their quiz. They plan their quiz to develop their understanding of using selection and repetition. They are introduced to using variables to keep score.
• There are many websites and apps that contain quizzes. The 'Wildlife Detective' app involves spotting animals and keeps a score, while using a countdown timer. The score is a variable, which increases by one each time an animal is found. The countdown timer is a variable, which decreases by one every second. Looking at other quizzes is important for the children to learn about the structure, features and rewards of quizzes and will improve their own designs.

Resources
• 'BN Rainforest' app (by MeSixty); 'Wildlife Detective' app (by Snepo Research)

Lesson activities
• Using the rainforest theme, the children research questions for their quizzes using a rainforest tourism app or tourism website. The 'BN Rainforest' app takes the children around Brunei and they can collect text and screenshots for their quiz.

• Using the 'Wildlife Detectives' app or a similar 'hidden object' app, the children see how a score can increase as the objects are tapped (a variable is increasing by one each time). Also, as they play, they can see how the timer counts down to increase the element of competition (a variable is decreasing).
• Use the game as an example to inform their planning or improvement of their quiz.

Using the 'BN Rainforest' app on the iPad
1. Open the BN Rainforest app.
2. Swiping through the pages, the children can find out information about the different sites in Brunei.

Using the 'Wildlife Detective' app on the iPad
1. Open the 'Wildlife Detective' app. Select 'Play now'. Choose 'Day' or 'Night'.
2. Tap on the screen on one of the hidden animals and the score goes up by one.
3. A countdown timer encourages them to work quickly.
4. When the time is up, the animals are displayed and more information can be read.

Year 4 Summer 2: Rainforests (2)

Overview
• Using a rainforest theme, the children have been using search engines to find accurate information to use in their quiz. They plan and create their quiz to develop their understanding of using selection and repetition. They are introduced to using variables to keep score. There are programming languages that work on tablets, for example, SNAP! (http://snap.berkley.edu). The Hopscotch app looks similar to the 'Scratch' software and takes advantage of the tablet's sensors, for example, the gyroscope and microphone.

Resources
• 'Hopscotch' app (by Hopscotch Technologies)

Lesson activities
• The children use a software app to create a quiz. .
• 'Hopscotch' is an iPad app or SNAP! could be used to create a simple quiz, using variables.
• The score needs to increase each time the answer is selected and the quiz needs a time limit.
• Ask the children to review working with different software. Could they transfer their learning?

Using the 'Hopscotch' app on the iPad
1. Open the app and select 'New project'.

2. From the 'Add an object' menu, select the Monkey and 'Start'.
3. Select the '+' at the top, to add an object. Add a 'Text object' and enter a quiz question 'What do I like to eat?'
4. Swipe down to reveal the grid of the display. Drag the question to the middle of the screen.
5. Add three more text objects, for 'Banana', 'Curry' and 'Score'
6. Select the 'What do I like to eat?' question from the tab at the top. Drag 'set value' to under 'When play button is pressed'. Select 'Add value' and type 'Score' and change the value to 0.
7. Select 'Banana' then 'When Banana is tapped'. Drag 'Change value' under it and drag the 'Score' from the values menu on the left. So, it will read 'Change value Score by 1'. Drag 'Set text' under it and type 'Correct'.
8. Select 'Curry' and from the drop-down menu, select 'When curry is tapped', then drag 'Set text' under it and type 'Incorrect'.
9. Select 'Score' from the tab at the top. Under the heading 'When play button is tapped', add these instructions: *repeat 200; set text to Score; end; set text to 'Time up!'; wait milliseconds 1000; set text to Score.*
10. Press Play and test the program.

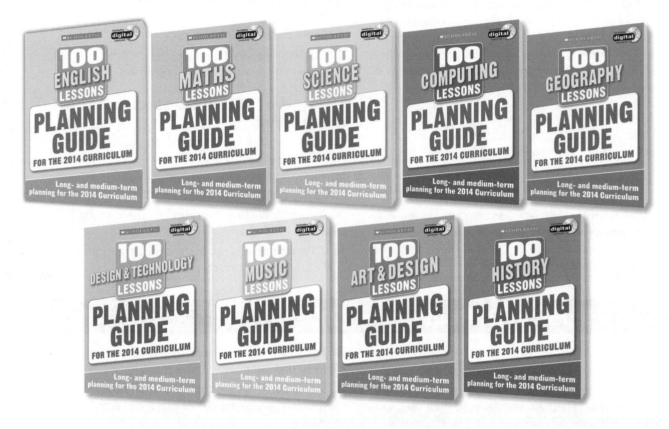